Assessment as Information Practice

Assessment as Information Practice provides information about a range of collection and service-based assessment approaches that can be applied in different contexts to benefit institutions and the users they serve by enhancing quality, efficiency, and effectiveness.

With contributions from practitioners and researchers in Australia, New Zealand, Thailand, and the United States, the chapters discuss practical and theoretical aspects of assessment in collecting institutions. Each chapter focuses on specific assessment approaches or contexts while providing guidance on method and use. The chapters can be read alone or as a series to gain an appreciation of assessment approaches, including assessment-oriented research; storytelling; design thinking; data visualisation; mixed methods assessment for digital resources; data for institutional repository assessment; bibliometric methods; and impact assessment.

Assessment as Information Practice serves as a resource for practitioners involved in assessment activities. Detailing the processes and considerations that will contribute to more effective and sustainable assessment programmes, the book is also relevant to faculty, researchers, and students working in the information sector.

Gaby Haddow is Associate Professor in Libraries, Archives, Records, and Information Science in the School of Media, Creative Arts, and Social Inquiry at Curtin University, Australia. Her research includes research assessment in the humanities and social sciences, bibliometrics and scholarly communication, the communication of research to practice, and research support in academic library environments. She was the co-editor of the *Journal of the Australian Library and Information Association*, co-edited a special issue of the *IFLA Journal*, and is a member of several journal editorial boards.

Hollie White is a Senior Lecturer in Libraries, Archives, Records, and Information Science in the School of Media, Creative Arts, and Social Inquiry at Curtin University, Australia. She holds a Ph.D. in Information and Library Science from the University of North Carolina at Chapel Hill, USA, a Master of Science in Library and Information Science from the University of Illinois at Urbana-Champaign, USA, and a Master of Arts in English from the University of Georgia, USA. Before moving to Australia from the United States, Hollie was Digital Initiatives Librarian at the J. Michael Goodson Law Library at Duke University, USA. Her research is around information organisation, institutional repositories, and library assessment.

Routledge Guides to Practice in Libraries, Archives and Information Science

This series provides essential practical guides for those working in libraries, archives, and a variety of other information science professions around the globe.

Including authored and edited volumes, the series will help to enhance practitioners' and students' professional knowledge and will also encourage sharing of best practices between different countries, as well as between different types and sizes of organisations.

Titles published in the series include:

Guidance for Librarians Transitioning to a New Environment
Tina Herman Buck and Sara Duff

Recordkeeping in International Organizations
Archives in Transition in Digital, Networked Environments
Edited by Jens Boel and Eng Sengsavang

Trust and Records in an Open Digital Environment
Edited by Hrvoje Stančić

Assessment as Information Practice
Evaluating Collections and Services
Edited by Gaby Haddow and Hollie White

For more information about this series, please visit: https://www.routledge.com/Routledge-Guides-to-Practice-in-Libraries-Archives-and-Information-Science/book-series/RGPLAIS

Assessment as Information Practice
Evaluating Collections and Services

**Edited by
Gaby Haddow and Hollie White**

LONDON AND NEW YORK

Cover image: © gremlin / Getty Images

First published 2022
by Routledge
4 Park Square, Milton Park, Abingdon, Oxon OX14 4RN

and by Routledge
605 Third Avenue, New York, NY 10158

Routledge is an imprint of the Taylor & Francis Group, an informa business

© 2022 selection and editorial matter, Gaby Haddow and Hollie White; individual chapters, the contributors

The right of Gaby Haddow and Hollie White to be identified as the authors of the editorial material, and of the authors for their individual chapters, has been asserted in accordance with sections 77 and 78 of the Copyright, Designs and Patents Act 1988.

All rights reserved. No part of this book may be reprinted or reproduced or utilised in any form or by any electronic, mechanical, or other means, now known or hereafter invented, including photocopying and recording, or in any information storage or retrieval system, without permission in writing from the publishers.

Trademark notice: Product or corporate names may be trademarks or registered trademarks, and are used only for identification and explanation without intent to infringe.

British Library Cataloguing-in-Publication Data
A catalogue record for this book is available from the British Library

Library of Congress Cataloging-in-Publication Data
Names: Haddow, Gaby, 1958- editor. | White, Hollie, 1980- editor.
Title: Assessment as information practice : evaluating collections and services / edited by Gaby Haddow and Hollie White.
Description: Milton Park, Abingdon, Oxon ; New York, NY : Routledge, 2022. |
Series: Routledge guides to practice in libraries, archives and information science | Includes bibliographical references and index. |
Identifiers: LCCN 2021031822 (print) | LCCN 2021031823 (ebook) | ISBN 9780367539948 (hardback) | ISBN 9780367533342 (paperback) | ISBN 9781003083993 (ebook)
Subjects: LCSH: Collection development (Libraries)--Evaluation. | Public services (Libraries)--Evaluation. | Collection development (Libraries)--Evaluation--Case studies. | Public services (Libraries)--Evaluation--Case studies.
Classification: LCC Z687 .A83 2022 (print) | LCC Z687 (ebook) | DDC 025.2/1--dc23
LC record available at https://lccn.loc.gov/2021031822
LC ebook record available at https://lccn.loc.gov/2021031823

ISBN: 978-0-367-53994-8 (hbk)
ISBN: 978-0-367-53334-2 (pbk)
ISBN: 978-1-003-08399-3 (ebk)

DOI: 10.4324/9781003083993

Typeset in Times New Roman
by Taylor & Francis Books

Contents

List of illustrations vii
List of contributors viii
Foreword xi
Acknowledgements xiii

1 Assessment as information practice 1
  GABY HADDOW

2 Research design and the relationship between assessment and research 12
  STARR HOFFMAN

3 Storytelling for the evaluation of GLAM programmes and services 29
  ANNE GOULDING

4 Facilitating iteration in service design in libraries 53
  SONGPHAN CHOEMPRAYONG

5 The assessment and analysis of materials availability: a mixed-methods approach 76
  DAVID WELLS

6 Data visualisations for library collections: applying an inquiry-based approach 91
  SUSAN PAYNE, DAVID DUDEK, BONNIE WITTSTADT, MARK CYZYK AND TOM EDWARDS

7 Moving beyond downloads and views when assessing digital repositories 107
  HOLLIE WHITE

8 Taking a quantitative approach to collection assessment: an
   introduction to bibliometrics in practice   118
   GABY HADDOW

9 Assessment in practice: effectiveness and impact   132
   GABY HADDOW AND HOLLIE WHITE

   Index   144

Illustrations

Figures

4.1	An example of the one-and-done approach in a service development project	54
4.2	The Double Diamond framework	58
4.3	Prototyping and testing process	69
4.4	Iterative process for rapid prototyping	69
6.1	2018 collection size and usage comparison	96
6.2	D-level heat map	100
7.1	Repository assessment programme development steps	112
8.1	*Web of Science* data	127

Tables

2.1	Potential research methods and practices	17
4.1	Example of design methods and tools in different service design phases	61
5.1	Summary of materials availability surveys run at Curtin University Library	80
5.2	Error types and areas of remediation	83
5.3	Availability errors and assessment methods	85
6.1	2018 collection size and usage comparison	98
8.1	Citation data required for analysis	127

Contributors

Songphan Choemprayong is an Assistant Professor in the Department of Library Science and a principal researcher at the Arc of Memory research unit, Faculty of Arts, Chulalongkorn University in Bangkok, Thailand. He holds a Ph.D. in Information and Library Science from the University of North Carolina at Chapel Hill, USA. He has been working with academic and special libraries in Thailand in applying design thinking and service design approaches to improve their services. At Chulalongkorn University, he teaches courses on information systems in humanities, evidence-based practice, and human information interaction. His current research interests include digital humanities, human-centered design, and accessibility of minority collections.

Mark Cyzyk, M.A., M.L.S., is a software engineer and librarian in the Library Applications Group, The Sheridan Libraries, Johns Hopkins University, USA. He is responsible for running and maintaining all library instances of WordPress (including the main library website), all instances of Omeka (including the official Libraries and Museums instances as well as an array of instances for use in instruction), for instances of ArchivesSpace, for an instance of Open Journal Systems, for all the various Springshare applications, as well as special projects. He has a passion for technology, for libraries, and for the noble mission of higher education. After a quarter century in technology, libraries, and higher education, if he can be said to be expert at anything, it's tenaciously troubleshooting things that spontaneously break.

David Dudek is the Collection Analyst, Services Librarian at Johns Hopkins University, USA. He is responsible for collecting data on e-journal subscriptions and databases, and circulation data for the print collection. The data is used to assess patron use and to assist in collection development. David is involved in a current project to identify 500,000 print items to be relocated from the main library to an offsite facility. The goal is to remove materials that are not used or rarely used, and maintain an onsite collection that matches patrons' needs and expectations. At the time of publication, David is now the Manager of Collection Services and the Library Services Center (offsite facility).

List of contributors   ix

Tom Edwards has worked in various capacities at Johns Hopkins Sheridan Libraries, USA, for nearly 20 years, instituting new workflows and policies with the Entrepreneurial Library Program for Capella University's online students (USA), completing transitions from print to electronic in GPO and microform materials for the Government Publications/Maps/Law Department, and online posting of Baltimore and Maryland maps to the JScholarship university digital repository. Tom now works with the Collection Management Council and the Assessment and User Experience Department. At the time of publication, Tom has now retired, but continues to work with JHSL on editing Chapter 6 of this book. This chapter would not have come together without his tireless efforts in collecting writings from all of us and pointing out areas needing improvement.

Anne Goulding is Professor of Library and Information Management in the School of Information Management, Victoria University of Wellington in Aotearoa, New Zealand. Her research interests lie primarily in the area of the management of library and information services and her main focus is on the management of public libraries. She has a particular interest in how GLAMR (galleries, libraries, archives, museums, and records) organisations demonstrate the impact of their service, activities, and programmes, and has undertaken a range of studies focusing on the evaluation of library programmes and services. She has published widely in the field and is Editor in Chief of the *Journal of Librarianship and Information Science*.

Gaby Haddow is Associate Professor in Libraries, Archives, Records, and Information Science in the School of Media, Creative Arts, and Social Inquiry at Curtin University, Australia. Her research includes research assessment in the humanities and social sciences, bibliometrics and scholarly communication, the communication of research to practice, and research support in academic library environments. She was the co-editor of the *Journal of the Australian Library and Information Association*, co-edited a special issue of the *IFLA Journal*, and is a member of several journal editorial boards.

Starr Hoffman (Ph.D., M.L.S, M.A.) coordinates assessment, strategic planning, and data reporting as Director of Planning and Assessment at the University of Nevada, Las Vegas Libraries, USA. She has presented on assessment-related topics at many national and international conferences, including workshops on data inventories presented at the International Conference on Library Performance Metrics in 2017 and 2019. Starr edited the book *Dynamic Research Support for Academic Libraries* (2016) and speaks, consults, and publishes on a variety of topics, including assessment, strategic planning, research support, and academic library leadership.

Susan Payne holds a master's degree in Science of Information from University of Michigan, USA. Since 2016, she has been the Head of Assessment and User Experience in the Sheridan Libraries at Johns Hopkins University, USA. With over 18 years of experience in academic libraries,

Susan has served in various other roles, such as library director, entrepreneurial virtual services librarian, and liaison librarian. In her current role, she applies assessment, data analysis, and design thinking approaches to both projects and ongoing work that spans library departments and divisions. Previous publications and conference presentations include relating to visualising collection evaluation decisions; information research fluency; and creating stronger student outcomes through collaboration and assessment. In 2013, she co-presented on an ACRL panel about creating a culture of innovation, inspiration, and entrepreneurialism. At the time of publication, she is now the Manager of Access, Assessment, and User Experience for the Sheridan Libraries.

David Wells is Manager, Collections, at Curtin University Library, Australia, where his responsibilities include collection development and the management of the library's systems for the discovery of information resources. As well as materials availability his interests include the evaluation of technical services work more generally. He has also written on OPAC and discovery system design, and on patterns of adoption and challenges in the acquisition of ebook and streamed video material. His recent book, *The Russian Discovery of Japan, 1670–1800* (Routledge, 2020), explores questions of information transfer in eighteenth-century Russia.

Hollie White is a Senior Lecturer in Libraries, Archives, Records, and Information Science in the School of Media, Creative Arts, and Social Inquiry at Curtin University, Australia. She holds a Ph.D. in Information and Library Science from the University of North Carolina at Chapel Hill, USA, a Master of Science in Library and Information Science from the University of Illinois at Urbana-Champaign, USA, and a Master of Arts in English from the University of Georgia, USA. Before moving to Australia from the United States, Hollie was Digital Initiatives Librarian at the J. Michael Goodson Law Library at Duke University, USA. Her research is around information organisation, institutional repositories, and library assessment.

Bonnie Wittstadt holds a master's in Library Science, with a specialisation in Digital Technology Services, from Drexel University, Philadelphia, USA, and a master's in GIS from Johns Hopkins University, USA. She received her GIS Professional in 2015 with 15 years of work in the industry. She became the first Geospatial Services Librarian/Consultant for Johns Hopkins University in 2014, working on faculty research projects and teaching GIS to students. After developing the library GIS basemap, she worked with the library collection's data to show the most heavily circulated resources to help determine what could be discarded based on usage. Her research interests include food security, neighbourhood redevelopment projects, instructional design, and pretty much anything data.

Foreword

In 2018 we presented a paper titled "User-Focused Mixed Methods Approaches to Assess Collections" at the International Federation of Library Associations and Institutions (IFLA) World Library and Information Congress, which was held that year in Kuala Lumpur, Malaysia. Our presentation was part of a session – Being Guided by Our Users: Using Assessment to Build User-Focused Collections – that comprised a group of people passionate about sharing their experiences to help others. Based on what we heard that day from our fellow presenters and the audience, we knew we could do more to contribute to the increasingly important information practice that is assessment.

Developing out of the IFLA presentation, and expanding in scope, this book focuses on assessment approaches to collections and services. It draws from a geographically diverse set of authors, from the academy and practice, and their lived experiences as information professionals and researchers. Both of the editors have worked as library practitioners and understand the demands, priorities, and stresses of that environment. Many of the authors are current practitioners who deal with these imperatives on a daily basis, yet they have devised and implemented assessment activities in order to better understand how their organisation is meeting the needs of users. The academic authors in this volume have written their chapters from a position of collaboration and personal experience. Some of the approaches presented in the book may be familiar, while others will be more challenging to conceive of as an assessment method that could be implemented in different workplaces. We encourage you, the readers, to explore this book and all it has to offer. We hope that by presenting a range of real assessment approaches, information professionals will find inspiration and an appreciation of how the different approaches can be of benefit to information practice, institutions, and users by enhancing quality, efficiency, and effectiveness.

The information profession, and our cultural institutions more generally, are operating in an age of unprecedented demand for accountability and evidence of benefit. We need to make sure that our information work and our actions in practice demonstrate value and meaning. Assessment allows us to know that value and meaning – to quantify it, understand it, discuss it, and promote it.

Gaby Haddow and Hollie White, Co-editors

Acknowledgements

The editors, Gaby Haddow and Hollie White, are grateful for the support provided by the School of Media, Creative Arts, and Social Inquiry at Curtin University. We would also like to thank the contributing authors to this book, who faced numerous challenges in 2020 as the world grappled with the COVID-19 pandemic. Their commitment to meeting deadlines is much appreciated.

1 Assessment as information practice

Gaby Haddow

Introduction

Assessment of collections and services is now an established and expected component of professional practice in the information sector. Assessment or evaluation – both terms are used – is a means to test how effectively resources are being managed, whether users are satisfied and to demonstrate accountability and impact. The importance of assessment is not unique to the information sector, as Dahler-Larsen (2012, p. 1) writes, "we live in the age of evaluation".

The 'age' demands that assessment goes beyond counting volumes in a collection or users through the door, although these data may also play a role. The information sector is faced with questions such as how a collection or service makes a difference to the community they are designed to serve (Creaser, 2018). Fortunately, the age is one of increasingly sophisticated tools and technologies that can support assessment activities and generate data that will inform and 'account' in meaningful ways.

This book was conceived around the notion that well-considered assessment of collections and services is inherently useful. Assessment can be critical in justifying and accounting for resources and, in extreme cases, existence. It is also a key to the daily activities of practitioners responsible for delivering the best possible information and services to their communities. The overarching aim of the book is to encourage ongoing and sustainable assessment so that it is a part of everyday information practice, rather than viewed as an additional activity. By presenting a range of different approaches that can be applied across a diverse sector, information professionals can adopt assessment practices that are the best fit for their particular environment.

For the purposes of this book, the terms collecting institutions and the information sector, which includes libraries, archives, and digital libraries and collections, are used to describe the environments being discussed. The GLAM (galleries, libraries, archives and museums) sector is the subject of a chapter on the storytelling assessment approach, but, to date, cultural heritage digital libraries, which includes galleries and museums, have applied evaluation techniques that are very similar to those used for digital libraries (Villaneuva & Shiri,

2021). Given that large cultural heritage digital collections, such as Europeana, are still developing appropriate frameworks for evaluation (Europeana, 2014), it is not surprising that assessment in the GLAM sector is still evolving. For this reason, and because the editors' experiences are in the physical and digital collections and services of libraries, it is library environments on which the book focuses.

However, several chapters discuss assessment activities that are applicable across all types of collecting institutions and it is this collective presentation of different approaches that binds the book. Qualitative, quantitative and mixed method approaches are described, to guide information professionals in the why and how a particular form of assessment is relevant and of the context in which it is most suitable. Four chapters are more focused on collections and two chapters specifically discuss services. The book does not include assessment of instructional programmes intentionally, as it has been and continues to be the subject of numerous journal articles and books.

What is assessment and why do it?

The aim of collection assessment has been defined by Johnson (2018, p. 281) as "to determine how well the collection supports the goals, needs, and mission of the library or parent organization"; a definition that applies equally to assessment of services. Johnson goes on to differentiate assessment from evaluation, describing the latter as "more abstract and theoretical". However, many years earlier Baker and Lancaster had used the term 'evaluation' in their 1977 book title, with no explicit definition. The International Federation of Library Associations and Institutions (IFLA) also uses 'evaluation', while 'assessment' appears to be the preferred term in the United States, and both terms are used in the archives and digital collections fields.

In this chapter both terms are used without differentiation. The differences in terminology appear to be an historical artefact and have no real bearing on how the information sector thinks about assessment and evaluation of collections and services. It is, however, useful to consider what the activity involves. According to eminent evaluation scholar Peter Dahler-Larsen (2012, p. 9), there are four components of evaluation:

> (1) an evaluand [the entity being evaluated], (2) some assessment based on some criteria, (3) a systematic approach or methodology to collect information about how the evaluand performs on these criteria, and (4) a purpose or intended use.

While all four factors are important, the "purpose or intended use" of an assessment is the key to determining how an assessment is carried out and what information is needed in that process. In a general sense, assessment is conducted to "affect decisions or actions" relating to the entity being assessed (Dahler-Larsen, 2012, p. 9). Dahler-Larsen describes it as "an artificial or consciously constructed mechanism for creating meaning" (p. 13). The notion of 'meaning' is included in Baker and Lancaster's (1991, p. 1) purpose of evaluation; that for organisations it "must indicate, in some meaningful and measurable way, the results of their services". Baker and Lancaster refer to an earlier work (by Weiss in 1982) that lists the types of decisions an evaluation might inform, generally encompassed by whether to continue a programme; improve or change practices; and allocate resources (p. 2). Resource allocation or "demonstrating value for money spent" (Saponaro & Evans, 2019, p. 180) is frequently mentioned as a reason for assessment and evaluation, but increasingly the information sector is looking for ways to demonstrate impact; that is "what difference does the library service make to an individual or a community?" (Creaser, 2018, p. 87).

Meaningful assessment is not box-ticking. It should "judge, improve, and inform" (Dahler-Larsen, 2012, p. 7) and produce benefits at all levels, from parent institutions to individual staff members, and for the wider community to a single user. Meaningful assessment demonstrates to funding bodies and stakeholders that a collecting institution is paying attention to how effectively it is managing day-to-day operational activities while ensuring the bigger picture is not lost. It is important for accountability sakes, but equally important for development and improvement in an 'age' of constant change.

In practice, assessment is likely to be conducted for discrete components within the broad systems in which information professionals work. For example, effective use of resources may be assessed in relation to expenditure and access to collections, use of space or programme development. Further narrowing is then required, so that an assessment of expenditure on collections will almost certainly focus on a particular part of a collection. Similarly, an assessment to understand impact will have to identify specific programmes to investigate. The initial planning, defining focus and deciding on appropriate methods all contribute to create an assessment exercise that is feasible and sustainable.

History of assessment

Assessment is a relatively new phenomenon for collecting institutions. It loosely parallels declining funding in the sector that occurred post-World War II (Heath, 2011). Standards, which Heath (p. 9) describes as "remarkable in their brevity and explicitness", had been developed for college and university libraries by the Carnegie Corporation by 1935. These standards related to minimum expectations, such as numbers of seats for the student cohort, numbers of volumes and acquisitions spending per student. While this development created a benchmark of sorts, meeting standards of this nature is far removed from providing meaningful information about the performance of a collecting institution that might be expected today. A sophisticated quantitative method for assessing a collection of chemistry journals had been published prior to the release of the Carnegie Corporation standards (Gross &

Gross, 1927), however, collection assessment appears to have been established much earlier, with Johnson (2018, p. 285) noting antecedents back to 1849.

Generally, quantitative approaches to assessment dominated until the late 1970s when F. Wilfrid Lancaster published the first edition of *The Measurement and Evaluation of Library Services* (Heath, 2011). Around this time there was a shift to considering qualitative aspects, such as user satisfaction, so much so that by 1996 Nitecki (p. 181) wrote: "A measure of library quality based solely on collections has become obsolete". The intervening years had also seen increased interest in assessment and evaluation in public, special and school libraries (Baker & Lancaster, 1991).

Assessment and evaluation activities (and its literature) took off in the 1990s. In Europe, *performance measurement* was the term adopted for the first biennial conference on the topic (Heath, 2011). There is a sense in the literature that libraries were a little reluctant to conduct assessment activities prior to this period (Baker & Lancaster, 1991), however that situation changed as "economic conditions necessitated closer control of resources and justification of services" (European Commission, 1995, p. 1).

The development of digital libraries and later digital humanities, which encompasses cultural heritage digital collections and archives, created the need for assessment approaches that addressed criteria unique to their aims and characteristics. In 2000, Saracevic noted the lack of work in evaluation of digital libraries and proposed a conceptual framework to develop assessment criteria based on existing approaches:

- *User-centred*: impact at the social, institutional and individual levels, and usefulness of the interface;
- *System-centred*: performance of the system, processes and content selection, representation, organisation and structure;
- *Traditional library criteria*: collection, information, use and standards;
- *Traditional information retrieval criteria*: relevance, satisfaction, success, index, search and output features; and
- *Traditional human–computer interaction criteria*: usability, functionality, task appropriateness, failures, connectivity, reliability, design features, navigation, browsing, services and help.

(Saracevic, 2000)

A few years later, Saracevic (2004) investigated the types of assessment approaches that had been used in digital library evaluation. He concluded that issues such as the complexity, stage of development, funding and lack of an evaluation culture in digital libraries had resulted in scant attention and no cohesive approach.

In the years that followed the number of digital collections grew exponentially and the term digital humanities emerged. Gooding (2020) argues that digital humanities is increasingly a component of large libraries, and that library and information science has made an important "intellectual contribution" to the digital humanities. This suggests that Saracevic's conceptual framework for digital library evaluation (2000) is appropriate in the wider collecting environment. However, Villaneuva and Shiri (2021), who carried out a systematic review of evaluation studies of cultural heritage digital libraries, recommended that more attention to cultural aspects was needed. The authors argued that while existing frameworks were useful, they needed to be adjusted and adapted to incorporate cultural components central to these collections.

The extensive financial costs involved in developing digital collections suggests that information professionals working in these areas need to explore the best possible methods available to undertake effective assessment in their particular context. A key question to bear in mind was posed by Saracevic (2000, p. 368) in relation to digital libraries, but is equally valid for other GLAM collections: "How are digital libraries transforming research, education, learning and living?"

In 2021, assessment and evaluation are widely understood to be an important component of information practice across a diverse sector: several conferences are now established events, IFLA has a section focused on 'Statistics and Evaluation' and a journal wholly focused on the topic, *Performance Measurement and Metrics*, is in its 20th year of publishing.

Types of assessment

As assessment and evaluation gathered momentum in the information sector, the approaches and tools that could be used also multiplied. Some tools are well known, such as LibQUAL+, which is used by hundreds of libraries to assess service quality, while others are bespoke activities designed for a specific environment and purpose. This discussion, and the following chapters, illustrate the diversity of assessment approaches to enable information professionals to select the most appropriate and relevant methods for their workplace.

Rather than list all the different approaches that can be used in assessment, this discussion explores the ways that *types* of assessment can be conceived. Baker and Lancaster (1991, p. 7) discuss evaluation in terms of scale (macro and micro) and the measure that is sought (effectiveness, cost-effectiveness and cost-benefit). They argue that at the broader level, a *macroevaluation* will indicate whether a 'benchmark' is being achieved, but will not explain "why the system operates at this level or what might be done to improve performance". On the other hand, *microevaluation* "is diagnostic in nature" (p. 9). This approach will provide explanations about performance that can inform decisions about the actions required to make improvements.

Baker and Lancaster (1991, p. 10) also note the difference between *subjective* and *objective* evaluation, with a caution to ensure subjective information is supported by data drawn from other sources. Their example of a subjective evaluation is a subject expert being asked to assess the value of a collection in their discipline. Another example would be asking staff to assess the satisfaction of users after an interaction. In both cases useful information is gathered, but it speaks to only one perspective and is not adequate, alone, for meaningful assessment.

The kind of data gathered is another way to think about types of assessment. *Quantitative, qualitative* and mixed methods are typically described in the literature (Heath, 2011) and there is a place for both approaches in an assessment activity. Some assessment activities, such as those relating to expenditure and extent of use, will naturally demand quantitative data. Others, for instance assessing impact or value to users, will require qualitative information; and many assessment activities will benefit from a combination of the two. Possibly the most important factor to consider in deciding what data are required is that the assessment outcomes will "gain legitimacy" (Dahler-Larsen, 2012, p. 7), and some data will be more appropriate than others in different contexts. This is critical if those outcomes are going to be used to justify changes to services or as the basis for a request for additional funding.

How the outcomes of an assessment activity will be used is directly related to the purpose of an assessment and the measures that are being applied. Returning to Baker and Lancaster's (1991, p. 7) types of evaluation, those measures can be *effectiveness, cost-effectiveness* and *cost-benefit*. Later literature adds *service quality* and *impact* (Creaser, 2018; Heath, 2011). For example, an *impact analysis* by Suffolk Libraries (2019) illustrates how social impact can be measured alongside expenditure, using both quantitative and qualitative data. In many cases the cost of delivering a service or of developing and/or maintaining a collection will be an important factor. However, cost alone, just as opinion alone, will not provide the broader context and perspective needed for decision-making. An example is provided by Carrigan (1996, p. 274), who discusses another measure, *opportunity cost*, in relation to collections. The measure translates just as well to services and, in essence, is the cost to users when expenditure is used for a particular acquisition or service and not on an alternative acquisition or service that may be of equal value to users.

Assessment can also be viewed in terms of time. Baker and Lancaster (1991) differentiate between *formative* and *summative* evaluation. The decision as to which is most appropriate depends upon the purpose and subject of an assessment. That is, formative assessment is undertaken to collect information during the development of a service or programme, whereas summative assessment is used to gain information about a service or programme following implementation. Both forms of assessment will be useful in different situations.

Assessment today

As discussed earlier in this chapter, assessment is an accepted and expected component of management practices in the information sector and beyond.

Changes to the way collecting institutions operate influence the purpose of and methods applied in assessment activities, as do social values. These changes include:

- The ability to make collections available and to deliver services in an online environment;
- Communication and dissemination options for both scholarly and popular forms of information;
- The potential for global access to resources that were once location-specific;
- Automated data collection and reporting systems;
- Publisher and subscription models; and
- The needs and expectations of communities and users.

Although many of the points above are related to technological changes, which can make assessment activities easier and also more challenging, the final point is at the core of why evaluation and assessment is important. First and foremost, collecting institutions operate to serve communities and these are dynamic social entities. Changes to demographics, social norms and workplace roles will affect a community's expectations and needs, and assessment activities should ensure that these are recognised and acted on. The alternative is building collections and delivering services that become less and less relevant.

Similar considerations apply to the organisational environment in which collecting institutions operate because "evaluation is strongly dependent on its social and organizational context" (Dahler-Larsen, 2012, p. 34). That is, the collecting institution, its parent organisation and stakeholders will have goals, processes and constraints that influence the assessment aims, the resources available and the use of outcomes from an assessment activity. In addition, an institution and the individuals managing assessment processes will work within certain values that have the potential to affect an assessment's purpose and approach. Acknowledging these values and any assumptions that are built into an assessment activity will contribute, like the methods used, to the 'legitimacy' of the outcomes.

Assessment is not without its challenges and several were identified in a study of Digital Library Federation members' concerns about assessment:

- Focusing efforts to collect only meaningful, purposeful data;
- Developing the skills to gather, analyse, interpret, present and use data;
- Developing comprehensive assessment plans;
- Organising assessment as a core activity;
- Compiling and managing assessment data; and
- Acquiring sufficient information about the environment to understand trends.

(Covey, 2002, p. 2)

8 *Gaby Haddow*

These challenges are interwoven. The generation of meaningful outcomes relies on a sound assessment plan and the skills to carry out data collection and analysis. In order to assess trends, an ongoing assessment programme is required. Feasibility and sustainability present as issues that need to be addressed, but finding a balance between applying the most appropriate method(s) within resourcing constraints will challenge most collecting institutions. All the issues listed above are relevant beyond digital libraries and are components of different chapters in this book.

A good assessment plan is the overarching framework to counter these factors. It will document and guide an assessment process, ensuring focus and purpose are maintained within the limits defined for the assessment activity. It should also identify the skills and expertise required and a communications plan that ensures staff are aware of why an assessment is important and how it will be carried out. There are numerous templates and models of assessment plans available, and most will include the following:

1 Purpose, rationale and scope (including links with strategic plans);
2 Resources required and staff responsible (including expertise, budget);
3 Data collection methods (including data collection tools);
4 A timeline (including plans for future assessment);
5 Data collection, analysis and interpretation methods;
6 Reporting/dissemination methods and audience; and
7 Responsibilities for translating outcomes to practice and implementing changes.

(Covey, 2002, p. 45; Tatarka, et al. 2010)

Several of the chapters in this book emphasise the importance of an assessment plan; all present ideas that information professionals can use in their assessment practice. The diverse foci and assessment approaches discussed in the different chapters are designed to explain, guide and spark enthusiasm for assessment across the information sector. The authors' examples of why and how an assessment has been conducted will enable readers to determine if a particular approach is suitable for their assessment activities or borrow components for adapting in their environment.

Hoffman provides an excellent overview of the differences between assessment and research in Chapter 2. These distinctions are important because while either form can be used to evaluate collections and services, a decision to use one or the other will impact on planning and processes. Using examples to illustrate assessment and research activities, the chapter steps through the main issues to be considered. Aspects such as the need to gain ethics approval for research, feasibility and sustainability are presented to assist information professionals in making good choices in the planning and execution of an assessment or research activity.

In Chapter 3, Goulding describes how the storytelling method of evaluation can be used and in what context it is an appropriate approach. With a focus on GLAM activities, the chapter emphasises the need for assessment of quality, effectiveness and impact to achieve a 'meaningful' understanding of how users engage with programmes and services. This qualitative approach can make a significant contribution to assessment activities, however, like all approaches, it can present some challenges. Goulding provides an overview of these along with suggestions for minimising them, and concludes with a discussion of the most useful data collection techniques.

Service design and the importance of iteration in assessment is the subject of Chapter 4 by Choemprayong. The author contrasts a typical assessment activity, which may include repeat cycles, with a service design model. This approach sees development, assessment, analysis and refinement occur over multiple cycles until a service is ready for full implementation. It is a way of thinking about assessment in a constantly changing environment and involves prototype testing as an assessment method. The chapter concludes with case studies to illustrate how service design can be applied in practice.

Very few assessment activities are perfect on their first outing and Wells, in Chapter 5, describes the continual improvement of an evaluation of materials availability. Wells shares the experience of an academic library over a period of 15 years, during which time data collection tools were developed, revised and supplemented in order to understand the complex access environment for users. Surveys, focus groups, system logs, document-delivery requests and reports of system problems formed the basis for the multi-methods assessment approach. The author's analysis of the different methods and their contribution to a better understanding of materials availability is likely to be especially useful for readers.

Chapter 6, by Payne and colleagues, provides a detailed discussion about the creation of visualisations for collection evaluation activities. Multiple tools were employed to create a data set that could answer specific questions relevant to the collections team. Information about collection size, borrowing, document delivery and vendor statistics are just some of the data that contributed to the visualisations. The authors describe the major challenges involved in bringing data from different sources together, including the cleansing of data. However, the work has ultimately resulted in effective visualisations that inform, most significantly, the library's understanding of usage of print and electronic resources.

Repository assessment development is the subject of White's Chapter 7. The author gives a brief history of repositories and explores the difference between repository downloads, views and use. Drawing from a project that sought to develop a guide for repository metrics programmes for law libraries, the repository assessment steps include mixed methods that incorporate stakeholder input and repository data. Together, the series of steps and accompanying practical advice provide a plan that can be used to guide a repository assessment activity.

In Chapter 8, quantitative data takes centre stage. Haddow uses a case study to demonstrate that bibliometric approaches to collection assessment are feasible and remain an important source of data to inform decisions about journal collections. With antecedents in the first half of the 20th century, a systematic bibliometric analysis can contribute to a better understanding of whether collections are meeting the teaching and research aims of an institution, if a collection is cost-effective and if backfiles are required. Haddow concludes the chapter by discussing the challenges and limitations of bibliometric approaches.

In the final chapter, Haddow and White bring the earlier chapters together to discuss common themes in the different discussions of assessment. These themes are planning and taking a systematic approach, incorporating iterative processes in assessment activities and using multiple methods to collect data. The authors then go on to discuss impact assessment, an increasingly important consideration for collecting institutions. Impact assessment seeks to identify how services and/or collections make a difference to individuals, groups and communities. It is through impact assessment that collecting institutions can understand how they are contributing to the knowledge and skills, quality of life, and social and economic wellbeing of their communities.

The chapters in this book illustrate how assessment practices have developed from simple notions of benchmarking and counting with a focus on libraries to sophisticated assessment techniques and methods relevant to the broader GLAM sector in which information professionals work today. Two chapters are based on assessment activities in Australia and the United States, however all the assessment approaches discussed in this book are transferrable and not bound by national issues. Some chapters are focused on qualitative methods, others on quantitative approaches, and many describe an activity that incorporates both. The choices open to information professionals are numerous, but several key considerations are common to all. Assessment should be planned, purposeful and meaningful, as Dahler-Larsen (2012, p. 226) argues: "it is a broad social responsibility to think cleverly about evaluation and use it intelligently".

Bibliography

Baker, S.L. & Lancaster, F.W. (1991). *The Measurement and Evaluation of Library Services*. 2nd ed. Arlington, VA: Information Resources Press.

Carrigan, D.P. (1996). Collection development – Evaluation. *The Journal of Academic Librarianship*, 22(4), 273–278.

Covey, D.T. (2002). *Usage and Usability Assessment: Library Practices and Concerns*. Washington, DC: Digital Library Federation. https://www.clir.org/wp-content/uploads/sites/6/pub105_57d70f701af96.pdf.

Creaser, C. (2018). Assessing the impact of libraries – The role of ISO16439. *Information and Learning Science*, 119(1/2), 87–93.

Dahler-Larsen, P. (2012). *The Evaluation Society*. Stanford, CA: Stanford University Press.

Europeana (2014). Europeana Strategy 2015–2020, Impact. https://pro.europeana.eu/post/europeana-strategy-2015-2020-impact.

European Commission (1995). *Library Performance Indicators and Library Management Tools*. Luxembourg: European Commission.

Gooding, P. (2020). The library in digital humanities. In (Eds K. Schuster & S. Dunn) *Routledge International Handbook of Research Methods in Digital Humanities*. Abingdon: Routledge.

Gross, P.L.K. & Gross, E.M. (1927). College libraries and chemical education. *Science*. 66(1713), 385–389.

Heath, F. (2011). The way we have grown. *The Library Quarterly: Information, Community, Policy*, 81(1), 7–25.

Hughes, L.M., Ell, P.S., Knight, G.A.G., & Dobreva, M. (2015). Assessing and measuring impact of a digital collection in the humanities: An analysis of the SPHERE (Stormont Parliamentary Hansards: Embedded in Research and Education) project. *Digital Scholarship in the Humanities*, 30(2), 183–198.

Johnson, P. (2018). *Fundamentals of Collection Development and Management*. 4th ed. Chicago: ALA Editions.

LibQUAL+ (n.d.). LibQUAL+: Charting library service quality. https://www.libqual.org/home.

Nitecki, D.A. (1996). Changing the concept and measure of service quality in academic libraries. *The Journal of Academic Librarianship*, 22(3), 181–190.

Saponaro, M.Z. & Evans, G.E. (2019). *Collection Management Basics*. 7th ed. Santa Barbara: Libraries Unlimited.

Saracevic, T. (2000). Digital library evaluation: Toward an evolution of concepts. *Library Trends*, 49(3), 350–369.

Saracevic, T. (2004). Evaluation of digital libraries: An overview. Paper presented at the DELOS Workshop on the Evaluation of Digital Libraries, Padua, Italy. https://tefkos.comminfo.rutgers.edu/DL_evaluation_Delos.pdf.

Suffolk Libraries (2019). A predictive impact analysis. https://www.suffolklibraries.co.uk/assets/pdf/suffolk-libraries-a-predictive-impact-analysis.pdf.

Tatarka, A., Chapa, K., Li, X., & Rutner, J. (2010). Library assessment plans: Four case studies. *Performance Measurement and Metrics*, 11(2), 199–210.

Villaneuva, E. & Shiri, A. (2021). Methodological diversity in the evaluation of cultural heritage digital libraries and archives: An analysis of frameworks and methods. *Canadian Journal of Information and Library Science*, 43(3), 316–342.

2 Research design and the relationship between assessment and research

Starr Hoffman

Introduction

This chapter addresses the commonalities and differences between assessment and research, looking at the context and purpose of each. Distinguishing whether a given project is research or assessment can assist in selecting an appropriate study design, identifying if and how results should be shared, contextualizing it for various audiences, and determining whether it needs review from a research ethics committee. For instance, clarifying that a project was performed as a local assessment to solve a specific issue may help an audience understand and approach it differently than if it is presented as a rigorous research study intended to make broad generalizations across libraries. Both projects are valuable and are meaningful to share, but each have different intended outcomes.

The terms "assessment" and "research" are increasingly common across librarianship, particularly as the field of library assessment grows (Oakleaf & Kyrillidou, 2016; Killick & Wilson, 2019; Association of Research Libraries, 2020). Since the meaning of these terms varies according to context, I will define their use in this article. Fundamentally, research is intended to contribute generalizable knowledge to a field of study. Assessment's purpose is to evaluate services, spaces, or resources in order to continuously improve them. Assessment-oriented action research aims to fulfill both of these goals.

It is worth noting that many of the research and assessment practices discussed here depend on context, tradition, or local practice. This chapter's discussion should be used as a starting point for developing assessment or research guidelines rather than being applied as strict rules. Social science scholarship often involves ambiguity and judgement calls; this chapter is intended to be informative rather than prescriptive.

Assessment, research, and action research

What is assessment?

I view assessment as a practice that emphasizes the measurement and evaluation of services, resources, and performance for their improvement. In libraries, a culture of assessment emphasizes user needs, facilitates evidence-based decision making, measures what is meaningful, demonstrates value, and seeks to continuously improve (Matthews, 2005; Oakleaf, 2017; Killick & Wilson, 2019). Assessments are often local (geographically bound) and intended to solve a specific problem or inform a decision quickly. When conducted within a single organization the results might remain internal or may be shared more broadly across the field of librarianship. The stages of assessment are cyclical and iterative:

- measure;
- evaluate;
- interpret;
- improve;
- reflect; and
- back to measure.

What is research?

The role of research is to add to an existing body of knowledge. This contribution is usually formalized (as well as made available for critique and replication) through the publication or presentation of results (Shavelson & Towne, 2002). Research in library science makes generalizations about libraries broadly, unlike assessment, which is typically limited to one locale (qualitative research, which is often contextualized locally, is an exception). Researchers may also connect their work to theory. In the social sciences, theory serves the same purpose as laws in natural science, to explain how or why something happens (Shavelson & Towne, 2002).

A research project usually begins by defining the research question to be explored (Hatch, 2002; Shavelson & Towne, 2002; Creswell, 2009; Pickard, 2013). This step often occurs simultaneously with an exploration of existing literature (which can pave the way for an eventual literature review). This is important to contextualize the work and clarify the current research question – to define what is unknown that the researcher desires to discover. The next step may be to define a theoretical framework, however, some research intuits theory at the end (grounded theory), while some does not explicitly connect to theory (Pickard, 2013). Selecting the research design (as well as the methodology, instrument, analysis, variables, or other measures) often follows the identification of a theoretical framework. Next is usually the data collection itself, after which follows analysis and interpretation. The final step is dissemination of results, often in the form of a publication or presentation.

What is action research?

"Action research" is a term for research that is intended to be applied; it aims both to solve a specific problem and to contribute to an existing body of knowledge. Action research is often local or has a local component, and may also be time-bound, similar to many assessment projects. Action research is intended to inform iterative cycles of evaluation (Pickard, 2013). This is similar to assessment's improvement-oriented iterative cycle (although not all action research is assessment-specific). What makes action research "research" is its goal to build on existing knowledge while solving a local problem. Action research balances the goals of local improvement and broader application to the field of librarianship. However, because action research is focused on applicability, not merely broad theory, its research questions tend to be more immediate or direct than typical research questions.

Because action research incorporates aspects of both research and assessment (or other problem-solving applications), the steps in this process may vary. However, to define action research simply, it often consists of the following broad stages:

1. Identify the problem
2. Evaluate the problem
3. Plan the action
4. Implement the action
5. Evaluate the action
6. Reflect
7. (May return to Step 2, as a cycle)

The sequence above may involve several steps from the research process or the assessment cycle, depending on the project. For instance, Step 1 above, "Identify the problem," may involve selecting an appropriate measure (assessment cycle), creating a research question (research process), and investigating related literature (research process).

Differences and commonalities between assessment and research

Context and purpose may distinguish differences between assessment, research, and action research. Assessment is usually performed in one specific context – for instance, at a particular library (local). Because research seeks to generalize from a sample, often that sample involves multiple locations or institutions. Action research's scope may be either local or broad. In terms of purpose, assessment seeks to improve a service, space, or resource, while research seeks to add to a body of knowledge. Action research seeks to contribute knowledge to the field that is also applied to solve a specific problem (local or otherwise). Determining the nature of a given project has significant implications about its procedure and outputs.

Determining if a project is assessment, research, or action research

The purpose of a project often provides telling clues about its type. If the purpose of the study is to make local improvements, to move quickly, or to continuously improve and adjust, then that project is likely geared toward assessment. If the purpose is to make improvements across the field of librarianship, to discover why something happens, to improve practice in a broad context, or to perform a rigorous investigation, then the study is likely research-oriented. If the project's purpose is to make actionable discoveries, such as determining why something happens and then applying that knowledge to solve a local problem, it may be classified as action research.

When determining if a project is assessment, research, or action research, consider the following questions:

- Is the project's purpose to solve a local issue, to examine a problem across the profession, or both?
- Is information needed quickly in order to make a local improvement?
- Are you interested in discovering why or how something happens?
- Who is the primary audience (one library, all librarianship, or both)?
- How do you envision sharing results?

The three examples below illustrate projects that fall into each category.

Assessment example

A university library surveyed students to inform the choice of new library chairs. The survey results were shared locally (at a library staff meeting) and were not published. Because this project was performed for a specific local use (the improvement of a space), was performed at a single location, and wasn't publicly shared in a research article or presentation, it was deemed assessment.

Research example

An academic librarian studied how space is used in libraries across the United States by analyzing floor plans and surveying librarians at over 100 libraries. They then published the results in an article that broadly categorized library spaces. This qualified as a research project because it produced generalized knowledge (often signified by a large population sample or using a common survey instrument) and contributed to the body of research by being published or formally presented.

Action research example (both)

A university library administered LibQUAL+, a common satisfaction survey, to their users. In the case of a common survey instrument, while it may be conducted primarily to inform local changes (assessment), if those results are shared, they also add to generalizable knowledge (research). In this case, library staff specifically used respondents' feedback in the survey section on library space to make changes, such as adding more comfortable chairs to an open area and replacing small tables with those that seat large groups. Library staff then presented the survey results and the changes they implemented at an academic conference, and later published an article. Thus, this project could be classified as action research, assessing in order to make local improvements (improved library space) while adding to the body of knowledge (used a common instrument, produced comparable results, and published results).

Design and methodology

After determining the project's purpose (which may involve writing specific research questions) comes the design phase. Assessment usually proceeds by choosing a metric, while the next step for research is the selection of a research methodology. Action research may involve either of these approaches.

Choosing a relevant metric

Selecting a metric is key to assessment because the metric measures what is being examined – a service, space, or resource. This metric should inform the decision to improve a service or space, to continue or stop an action, or to pivot to something new. When selecting a metric, consider the following:

- What do you want to know?
- What problem are you trying to solve?
- What type of decision are you trying to inform? What information will help you make that decision?
- How do you plan to use this assessment data to make changes?
- What related data do you already gather?

There may be several options for a metric, including pre-existing data related to the project, either from a national dataset or locally gathered data. However, pre-existing data might be a less specific or direct measure of a project's purpose than creating a new metric. Consider which is more important for this project's context: easy-to-obtain existing data with years of past data for comparison? Or specific and meaningful data, even if that means starting from scratch with a new data collection procedure? Examining library literature for example metrics is also good practice and can help identify similar assessments and survey questions. Selecting a metric used by others may make results more comparable across librarianship. If possible, strike a balance between meaningfulness and feasibility.

Choosing a methodology

When designing an assessment project, methodology is not always formally selected, but it may still be a subconscious choice. Often the methodology is determined or highly influenced by the choice of metric, as described above. In a research project, methodology selection generally leads to the choice of data collection, variables, and analysis. The methodology may be as significant as the specific variables chosen to study, because how the research is conducted (method) affects its generalizability and its relationship to past research.

My aim is not to be exhaustive but to provide a brief overview of things to consider when designing a project; there are many thorough sources on research design and methodology (Shavelson & Towne, 2002; Huck, 2008; Lunenburg & Irby, 2008; Creswell, 2009; Pickard, 2013. Additionally, the research methodologies to which I refer here are long-established Western traditions, and do not encompass emerging and other equally valid methods of research, such as community-based participatory research, critical race theory, indigenous methodologies, and others (Becvar & Srinivasan, 2009; Hacker, 2013; Schroeder, 2014; Lilley, 2017; Nicholson & Seale, 2018). What is presented here is only the barest hint of what is possible.

Table 2.1 provides a simplistic (far from exhaustive) look at some potential research methods and practices to illustrate how methodology informs data collection and analysis.

A research design may be quantitative, qualitative, or mixed (aspects of both). Quantitative design seeks to quantify, that is, to ask questions about how many, how often, or when. It often involves numeric data and statistical analysis. It stems from a positivist paradigm that social reality, including human behavior, is tangible and thus knowable (Pickard, 2013). Qualitative design asks the questions why and how, and measures things such as quality, opinion, or feelings. It originates from an interpretivist paradigm that believes reality is constructed by social context and is thus subjective – only knowable in a specific context (Pickard, 2013). Mixed method design takes a post-positivist stance, acknowledging that while human behavior and social reality are tangible, our perception of them and discovery itself are subject to interpretation. This design seeks objectivity in

Table 2.1 Potential research methods and practices

Design	Methodology	Data Collection	Data Analysis
Quantitative	Survey	Questionnaire	Cross-tabulation, correlations
Quantitative	Usability testing	Focus group	Descriptive statistics
Quantitative	Experimental research	Questionnaire (pre-test, post-test)	Hypothesis testing
Qualitative	Ethnography	Observation	Narrative analysis
Qualitative	Case study	Photo diaries	Coding and themes
Mixed Method	Surveys + Ethnography	Questionnaire + Observation	Comparison of conclusions (descriptive stats, narrative)

research as a goal but also views the role of interpretation as significant (Pickard, 2013). Thus, mixed methodology balances a quantitative and qualitative approach.

Surveys are often considered quantitative because their results are easily quantifiable (for instance, Likert items). However, surveys can also measure opinion or feeling, and may be used in any project design. The type of analysis and interpretation of results are what illuminate the purpose behind a chosen project design.

Overview of specific methodologies

Since there are many methodologies in formal research, a few that are also common to assessment or action research are explored below.

Survey research

Surveys are particularly useful for research projects when there is a common instrument (such as the LibQUAL+ user questionnaire) to compare trends across locations or across time. Surveys can obtain information from a large number of people in a relatively short amount of time (compared to focus groups or interviews). However, surveys are best at obtaining simple, straightforward information; for rich data on complex attitudes, use focus groups or interviews. The number of questions and sample size greatly affect the time needed to administer and analyze a survey. Likert-style items present their own advantages and disadvantages (Willits, Theodori, & Luloff, 2016).

In assessment, it is best to evaluate only what can be used to either make a change or a decision. Library surveys often fail this test, asking questions about issues outside of the library's control. To honor participants' time and ensure the relevancy of results, each survey question should serve a specific purpose – thus, questions about unchangeable things are best eliminated. However, in some specific cases there may be reasons to include questions of this kind, including letting people feel heard or gathering evidence to push for change outside the library. The key is to make informed decisions about what is asked, particularly if it is about something that is outside the library's control. Examining each question by considering how a response might be used or responded to may help prioritize which questions are the most relevant and useful.

Ethnography: Observation studies

Observation studies can be rich sources of data on user behavior and are particularly meaningful for assessing how users move through or behave in a space (Foster & Gibbons, 2007). Observations may take the form of written narratives or may be recorded as notes on floor plans that indicate users' locations and activities. These studies are often time consuming due to repeated observations (for instance, once an hour; during business hours; for a week) and the time spent on analysis. However, the process can be streamlined, such as using tablets with customized data entry forms and delegating data collection to multiple people.

Assessment projects can also utilize small-scale observations. For instance, observing users in line at a service desk at different times over the course of a week could inform of desk staffing levels, or perhaps how the line might be better managed within the space (perhaps by adding stanchions). Even such informal observations, performed regularly and recorded, provide insights beyond those obtained from anecdotal evidence.

Focus groups or interviews

Conducting in-person or remote interviews with individuals or facilitating focus group conversations provides detailed, nuanced information. Direct interaction with research participants enables researchers to ask follow-up questions or explore unanticipated comments, leading to unexpected discoveries. This makes these methods ideal for exploring emerging or unpredictable topics.

However, it is time consuming and often expensive to arrange such interactions and may be difficult to recruit participants. Additionally, while the data provided is often rich, it can also be overwhelming in its quantity and in the time needed to analyze it. Skillfully facilitating interviews and focus groups may require training. If performing interviews or focus groups for the purpose of assessment, training may be less important, but reading best practices is recommended. These methods are best used for emerging topics, if the topic of interest is related to attitudes or complex practices, or if surveys will not provide sufficient insight.

Quantitative: Usage data analysis

Many studies are performed with existing data, particularly around use: circulation statistics, full-text downloads, reference statistics, etc. Since this data is used in the normal course of library operations and does not involve human subjects it may be exempt from ethics review, but it is wise to double check with the local ethics committee. This type of research can often be conducted quickly and may be relatively easy to compare across locations. For instance, usage statistics for circulation may be compared for all academic libraries in the United States via publicly available statistics from the National Center for Education Statistics (NCES). Whether used for assessment or research purposes, usage data is often a quick way to examine a topic.

Ethics committees and research oversight

If research involves human subjects (that is, studying people through a survey, observation, or other means) it usually requires oversight from an ethics committee – a group that reviews proposed research under the auspices of a professional organization, educational institution, or government body (Fischer, 2006; Emanuel, et al., 2008). In the United States, they are called Institutional Review Boards (IRB); in the United Kingdom, they are Research Ethics Committees (REC); in Australia, they are Human Research Ethics Committees (HREC). Such review is required as part of government regulation on the oversight of research on humans, including surveys, to ensure ethical practices. Ethics committees seek to ensure that research subjects have voluntarily provided informed consent (and are competent to do so), are treated respectfully, are protected (benefits outweigh the risks of research), are informed about its purpose, and that the research is conducted ethically (Pickard, 2013).

Assessment performed as part of the normal course of library operations is usually not considered research, even when it involves human subjects. However, some assessment projects, particularly those performed in a college or university library setting, may require an ethics review. Recommended practice for academic librarians is to investigate with their college or university regarding each project that involves human subjects (such as a survey). Some ethics committees provide options for an expedited review process for projects in the social or behavioral sciences, or may designate projects performed as part of library operations as exempt. It is good practice to become familiar with the practices of the local ethics committee, and to proactively ask them questions when beginning a new project. This not only ensures that the work meets any local or national requirements but also signifies a responsible and ethical way to approach each project.

Ethics committees use specific definitions to determine what qualifies as research on human subjects. The United States government defines a human subject as "a living individual about whom an investigator (whether professional or student) conducting research obtains: (1) Data through intervention or interaction with the individual, or (2) Identifiable private information" (Protection of Human Subjects, 2016). Australia's National Health and Medical Research Council (2018) more simply defines human research as "research conducted with or about people, or their data or tissue". Thus, a project that gathers information about an individual can be considered research on a human subject.

Although academia abounds with tales of ethical review taking months and causing research delays, this need not be an intimidating process. The foremost practice is to apply for review early, check local review timelines, and build review time into the research plan. It helps to be familiar with the local group's procedure, particularly if they offer training or online guidelines. Contact the ethics committee with any questions before submitting an application, to ensure that it is relevant and follows procedure, and to avoid follow-up questions from the group which could cause delays. Throughout the process, keep in mind that the purpose is to protect human subjects, and to ensure that the research method is relevant and appropriate to its purpose. The ethics committee ultimately exists not to penalize researchers but to make research stronger.

Keep your own values in mind so that the work follows your personal ethical code, regardless of whether any governing body considers it assessment or research. For instance, let's suppose that one of your personal values is the privacy of your subjects. Make it part of your own personal practice to gather as little identifiable information as possible, to keep it stored securely, and to share the results in an aggregated form. Other common research-related ethics are to do no harm; create benefit for research subjects; respect the subjects' time and effort; and consider multiple populations and perspectives. Defining a personal ethical code, even informally, will help ensure your work is done in a respectful and responsible manner.

When assessment becomes research "after the fact"

Sometimes a project begins as a local assessment but then the results are so interesting that they should be shared across librarianship. This is why it is good practice to seek advice from a local ethics committee for assessment projects ahead of time (if they involve human subjects). However, if approval was not sought initially, a formal post-assessment review might still be obtained.

Some ethics committees allow review for existing data gathered in the course of professional practice. To clarify, this is not seeking approval for an obviously research-oriented project after it has already been conducted. Rather, this is seeking approval to use data or other information that was gathered in the general course of library operations for the added purpose of research. There may be limits on what data is used, how it is used, and how it is shared. It is, therefore, important to seek this research ethics approval before sharing results, particularly if publication in a peer-reviewed journal is desired (some journals require evidence of approval from a research ethics committee).

There are some grey areas when sharing results. For instance, publishing results in a descriptive "how we did it" article, particularly in a non-peer-reviewed journal, is quite different from publishing a research article. Similar examples include newsletters, blog posts, posters, and presentations for conferences that do not require accompanying papers. It is good practice to contact the local research office and ask questions about each specific circumstance.

For librarians working at libraries without research offices (for instance, public librarians), this may be more challenging. If seeking input on research practices or rigor, discuss the situation with colleagues, both your local library colleagues and those at other institutions. If planning to seek publication or presentation, contact the journal editors or conference organizers for advice; they may have specific policies dealing with these situations. Another option is to partner on such a project with an academic librarian with access to a research office; the project would then be guided by their local ethics committee. Pickard (2013) also provides further tips on creating ethically responsible research, even when an ethics committee is not involved.

Finally, many assessment projects don't involve human subjects. If the assessment project doesn't involve a survey or observation (for instance, checking circulation statistics or assessing collection development procedures), then "transforming" it into research may involve little fanfare. The United States' Office for Human Research Protections (2018) provides a decision tree for how to determine if a project is 1) research and 2) involves human subjects. However, be aware that some institutions require all projects to be vetted through an ethics committee, rather than making individual determinations of what constitutes "research" or "human subjects".

Data collection

In research and action research, selecting a methodology highly influences how data is collected. In assessment, choice of a metric (as described above in the design phase) guides data collection. Therefore, the data collection phase may be straightforward, carrying out the process of obtaining the data as was decided in the design and methodology phase. However, sometimes these stages are reversed – for some projects, deciding what data to collect occurs before choosing a methodology. Research and assessment processes are fluid and varied, rather than following the discrete stages I have described. They are presented here in a linear format for the sake of clarity and to follow conventions of research publication, but, in practice, they may overlap or occur in different orders. When considering what data to collect for a project, consider:

- What data is most meaningful or relevant to the current study?
- What data is easy or quick to gather?
- What data might already exist?

In particular, there are several reasons to consider using pre-existing data. First, if performing local assessment or action research, it's possible that your library already gathers data related to your project. Repurposing data for multiple uses is more efficient and better practice than gathering new data for each new assessment or research project. It is also faster to complete projects if a new data collection procedure doesn't need to be implemented. Second, using pre-existing national datasets, such as those gathered by national departments of education or library associations, ensures that research is more broadly applicable and directly comparable to other research that uses the same data. Third, using widespread data can make even local assessment more broadly applicable. For instance, by using data that is known to be collected by most or all libraries, such as reference statistics or number of visitors, even local assessment can be transformed into action research (contributing to broad knowledge of librarianship) by being comparable to other libraries that gather that same data. Even if such data isn't an exact match for the project's purpose or research question, if it is related and is regularly gathered by many institutions in a specific way (for instance, in the case of government-mandated statistics), then the results may be more broadly relevant than creating a new variable.

After deciding what data to collect, a data collection instrument must be selected. As the example in Table 2.1 shows, this may take the form of a survey questionnaire, a photo diary, or many other forms. Pre-existing instruments may be located in published research literature, measurement databases such as APA PsycTESTs, or community sources such as list-servs and repositories. For instance, assessment instruments may be found in the Library Assessment Repository (ALA-Core, 2020) or by requesting examples on the ARL-ASSESS email list-serv. Instruments may also be altered or designed from the ground up.

Considering how the results will be used can also inform the adjustment of a data collection instrument so it is more relevant. For instance, when seeking student input on new chairs for a study room, one's instinct might be to ask students which chair they like best, or which is most comfortable, without further specification. Writing out criteria that would be helpful for decision-making about the chairs may reveal if that instinct will provide relevant results. Perhaps the actual information needed is what types of activities the students plan to do in the spaces where chairs will be installed. If students want to stay awake and study, perhaps asking if the chair is "comfortable" doesn't provide enough information. One chair might be comfortable for relaxing but might not be suitable for maintaining alertness while studying. This example also shows why it is good practice to share a project's purpose with participants. It is not only good ethical practice; it helps participants understand how to provide the most relevant information.

Data analysis

Data analysis is often one of the most time-consuming phases of any project, be it assessment, research, or action research. Thus, it is important to plan enough time for this stage. Analysis will be very different depending on the project's design. It might be simple; assessment analysis might produce a few bar graphs of basic counts or a short narrative description of results. Research might be similarly limited to basic descriptive statistics or might involve more complex inferential statistics or complex qualitative analyses. Selecting a specific statistical analysis may be determined by characteristics of the data variables that are studied (Creswell, 2009; UCLA Statistical Consulting Group, 2020).

The initial step in analysis is cleaning the data. For research using numeric data, this may involve a variety of processes such as checking for errors, dealing with missing data, formatting data types, performing calculations, and reshaping (Osborne, 2013). When working on qualitative projects, in which data might be text, photographs, or other non-numeric content, the ways this data are processed are even more complex. However, a basic step common to many qualitative analyses is coding – categorizing data into various themes related to the project (Saldaña, 2016). Analysis for assessment projects may be simpler, although it may still be time consuming (Matthews, 2014). This may involve aggregating survey responses, calculating percentages or totals, and formatting results in a narrative, tables, or charts.

Visualizing data may be as simple as creating a bar chart of counts, or may be a complicated process involving multiple data points depicted by various characteristics, such as color, shape, location, size, etc. (Tufte 1990; Tufte 2002). Data may be visualized using spreadsheet or statistical applications (Microsoft Excel, R, SPSS, etc.), visualization programs (Tableau, Microsoft Power BI), graphics programs (Adobe Illustrator), or a combination of these. However, the value in a visualization lies not in its complexity but in how effective it is at making the analysis easy to understand. Visualizations should explain results, not complicate them.

The most important part of data analysis, regardless of the project, is thinking through it ahead of time – ideally, even before deciding what data to collect. Initially anticipating the analysis is one of the best ways to obtain relevant, efficient results. This principle may seem obvious, but this approach is not common. I find it helpful to sketch out the types of data visualizations (charts, tables, etc.) that I desire, or to write out example sentences for an article or final report. For example, for an assessment project, desired statements might be, "[X%] of students indicated they are very satisfied with the library's document delivery service," or "Graduate students in business and law showed [greater or lesser] interest in expanding inter-library loan services than those in other disciplines." Writing these statements informs the researcher what to ask and how, such as choice of wording, question types, answer options, and relevant demographic data to gather (Fowler & Cosenza, 2009).

Final stages

In assessment, data analysis leads to interpreting the results and then using them to inform making improvements. For instance, if a space assessment shows that more users are occupying group tables and not using single-occupant desks, an improvement might be replacing more desks in that area with large tables. Continuing to observe the area after the improvement is made restarts the assessment cycle, ensuring that the space will continue to adjust and improve as needed.

In research, the interpretation of data analysis leads to conclusions about what the study results mean in the broader context of the field. These conclusions are then shared, usually in the form of a poster, presentation, or publication (such as a research article). Sharing results not only adds to the existing body of knowledge – the very point of research, as mentioned earlier – it also enables other researchers to review, replicate, and/or critique the work. This process is designed so that shared research is rigorous, verifiable, and vetted by a community of peers.

Conclusion

Implications for the practice of assessment, research, and action research

Determining at the outset whether a given project is intended as assessment, research, or action research can guide the selection of an appropriate methodology and the most relevant and useful output for results. This isn't to say that research can't later be used for the purpose of assessment, or vice versa, but considering the primary purpose of the project will lead to selection of the most appropriate method.

It is good practice to document all projects thoroughly, regardless of type. Record practices (steps taken throughout the project), methodologies, and responsibly capture and store data (whether that data is quantitative, survey responses, written notes, or something else). That way, whether planning a research project, doing an assessment that might be published later, or performing an assessment that is kept within the organization but may be repeated, the necessary information will be available. Thorough documentation helps in the research ethics review process, as well as ensuring sustainability of long-term assessments.

It is good practice for any research or assessment project that data containing identifying information should be carefully stored and protected, its access regulated, and should be de-identified and/or aggregated before being shared (Pickard 2013; Erway, et al., 2015). Any information gathered for analysis in an assessment or research project may be considered data – not only numeric data, but also survey results, written notes, and even images. Good data management should be practiced, ensuring that information is appropriately stored and shared so that it can be found again later. This enables replicative research studies or sustainable, comparable assessment results.

Reviewing related literature is important to connect new work to existing practice, research, or theory. This is true regardless of whether a project is assessment, research, or action research. Past work should ground and inform new projects and may also provide valuable lessons learned from others' experiences. Exploring the literature may also uncover existing instruments, such as surveys, that could be used in new projects and may make the process of an ethics review simpler. As such, a literature review is a significant benefit for any project. It can also be useful as a stand-alone work that contributes to broader research by synthesizing work and drawing larger conclusions from it (Boote & Beile, 2005; Grant & Booth, 2009).

Considering the intended audience is a key aspect of scoping each project appropriately. As mentioned in several sections above, choosing a primarily internal (assessment) versus external (research) audience impacts how work is conducted and shared. It should also affect the choice of metric, methodology, and analysis, as results should ideally be easy for the audience to understand and apply. Thus, it is good practice to consider the specific audience, the types of information they absorb best, and in what venues or formats they are most likely to seek out information.

Composing a specific research question helps clarify the purpose of a work, both for the author and the intended audience. Although not required for an assessment project, creating research questions can also help you determine the most appropriate metric or variable to study. Do not underestimate the importance of succinctly summing up a project's purpose in a sentence or two. It is surprising how the necessity of describing a purpose in a few words can illuminate the most relevant way to investigate it.

All of the practices above are provided to guide you, as smoothly as possible, through the assessment or research process, and to lead toward results that are most relevant for each particular purpose. Keeping the end purpose in mind, both when planning the project and throughout its execution, will ensure that each research or assessment project is relevant, realistic, and meaningful.

Bibliography

ALA-Core. (2020). Library assessment repository. Available at: https://ala-core.libguides.com/repository.

Association of Research Libraries. (2020). About page of the Library Assessment Conference. Available at: https://www.libraryassessment.org/about/.

Australian Research Council. (2018). State of Australian University research 2018–19: ERA national report. Australian Government, Canberra. Available at: https://dataportal.arc.gov.au/ERA/NationalReport/2018/.

Becvar, K., & Srinivasan, R. (2009). Indigenous knowledge and culturally responsive methods in information research. *The Library Quarterly*, 79(4), 421–441.

Boote, D. N., & Beile, P. (2005). Scholars before researchers: On the centrality of the dissertation literature review in research preparation. *Educational Researcher*, 34(6), 3–15.

Creswell, J. W. (2009). *Research design: Qualitative, quantitative, and mixed methods approaches*. Los Angeles, CA: Sage.

Emanuel, E. J., Grady, C. C., Crouch, R. A., Lie, R. K., Miller, F. G., & Wendler, D. D. (2008). *The Oxford textbook of clinical research ethics*. New York, NY: Oxford University Press.

Erway, R., Horton, L., Nurnberger, A., Otsuji, R., & Rushing, A. (2015). *Building blocks: Laying the foundation for a research data management program*. Dublin, Ohio: OCLC Research. Available at: http://www.oclc.org/content/dam/research/publications/2016/oclcresearch-data-management-building-blocks-2016.pdf.

Fischer, IV, B. A. (2006). A summary of important documents in the field of research ethics. *Schizophrenia Bulletin*, 32(1), 69–80. Available at: https://doi.org/10.1093/schbul/sbj005.

Foster, N. F., & Gibbons, S. L. (Eds.). (2007). *Studying students: The undergraduate research project at the University of Rochester*. Chicago, IL: Association of College & Research Libraries.

Fowler Jr, F. J., & Cosenza, C. (2009). Design and evaluation of survey questions. In: Bickman, L. and Rog, D. J. (Eds). *The SAGE handbook of applied social research methods*, 375–412.

Grant, M. J., & Booth, A. (2009). A typology of reviews: An analysis of 14 review types and associated methodologies. *Health Information and Libraries Journal*, 26, 91–108. doi:10.1111/j.1471-1842.20090.00648.x.

Hacker, K. (2013). *Community-based participatory research*. Thousand Oaks, CA: SAGE.

Hatch, J. A. (2002). *Doing qualitative research in education settings*. Albany, NY: State University of New York Press.

Huck, S. W. (2008). *Reading statistics and research* (5th ed.). Boston, MA: Pearson A&B.

Office for Human Research Protections. (2018). Human subject regulations decision charts: 2018 requirements. Washington, DC. Available at: https://www.hhs.gov/ohrp/sites/default/files/human-subject-regulations-decision-charts-2018-requirements.pdf.

Killick, S., & Wilson, F. (2019). *Putting library assessment data to work*. London, UK: Facet Publishing.

Lilley, S. (2017). Assessing the impact of indigenous research on the library and information studies literature. *Proceedings of RAILS – Research Applications, Information and Library Studies. Information Research*, 22(4). Available at: http://InformationR.net/ir/22-4/rails/rails1606.html.

Lunenburg, F. C., & Irby, B. J. (2008). *Writing a successful thesis or dissertation: Tips and strategies for students in the social and behavioral sciences* (1st ed.). Thousand Oaks, CA: Corwin Press, A SAGE Company.

Matthews, J. R. (2005). *Strategic planning and management for library managers*. Westport, CT: Libraries Unlimited.

Matthews, J. R. (2014). *Library assessment in higher education*. Santa Barbara, CA: ABC-CLIO.

National Health and Medical Research Council (2018). National statement on ethical conduct in human research 2007 (updated 2018). Canberra.

Nicholson, K. P., & Seale, M. (Eds.). (2018). *The politics of theory and the practice of critical librarianship*. Library Juice Press.

Oakleaf, M. J. (2017). *Academic library value: The impact starter kit*. Chicago, IL: ALA Editions, an imprint of the American Library Association.

Oakleaf, M., & Kyrillidou, M. (2016). Revisiting the academic library value research agenda: An opportunity to shape the future. *The Journal of Academic Librarianship*, 42(6), 757–764.

Osborne, J. W. (2013). *Best practices in data cleaning: A complete guide to everything you need to do before and after collecting your data*. Los Angeles, CA: SAGE.

Pickard, A. J. (2013). *Research methods in information*. London, UK: Facet.

Protection of Human Subjects, 45 C.F.R. § 46 (2016). Available at: https://www.govinfo.gov/content/pkg/CFR-2016-title45-vol1/pdf/CFR-2016-title45-vol1-part46.pdf.

Saldaña, J. (2016). *The coding manual for qualitative researchers*. (3rd ed.). Los Angeles, CA: SAGE.

Schroeder, R. (2014). Exploring critical and indigenous research methods with a research community: Part II–The landing. *In the Library with the Lead Pipe*. Available at: https://www.inthelibrarywiththeleadpipe.org/2014/exploring-the-landing/.

Shavelson, R. J., & Towne, L. (Eds.). (2002). *Scientific research in education*. Washington, DC: National Academy Press.

Tufte, E. R. (1990). *Envisioning information*. Cheshire, CT: Graphics Press.

Tufte, E. J. (2002). *The visual display of quantitative information*. Cheshire, CT: Graphics Press.

UCLA: Statistical Consulting Group. (2020). "Choosing the Correct Statistical Test in SAS, STATA, SPSS AND R." Institute for Digital Research & Education: Statistical Consulting. Available at: https://stats.idre.ucla.edu/other/mult-pkg/whatstat/.

Willits, F. K., Theodori, G. L., & Luloff, A. E. (2016). Another look at Likert scales. *Journal of Rural Social Sciences*, 31(3), 126–139. Available at: https://egrove.olemiss.edu/jrss/vol31/iss3/6.

3 Storytelling for the evaluation of GLAM programmes and services

Anne Goulding

Introduction

The GLAM (galleries, libraries, archives and museums) professions and academic literature have an ongoing preoccupation with identifying the most effective methods and techniques to capture the unique value that our cultural heritage institutions bring to communities and society more generally. Quantitative methods, such as Return on Investment, Contingent Valuation and performance metrics and analytics, have dominated attempts to demonstrate and quantify the value of the services that GLAM organisations provide to funders and other stakeholders (e.g. Yakel & Tibbo, 2010; Jantti & Heath, 2016; Agostino & Arnaboldi, 2018). This is unsurprising given a public sector assessment culture focused on efficiency and measurement. Goulding (2020) suggests, however, that a shift in emphasis in favour of the evaluation of outcomes, quality, effectiveness and impact, rather than just outputs, has led to the search for "more meaningful and context-relevant evaluation approaches" (p. 315). The increasing recognition that quantitative measures only tell part of the story of the value of GLAM institutions has prompted a new interest in narrative methods of evaluation, including storytelling.

Stories provide qualitative information about people's experiences with and perspectives of programmes and initiatives, and while it can be difficult to categorise and draw generalisations from this kind of anecdotal data, they often provide important insights into processes and outcomes and can be used to support numerical data to show impact and innovation. For organisations like GLAM institutions that focus on enhancing individuals' and communities' quality of life, many of the outcomes of the programmes and services they provide are subjective, difficult to measure and not routinely collected by existing data collection processes. Qualitative approaches like storytelling, it has been argued (Guijt et al., 2011), are better at addressing the complexity of the kinds of programmes and initiatives provided by GLAM institutions because they give access to more nuanced information, including the potential for unanticipated outcomes or benefits to be identified.

People's personal stories of how they interact with and experience programmes and services are an important aspect of evaluating the extent to

DOI: 10.4324/9781003083993-3

which they have fulfilled their aims and, outside the GLAM sector, storytelling approaches to evaluation have been used as a powerful way of enabling participants to talk about their own experiences of programmes or initiatives in their own ways. Stories are usually collected by evaluators through exploratory group or individual interviews and, as discussed later in the chapter, a range of techniques for drawing out people's stories and anecdotes about their experiences can be used, making storytelling a flexible and adaptable approach. The analysis of people's stories usually focuses on drawing out common themes and patterns across the different stories collected to give an overview of the key benefits and outcomes for individuals, groups and the community, but specific stories and separate cases can also be highlighted to illustrate notable programme successes and lessons learnt.

This chapter explains the place of storytelling in evaluation, outlines its strengths and challenges, describes and explains some common techniques that can be used for storytelling evaluations, and concludes with a discussion of some examples and applications in GLAM institutions.

Storytelling for evaluation

For the purposes of this chapter, storytelling is defined as the "sharing of knowledge and experiences through narrative and anecdotes" (Sole & Wilson, 2002, p. 6). The term "narrative" is also used in the literature to describe an approach to evaluation aimed at gathering people's "lived stories" (Clandinin & Connelly, 2000, p. 43). Baú (2016, p. 375) points out that while the terms storytelling and narrative are often used interchangeably, they differ in that the story is regarded as data while the narrative conveyed through the story is "the point of analysis"; stories are the containers for narratives that explain and make meaning of people's experiences.

The case for storytelling

Ospina and Dodge's (2005) discussion of the power of stories highlights the unique contribution they bring to evaluation, although they focus on the use of storytelling primarily for research purposes:

> Stories are compelling. When someone tells us a story about his or her experience, we become alert, tuned in, curious. … [S]tories contain within them knowledge that is different from what we might tap into when we do surveys, collect and analyze statistics.
>
> (p. 143)

Chelimsky's (1997) summary of the purposes of evaluation is widely accepted: for accountability; to provide new knowledge; and to improve capability. Storytelling is strongly aligned to the last two. In an evaluation context, the purpose of storytelling is to understand participants' experiences of a programme, initiative or of service delivery (new knowledge) so that changes for the better can be made (improved capability). The premise behind the use of storytelling in evaluation practices, therefore, is that people's stories can give powerful insights into how they use and understand public services and their experiences of social initiatives or programming, with the aim of improving them for all stakeholders.

Widdershoven (2001) notes that it is difficult to assess or improve practice without talking to the people involved, and Ryan and Destefano (2001) explain how a conversational or dialogic approach to evaluation legitimises the voices of marginalised stakeholder groups, particularly. Costantino and Greene (2003, p. 37) recommend the use of storytelling to gain an understanding of people's "contextualized lived experiences" of a programme, explaining how the approach can help programme designers and evaluators better understand "the nature and meaningfulness" of participants' experiences and the interplay of factors or dynamics within their environment that influence those experiences. Their study draws on the work of Kushner (2000, p. xiv), who argues for a personalisation of evaluation, contending that programmes are "subject to situation interpretation and contested meaning".. He suggests that rather than just focusing on and documenting the outputs and outcomes of a programme, evaluators should document the experiences of the people involved, which can then be used "to 'read' the significance and meaning of programs" (p. 11). Costantino and Greene (2003) explain that much of what is significant and meaningful to programme participants is embedded in the stories they tell about it and so the value of taking a storytelling approach to evaluation lies in its ability to help us see and understand the programme from the participants' perspective. Stories offer access to what people "know, think, believe, feel and remember" (Sherwood, 2018, p. 89).

Combining approaches

Despite the comment in the Introduction about a perceived shift away from an obsession with statistics and towards a more nuanced approach to evaluation, a focus on outputs and measuring remains prevalent in many organisations, including GLAM institutions. Poll (2018, p. 90) writes of the requirement of museums to provide "hard data", while Voorbij (2010, p. 274) found that cultural heritage institutions consider web statistics a "critical success factor". While the requirement by certain groups of stakeholders for figures and statistics has been noted (Goulding, 2020), GLAM organisations are also seeking ways to bring colour and a human face to the many facts and figures we collect about the use of our services. There is no doubt that statistics and metrics provide useful and easily analysed snapshots of engagement and satisfaction with GLAM programmes and activities. Schrag et al. (2015) suggest, though, that data in the form of statistics do not always explain the full impact of a programme or initiative, and using stories alongside numerical metrics can provide a compelling narrative of impact as perceived by participants and our communities. Individual users or community members telling stories about their experiences with programmes or services are likely to include different information than that provided through more conventional evaluation surveys often distributed, providing insights into perceptions and experiences that we might otherwise overlook. Another compelling reason for including storytelling alongside other data gathering in evaluation activities connects with the point made above about improving our users' experiences. As Goulding (2020) notes, GLAM organisations should be seeking not only to *prove* the value of the services or programmes we offer, but also to *improve* them, and this requires a move away from a summative approach, focused solely on measuring results, towards a formative stance, where the aim is to understand what changes we need to make to enhance people's experiences. Combined with statistics giving an overview of participant satisfaction and reactions, storytelling can provide us with a rich source of data that detail how, why and for whom programmes and services work, or do not.

The strengths of storytelling for evaluation

Within this discussion of the role of storytelling in evaluation, the advantages of incorporating the practice into our evaluation approach appear obvious, but they are further elaborated in this section with a focus on how storytelling can reveal different stakeholders' expectations and experiences of a programme or initiative, and how the deeper involvement of programme participants and community members in evaluation processes can ensure we privilege their voices. Finally, we consider how storytelling methods can enliven and bring variety to programme evaluation reports.

Clarifying complexity and establishing connections

Storytelling is beneficial in situations where we lack clarity or certainty about outcomes and why things are happening the way that they are, helping us build an understanding of complex dynamics between our users and our services that may not emerge through other methods. Stories can reveal ineffective practices, processes and policies, and may help us identify ways of overcoming them so that we can make a convincing case to senior management and funders about why and how things need to change. The benefits of the personalisation of evaluation have already been noted, and the subjective nature of stories is another strength often emphasised, with Wagenaar (2001, p. 112) suggesting that "the personal is a window onto the general" and that this kind of idiographic approach can help us capture insights into difficulties or issues that would be unlikely to emerge from the more conventional evaluation methods commonly used (e.g. post-programme evaluation questionnaires). Storytelling has long been acknowledged as a powerful way of addressing organisational problems because it helps raise awareness of differing perspectives within the workplace (Mitroff & Kilmann, 1975). Similarly, in an evaluation context, stories can deepen our understanding of the different realities of all our participants, helping us recognise that people within our communities are likely to perceive and experience programmes or services in diverse ways. A good example of this is explained in an article by Cieslik et al. (2020). They evaluated a project that involved local people of an Andean community in environmental monitoring of their own mountain ecosystem, including tracing rainfall, temperatures and wind power. To evaluate the success of the participatory monitoring, the team took a narrative approach that involved interviews with three groups of people: the researchers who designed the project; the environmental NGO that helped implement it on the ground; and members of the Andean community who were involved in the project or who had an interest in its outcomes.

Their quite simple approach to gathering the stories of their participants provides a good, clear model for exploring participant or community reactions to programmes or services in GLAM organisations. Beginning with a "narrative stimulus" – an initial open question – participants are invited to talk about their experiences in their own way, highlighting what is important for them:

- Could you tell me the story of [this project/service/programme/initiative]?

Participants can then be prompted to elaborate using questions such as:

- Describe, from your perspective:
    a   how/why it began
    b   what happened
    c   where it is supposed to lead.

As discussed in a later section, although this is a good open question, encouraging participants to focus on the most important aspects from their perspective, it may be a little daunting for some of our users in a GLAM context, particularly those not accustomed to speaking out or being asked for their opinions. Rather more "scaffolding" or gentler introductory questions may be required in those circumstances. Nevertheless, in Cieslik et al.'s (2020) study, the analysis of the narratives revealed through this approach identified notable discrepancies between the different stakeholders' perceptions of the purpose and outcomes of the project. While the researchers' focus was on the successful involvement of local people in a citizen science project, the people themselves were more interested in the results and what this meant for their livelihoods, and the NGO was concerned with the evidence of the damage to the ecosystem the project revealed and how this might raise local people's awareness of the need for sustainable practices.

This example is a good demonstration of the fact that different people, depending on their perceptions and values, will often have different perspectives and interpretations of incidents, and may even tell different versions of events when asked. In this way, stories can also be helpful for shedding light on the relationships between all the stakeholders and participants involved in a programme or initiative, as well as the different meanings that different groups of people attach to their experiences of GLAM services and programmes. Storytelling can thus be viewed as a participatory, collaborative approach to evaluation, and Cooper (2014) suggests that it is an inclusive approach that can help forge connections between participants and stakeholders, resulting in new and more rewarding interactions and communications between the different actors involved.

Democratising evaluation

Following on from this, storytelling is also considered an important way of democratising evaluation practice (Ryan & Defestano, 2001). Kushner (2000) notes how participants' or citizens' voices are often missing from programme evaluations, and this is particularly so for the "least powerful" (Cooper, 2014 p. 148), whose stories, once heard, can lead us to significantly improve practices and outcomes for their benefit. The storytelling approach may also be especially appropriate for the evaluation of GLAM programmes or services involving communities with strong cultural traditions of oral storytelling, particularly relevant for those working with Indigenous communities. Keene et al. (2016) draw on their experiences of tracking and reporting tribal demonstration programmes in the North American context that gave grants to Indigenous tribes to promote self-sufficiency and stability among needy families (Ahonen et al., 2016). They highlight how tribal communities have long used storytelling to transmit language, traditions and beliefs through the generations, and they encourage evaluators to make the most of this tradition by privileging the use of stories and storytelling to evaluate the implementation and outcomes of programmes and initiatives. The First Nations participants in Johnston's (2013) study of the evaluation methods used in a wide range of Canadian Federal programmes covering health, social welfare, social justice and education initiatives confirmed that they preferred a reciprocal, participatory evaluation process, ideally within their communities, based around storytelling, as this is an accepted and essential characteristic of First Nation learning and communication practices. The benefits of the sharing experience of storytelling were emphasised, as was its focus on context, whether that was the context for the individual, their family, First Nation or national.

Storytelling is therefore positioned as a culturally relevant approach and method for evaluation of programming among Indigenous peoples, and could be used to good effect when reflecting on the use of value of GLAM programmes and services for Indigenous peoples. Chouinard and Cousins (2007), reviewing the literature on culturally competent evaluation, recommend the use of participatory approaches like storytelling to enable those in Indigenous communities to be active participants in the process, rather than passive agents, and write that this can be achieved through engaging community members in reflective dialogue akin to their cultural oral traditions. Similarly, in Aotearoa New Zealand, Cavino (2013) notes that a culturally safe approach to evaluation includes responsiveness to context and, for Indigenous peoples, this means privileging data collection methods like storytelling and oral history. She gives an example of the evaluation of a programme for young urban Māori women that incorporated aspects of a *He Taniko* design, described as a "distinctly female framework based in the world of weaving" (p. 347). Represented by a weaving together of ideas and information within organised female peer groups, the approach enabled the discussion of a depth and breadth of issues important to the participating *wahine* (women) on their own terms, allowing them to share their *purakau* (stories) in the context of their family, culture and community support.

Introducing variety

Alongside these philosophical strengths of a storytelling approach to evaluation, there are other more practical benefits for GLAM organisations. Perhaps the most persuasive of these is that stories are interesting and engaging for participants, evaluators and decision makers. Survey fatigue can mean that programme participants or service users do not always complete the common, standard evaluation forms that are often distributed following a programme either with thought or, perhaps, at all. Similarly, the conventional evaluation techniques that often focus on "how many?" or "how much?", rather than evidence of how people's lives have been changed, can be frustrating for all those involved in running a GLAM programme or service. Focusing on the health context, Fadlallah et al. (2019) discuss how narrative information can be more useful and compelling than statistical data in some circumstances, and explain how personal stories of breast cancer have been instrumental in changes made to health policy in the United States. Although, in the GLAM sector, we collect reams of facts and figures on collection use and user behaviour, when it comes to programme or service evaluation, statistical data often lacks the nuance and sensitivity required to make good decisions about their further development or continuation.

Costantino and Greene (2003) found that the staff and participants of a programme that they were evaluating in rural mid-west USA turned naturally to stories to explain and describe their experiences, to the initial bewilderment of the authors who were undertaking semi-structured group interviews with a clear list of questions that they wanted answered. As Elliott (2012) suggests, most people like telling stories and anecdotes and enjoy being listened to. She describes how stories are inherently social and participants will often spontaneously provide stories during research or evaluation interviews, much as Costantino and Greene (2003) found. In their study, after their initial dismay at not having their list of questions answered directly, they decided to "Go with the flow" (p. 40) and let their interviews turn into mini-storytelling events that captured participants' experiences, meanings and emotions in relation to the programme.

Evaluation reports that include human stories evidencing the value and impact of GLAM programmes or initiatives can also make a welcome change for administrators and funding bodies. The inclusion of stories presenting the lived world of participants can facilitate a more in-depth appreciation and understanding of a programme or service's meaning for our communities and may be more accessible and readable (Costantino & Green, 2003). It is likely that the people we want to influence are more likely to pay attention to statistics and data if they first hear a story that appeals to their emotions. Sukop (2007) recommends incorporating excerpts or vignettes that highlight participants' growth and how programmes have helped them overcome difficulties in their lives. She suggests that compelling human-interest stories "speak to" funders and policymakers, capturing their interest and strengthening advocacy messages. Set alongside attractive visuals and summaries of statistical data, short extracts from stories or examples of key incidents can provide a rich experience for readers of GLAM evaluation reports.

The challenges of storytelling for evaluation

Despite the compelling reasons to use storytelling as part of our GLAM evaluation processes, highlighted above, the practice is not without its challenges. Keene et al. (2016) detail the common issues experienced by evaluators taking a storytelling approach, including negative perceptions of the validity and rigour of stories as evaluation information, the time it takes to gather and make sense of stories and the skill needed to draw people's stories out of them effectively. They also suggest ways in which the challenges may be overcome.

Legitimacy and representativeness

Perhaps one of the most difficult to address is that, although stories are engaging and can bring a human touch to GLAM evaluation practices, they can also be dismissed as mere anecdote and lacking the legitimacy of the more common quantitative approaches we often use in GLAM organisations. To some extent, the use of storytelling for evaluation involves a paradigm shift both for practitioners evaluating GLAM services or programmes and for those managing and funding them. Organisational culture is often resistant to change, and it is likely that some will argue that an individual story provides a snapshot of one person's experience, from one perspective at one point in time, rather than the statistically detailed reports of use and reach that are common across our sector. Although, as described above, the idiographic approach has been celebrated as a strength of storytelling, others will see it as lacking rigour and generalisability and likely to be biased. Cieslik et al. (2020)

argue that, in fact, a storytelling approach is *less* open to bias than more conventional interview-based evaluation methods because the participants focus on what is important to them about their experiences rather than the evaluator imposing an external protocol and structure. Drawing on their experiences of storytelling-focused evaluation, they also insist that the aim of this kind of narrative evaluation is not to reveal "the truth", but rather to gather a range of truths from programme participants that, so long as they are consistent, reasoned and coherent, are all legitimate.

Nevertheless, questions may be raised about the representativeness of the participants' stories. Krueger (2010) suggests that these queries can be answered through three strategies that should guide us when taking a storytelling approach in GLAM organisations:

1 Collect a sufficient number of stories so that patterns or trends across them can be identified.
2 Invite experts to comment on the extent to which the stories are representative. This could be GLAM service staff working closely with the communities/individuals involved, or those of other agencies.
3 Invite the storyteller to comment on how far they think their story fits with those of others, or the extent to which they felt fellow participants experienced the programme in a similar way.

Another response is to focus on the narrative contained in stories rather than the individual accounts themselves. Lessons learnt or common experiences should be drawn from across the stories to build evidence about a project or service and support the credibility of the approach. Keene et al. (2016) also recommend that we should be very clear about how stories were collected, interpreted and verified, and note that this can take time, which relates to the next challenge of storytelling.

Time consuming

Keene et al. (2016) note that stories rarely emerge in perfect form for sharing and they often require substantial editing, verifying and reworking to identify and clarify the key issues related to a programme's success, or otherwise. Costantino and Greene (2003) describe how they spent a considerable amount of time retelling their participants' stories to highlight the key elements appropriately while remaining true to the original telling, but note "the significant challenges of writing a good story, one that is engaging and compelling" (p. 48). They also raise the issue of "truthfulness", querying how we should handle stories that we know probably contain some exaggeration and "blarney" (p. 47), as well as stories that are boring or not told in an engaging manner. We know that our users often enjoy a good chat when making use of our GLAM services, but while most people may like telling stories about their lives and experiences, not everyone can do so in a way that captures our interest. The challenge here when writing up our report of a storytelling-focused evaluation is to find a way of raising awareness among our readers of the way that the story was told and the positioning of the teller, without casting doubt on their account or devaluing their experiences.

As well as the time taken to verify and frame the narratives appropriately, storytelling is not a quick and easy method of evaluation for GLAM organisations. To ensure a clear understanding of experiences, and to avoid some of the criticisms of rigour and representativeness discussed, we may need to involve a wide range and perhaps large number of service or programme participants, and collecting their stories will take time, as will the transcription and processing of those stories. Finally, while many of us tell and listen to stories in our everyday and work lives, as noted above, eliciting stories for evaluation purposes is a skill and may require training, particularly with some of the more structured and systematic approaches and techniques now considered.

Techniques used in storytelling for evaluation

It is important to note that although much of this chapter has focused primarily on the gathering of stories from GLAM programme or service users, all stakeholders involved in the service or programme being evaluated should have the opportunity to tell their stories about their experiences with the project or initiative. Those delivering programmes or services often know more about how they are run and how successful they are than their managers, and funders or administrators also have a unique strategic perspective. All programme or service stakeholders should therefore be involved in the storytelling process. Kreugar (2010 notes, though, that getting a good story out of someone is sometimes more difficult than we may anticipate and, as noted earlier in the chapter, asking a user to "tell me a story" may be met with a blank look. So, when evaluating GLAM programmes or services, we need to consider how best to encourage our participants to explain how something happened, what was meaningful and what did or did not work.

Individual and group interviews

Interviews, both individual and group, are generally a key feature of evaluations using storytelling. Individual and group interviews both have their advantages, with the former more appropriate when there is a power imbalance or potential for tension/conflict among participants and the latter helpful when our participants are nervous and feel more comfortable being one of a group – "safety in numbers" – and also when they can remind one another of incidents or confirm the sequence of events. As discussed, storytelling interviews differ from more formal evaluation interviews where there is a clear protocol and list of questions we want participants to address. While storytelling interviews still revolve around asking participants questions and using prompts to draw them out, the questioning is far more open-ended than in more conventional interview approaches, aiming to encourage our users to share stories from their perspective about their experiences. The questions should therefore be conversational, giving our participants a high degree of control and creating a space where their stories can emerge. Examples of questions we can use to encourage people to tell the story of their experiences with one of our programmes, services or initiatives include:

- Can you tell me a little about what led you to become involved with [the programme/service]?
- What were your past experiences of this type of programme/activity/service?
- What did you expect it to be like? Was the reality any different? How?
- Can you tell me about your involvement with [the programme/service]?
- What kinds of activities did you participate in during [the programme/service]?
- What did you learn/gain during [the programme] OR through using [the service]?
- What do you think was the best/worst thing about [the programme/service]?
- How would you change [the programme/service] if you could?
- What difference has [the programme/service] made to your life?

Keene et al. (2016) recommend story circles as a good group technique, especially among those from cultures with a strong oral tradition where they have long been used as a method for sharing perspectives and information. They explain that story circles can be considered a type of group interview, but instead of asking the group a series of questions, the evaluator asks the group to focus on one particular topic or theme. Although probably better for gathering users' experiences of one-off programmes, projects or initiatives, they could be used to evaluate on-going services in a GLAM context too, using prompts such as:

- The thing that led me to become involved in this programme/project was ....
- What I have learned from being a part of this programme/project is ....
- The reason I use this service is ....
- The benefits of this service for me are ....
- Some issues/challenges I have faced with using this service are ....

To use the story circle technique, there should be a group facilitator from the GLAM organisation or possibly an independent evaluator. In response to the prompts, the group leader or facilitator asks everyone in the story circle to share a story about their experiences from their personal viewpoints, one by one, and asks the other group members to listen without interruption or comment, except to perhaps say when it is their turn, "So-and-so's story reminds me of something that happened to me ...". After everyone has told a story, the facilitator should leave enough time for group members to comment generally on what others have said.

Critical Incident Technique

As already discussed, sometimes it is difficult to draw users' stories out of them, particularly if they are nervous or shy. To overcome this and to stimulate participants' reflection and storytelling more generally, we might want to use a couple of specific techniques during our interviews to help them recall and communicate their experiences. First, the Critical Incident Technique (CIT) (Flanagan, 1954) is a helpful way to encourage our participants to talk about any particularly notable experiences they had with a programme or initiative. After first putting the participant at ease, perhaps using some of the general questions about their involvement with the programme or use of the service listed in the previous section, we then move on to asking participants whether they can remember and describe an unexpected or significant event or incident that happened during the programme or service that made them feel particularly strongly positive or negative about it. Participants should be encouraged to describe the event/incident in as much detail as possible, helped by further questioning/ prompting if necessary to clarify what actually happened, who was involved, what was the cause, what were the consequences and, importantly, what it meant for them. Here, we are not only trying to hear and gather accounts or stories of our users' experiences, but also the meaning that they attach to them. The types of questions we can ask to encourage this include:

- Thinking about your experiences with [the programme], can you tell me about a positive or successful experience you had?
   a   What made this a positive/successful experience for you?
- Thinking again about your experiences with [the programme], can you tell me about a negative or unsuccessful experience you had?
   a   What made this a negative/unsuccessful experience for you?

To further probe or develop our participant's story of their critical incident, we can follow up with questions like:

- Can you give me a little more detail about what happened (the incident)?
- What led to the situation?
- What was your response?
- What was the result?
- How did it make you feel?

Using this kind of structure, we can use the CIT to provide an opportunity for programme participants to recall and articulate specific details, which can give us a valuable insight into their experiences of GLAM programming or services, enabling their voices and priorities to be heard.

Most Significant Change

The second technique that can help elicit users' experiences through storytelling is the Most Significant Change (MSC) technique (Davies, 1998). We can use the MSC technique to gather stories about changes that our participants have experienced during, and as a result of, a programme or initiative. It can be particularly effective at highlighting outcomes of personal significance and value for them and is often successful at revealing unexpected or unintentional impacts, beyond those envisaged by us as programme designers or project staff. Drawing on Cooper's (2014, p. 149) evaluation of a youth work initiative, a good open question focusing on a specific GLAM project, initiative or programme would be:

- Looking back over the last month or so, what do you think was the most significant change that occurred for you as a result of coming here/your participation in this programme?

It may be desirable to be a little more directive, as Choy and Lidstone (2011) were in their evaluation of a leadership capacity building course, by asking participants:

- What positive or negative changes have you observed as a result of your participation?
- Which changes do you consider most significant?
- Why do you consider those changes most significant?

A similar method is collecting "stories of change" (Roughley, 2009), based on the following series of questions:

- A beginning – What was the/your situation at the start of the programme?
- A middle – What happened as you became involved with the programme? What kind of activities did you become involved with? What support was provided and by whom?
- An end – What is different now compared to the beginning of the programme? What/who made the changes occur?
- Why this is significant – Why are these changes important to you?

Stories elicited through these techniques can help us demonstrate how GLAM programmes or services have impacted on the people most directly involved with them, and our communities more generally.

Digital storytelling and arts-based techniques

The techniques discussed so far involve in-person, synchronous communication, but another method we might use to allow GLAM programme participants to share their experiences is digital storytelling. A digital story is a short (two to three minute) multi-media video clip combining narrative, visual and performance media to express an individual or community story (Lal et al., 2015) and, as such, seems to align well with GLAM institutions' focus on the collection, curation and dissemination of stories about the lives of individuals, communities and whole nations. We can make use of digital storytelling to understand how individuals experience our programmes or initiatives and possibly as stimulus material for more in-depth evaluation processes. Mathison (2015) suggests that digital storytelling is a particularly useful method for undertaking evaluations of youth programming, but it is a relevant and useful technique for all ages, as demonstrated by the evaluation of a peer support project for Aboriginal adults living with diabetes in the Saskatchewan province of Canada (Public Health Agency of Canada, 2011). A workshop led by trained consultants created short (two to four minute) stories focusing on the storytellers' lives and how the programme had helped them. The stories were not only important for evaluation purposes but were also recorded and used to disseminate and promote the benefits of the programme among the target population.

A related method is PhotoVoice, a method commonly used in participatory research and evaluation. Here, participants are asked to represent their experiences and their feelings about those experiences by photographing scenes or events that capture their lives. This is followed by a discussion or conversation with evaluators or programme staff to explain and explore the photographs and the stories and meanings behind them. Another highly participatory method, PhotoVoice gives programme participants the opportunity to document their experiences and any concerns from their own perspective. As described by Hunter et al.'s (2020) use of PhotoVoice to evaluate a college preparation programme, programme participants are given a handout with instructions for the PhotoVoice activity and/or have it explained in person. The instructions ask them to take photographs in responses to one or two key questions. In a GLAM context these could include:

- What is digital technology for you?
- How do you use digital technology?

Krutt et al. (2018) used a series of prompts rather than questions, which, adapted for the GLAM context, could include:

- Take five pictures of what the [GLAM institution] means to you.
- Take five pictures that explain how you feel when you're at the [GLAM institution].

- Take five pictures of your favourite things about the [GLAM institution].
- Take five pictures of things you would like to see more of at the [GLAM institution].

Following the taking of the photographs, the discussion or conversation with participants asks them to:

- Describe the photo.
- Explain what is happening in the photo.
- Explain why they took the photo.

This could take place on an individual basis or in a group format, depending on the users involved and their confidence and comfort in both situations.

There are other arts-based methods for collecting stories that GLAM organisations could consider, as described by Keene et al. (2016) and Sukop (2007), including scrapbooking, story quilting and theatre or performance-based techniques. In all cases, participants are generally asked to respond to a question or a prompt, and the presentation of the final artwork can be followed by further discussion and storytelling. Again, in a GLAM context, these techniques may be particularly helpful and appropriate for those communities with rich traditions of telling stories through songs or poems and through crafting.

Analysing, writing up and presenting the stories

The analysis of stories is primarily determined by the objectives of the programme. In analysing the stories collected, we need to bear in mind the following:

- What did the programme aim to achieve?
- Is there evidence in the stories that the objectives were met? If so, how?
- If not, why not?

Other questions we may ask ourselves when reading through participants' stories are as follows:

- What was the context of this programme?
- Who did the programme work for? Why did it work for some and not others?
- Were there needs that were not anticipated?
- Were there significant key events?
- Were there any unintended or unexpected positive or negative outcomes?
- What kinds of emotions are expressed in the stories?
- What meaning did it have in participants' lives?

Pastor (2020) recommends a participatory approach to writing up the stories. She explains how she shares the transcript of the interview/conversation with her participants, who are invited to highlight extracts that stand out to them and explain why. She takes these into account when writing the evaluation story, a draft of which is given to the participants who can make changes until they are satisfied that the story conveys their experiences effectively. As noted previously, the presentation of the results of an evaluation involving storytelling is not straightforward. Sukop (2007) makes the important point that different approaches to disseminating the results of storytelling evaluation will be required for different stakeholders, relevant for those of us in the GLAM sector who often have multiple constituencies to consider, including users, staff, funders and often external partners and agencies too.

Costantino and Greene (2003) opened their official evaluation report with three stories and also included many quotes and story extracts alongside their key findings. Within evaluation reports, we should try to use stories to build evidence about programmes or services rather than just using them in isolation, although, as in Costantino and Greene's (2003) case, providing two or three longer stories with extracts and quotes from others to support points or to offer an alternative perspective can be a useful way of adding life and colour to a report on a programme or project. It is probably a good idea not to use all the stories collected, though, as advised by Keene et al. (2016), but rather highlight the stories that are notable for some reason, including those that capture common experiences of all/most participants and/or those that identify unexpected or unusual outcomes, as these can provide important lessons for future programme planning and design. Although we might want to edit some stories to make them easier to read (or to preserve someone's anonymity), it is important to try to convey participants' unique voices as accurately as possible, including presenting the stories in the first person.

As noted previously, using stories or even brief vignettes or extracts from stories alongside quantitative data brings life to the communication of key messages through statistics. Supporting the reporting of outputs and numbers with an account from a participant that reinforces the message gives a human face to collected data (Sukop, 2007). Vignettes can be short stories or strong personal statements from programme participants that encapsulate their experiences of the programme and its outcomes. Blodgett et al. (2011) explain three types of vignettes that can be usefully employed in programme or project evaluation reports:

1. Those that present a *portrait* of an individual programme participant – their character and experiences based on what they said in an interview or discussion.
2. A *shapshot* of what was observed in a particular situation during the programme or as a result of the programme.
3. A *composite* that amalgamates a range of programme participants' experiences into one holistic narrative.

Vignettes can provide a rich, vicarious experience for the reader about a particular participant's experience with a programme, and should provide an account of an individual's experience and include some appealing detail, characters and some plot (Fadlallah et al., 2019). As with all stories, vignettes should have a beginning, middle and an end, and be very clear as to how the anecdote explains or illustrates key findings of the evaluation.

Storytelling for evaluation in GLAM institutions

As long ago as 2003, Costantino and Greene noted the increase in interest in the use of narrative in evaluation, and yet there remain few examples of the practice within the GLAM sector, although their potential has been noted. In the library sector, Calvert and Goulding (2015) identify narratives as being simple to understand and able to capture value not easily measured, while Dando (2014) suggests that the use of stories, unlike raw statistics, can provoke an emotional response in the readers of evaluation reports. Schrag and colleagues (2015) also highlight the potential of storytelling in their discussion of the Global Libraries Data Atlas, which aims to present public library data in a dynamic, interactive way. While they focus primarily on describing the output-oriented "Common Impact Measurement System", devised for the Bill and Melinda Gates Global Libraries programme, the authors also emphasise the importance of adding "qualitative context" (p. 11) in the form of personal stories using some of the techniques discussed above, including digital storytelling.

Organisational storytelling in GLAM

Apart from these examples, there is scant literature and few examples of storytelling for evaluation in our sector. Searches in relevant bibliographic databases did reveal studies of organisational storytelling in GLAM organisations, however, indicating that storytelling techniques are not entirely unfamiliar to GLAM professionals and institutions. Eicher-Catt and Edmondson (2016) describe how, as part of a strategic planning exercise, narratives were collected from public library staff in York County, Pennsylvania. Although not an evaluation exercise, the authors argue that librarians are beginning to understand the value of stories to communicate with stakeholders both within and outside the library walls. They contend that, "Quantitative data do not typically speak to the heart of the listener" (p. 219), and argue for the development of persuasive narratives to reach out to funders and the wider community. The narratives they collected were solicited through interviews guided by eleven open-ended questions. Unfortunately, the questions asked are not all listed in the paper describing their experiences, but in their findings section they describe asking participants to narrate their experiences of going to a public library for the first time, and also asking, "In what ways has the library changed people's lives?" (p. 211). Another question asked the participants to tell them a story about a patron who had impacted them the most as a staff member. The authors identified that some of the narratives had characteristics of "sacred bundle" stories, described as representing the organisation's "heart and soul" – significant values and norms that have become embedded in the organisational identity (p. 213). Other stories were identified as "springboard stories" – stories that can spark action leading to organisational learning and change (p. 216).

In another account of organisational storytelling in the GLAM sector, Tilley (2016) describes her experience of gathering and using stories to connect with her library's users, in this case with university students in library instruction sessions. She gives examples of a range of stories she used in the sessions, which others in the sector could replicate or adapt, including this one:

> A few years ago, Abigail came to see me just one day before dissertation hand-in day with a query about a quote she was using that was crucial to her argument, for which she had all the bibliographic details, but not the relevant page number. If you were in this situation, what would you do?
> (Tilley, 2016, p. 183)

Tilley (2016) explains that she uses this story early on in the dissertation workshop and it seems to capture the students' imagination as they all want to know the outcome. She also notes that it allows others to air similar experiences and relax, facilitating more open group discussion overall. Tilley (2016) argues that stories change learners' behaviour, build community, and vary and enhance the librarian's teaching repertoire.

In the archives and museums sectors, oral histories are commonly collected from within communities, and there is increasing emphasis on participatory and post-custodial archival and museum practice to address the dominance of hegemonic forms of knowledge through the inclusion and privileging of the experiences of those who have been underrepresented or misrepresented (Duff & Harris, 2002). Community-based storytelling is a way in which multiple perspectives and the voices of non-dominant groups can be given space in the archive (Margolis, 2019), and other parts of the GLAM sector could usefully draw on oral history techniques to ensure that the views, experiences and perceptions of all parts of our communities are heard.

Participatory approaches in GLAM

Related to this is the argument that storytelling would fit well with the trend towards more participatory and collaborative programme and service development approaches across the sector generally. Design thinking, co-design, and UX research and design all aim to democratise services and institutions and have been used in a range of GLAM organisations to better understand user experiences, with the aim of improving them (Fuks et al., 2012; Meyerson et al., 2012; Nilsson, 2016; Rung, 2018). The use of storytelling fits particularly well with the UX approach, with its focus on ethnographic methods

(Appleton, 2018). Lanclos (2016) describes how the ethnographic approaches that feature in UX work gather stories that reveal patterns and are effective representations of service users' realities. She also emphasises that there is power in the stories of users' lived realities that cannot be represented effectively in statistics and charts, arguing that, "Numbers get in the way of our recognizing that we work with people" (p. 25).

The use of storytelling techniques in GLAM

Storytelling generally, whether for organisational/service development or for community participation, is a reasonably common practice within GLAM institutions. The discussion in the preceding paragraphs suggests that we have many of the skills and tools required in our sector. Similarly, many of the storytelling techniques described above have been used either in service provision or in academic research in the GLAM field. Digital storytelling is common in libraries (Detlor et al., 2018), local history contexts (Conrad, 2013), museums (Basaraba et al., 2019) and archives (Mukwevho & Ngoepe, 2019). PhotoVoice and photo-elicitation have been used extensively in studies of information behaviour (Hicks & Lloyd, 2018; Feng, 2019), as have the Critical Incident Technique (Jiang et al., 2020) and narrative approaches (Mansour, 2020). Marie Radford (2006) gives a very helpful overview of the use of CIT in our field, illustrated by an evaluation of a project that aimed to promote collaborations between schools and public libraries in New York. Although the evaluation did not take a storytelling approach, but instead gathered "incidents" through a questionnaire, the questions asked, and which follow, could be adapted to a more discursive conversational or interview approach:

- Think about times you have visited the public library. Remember a time when you had a good experience in the library.
    a   What was it that made this a good visit to the library?
- Now remember a time when you had an unpleasant or bad experience in the library.
    a   What was it that made this a bad or unpleasant visit to the library?

Within the GLAM sector, therefore, there appears to be both the skill and inclination to use storytelling for a range of purposes related to service development and design, but it remains a little-used approach for evaluation, which is regrettable given its applicability and potential contribution.

Conclusion

GLAM institutions, the services and programmes provided, and relationships with stakeholders are complex. Statistics and metrics alone cannot capture and demonstrate the true nature of the work taking place in our GLAM organisations nor their value for our communities, and so stories can be a valuable source of evidence of the human dimension of GLAM programmes, initiatives, projects, services and activities. Stories collected within our communities often provide profound insight and highlight areas of learning to improve provision for our users. With storytelling, the focus shifts from the perspective of the service providers to that of the service user, highlighting their unique experiences, knowledge and awareness of services, enabling us to evidence the difference our GLAM organisations are making within our communities and also to identify the lessons to be learned to take things forward. GLAM services are all about people and including storytelling approaches in evaluation practices can help us communicate a more holistic, dynamic and humanistic picture of their meaning and value in the lives of our communities.

Bibliography

Agostino, D. & Arnaboldi, M. (2018). *The role of big data analytics in museums: Balancing between contradictions and praxis.* 6th Workshop on Managing Arts and Cultural Organization. Oxford Saïd Business School, 30 November–1 December 2018, University of Oxford.https://re.public.polimi.it/retrieve/handle/11311/1125661/480289/AgostinoArnaboldi_Arts%20conference_full%20paper.pdf.

Ahonen, P., Buckless, B., Hafford, C., Keating, K., Keene, K., Morales, J., & Park, C. C. (2016). Study of coordination of tribal TANF and child welfare services: Final report. OPRE Report #2016–2052. Washington, DC: Office of Planning, Research and Evaluation, Administration for Children and Families, U.S. Department of Health and Human Services. https://www.acf.hhs.gov/opre/report/study-coordination-tribal-tanf-and-child-welfare-services-final-report.

Appleton, L. (2018). Qualitative methods for engaging students in performance measurement. *Information and Learning Science*, 119(1), 64–76. https://dx.doi.org/10.1108/ILS-09-2017-0093.

Basaraba, N., Conlan, O., Edmond, J., & Arnds, P. (2019). Digital narrative conventions in heritage trail mobile apps. *New Review of Hypermedia & Multimedia*, 25(1–2), 1–30. http://dx.doi.org/10.1080/13614568.2019.1642963.

Baú, V. (2016). A narrative approach in evaluation: "Narratives of Change" method. *Qualitative Research Journal*, 16(4), 374–387.

Blodgett, A. T., Schinke, R. J., Smith, B., Peltier, D., & Pheasant, C. (2011). In Indigenous words: Exploring vignettes as a narrative strategy for presenting the research voices of Aboriginal community members. *Qualitative Inquiry*, 17(6), 522–533. https://doi.org/10.1177/1077800411409885.

Calvert, P. & Goulding, A. (2015). Narratives and stories that capture the library's worth. *Performance Measurement and Metrics*, 16(3), 276–288. https://doi.org/10.1108/PMM-05-2015-0016.

Cavino, H. M. (2013). Across the colonial divide: Conversations about evaluation in Indigenous contexts. *American Journal of Evaluation*, 34(3), 339–355. https://dx.doi.org/10.1177/1098214013489338.

Chelimsky, E. (1997). Thoughts for a new evaluation society. *Evaluation*, 3(1), 97–109. https://doi.org/10.1177/135638909700300107.

Chouinard, J. A. & Cousins, J. B. (2007). Culturally competent evaluation for Aboriginal communities: A review of the empirical literature. *Journal of Multidisciplinary Evaluation*, 4(8), 40–57. https://uaf.edu/ianre/internal/reporting/programevals/aboriginal-eval.pdf.

Choy, S. & Lidstone, J. (2011). *Most significant change technique: A supplementary evaluation tool*. 14th Annual Conference of the Australian Vocational Education and Training Researchers Association, 28th–29th April 2011, Melbourne Australia. https://research-repository.griffith.edu.au/handle/10072/46565.

Cieslik, K., Dewulf, A., & Buytaert, W. (2020). Project narratives: Investigating participatory conservation in the Peruvian Andes. *Development and Change*, 51(4), 1067–1097. https://doi.org/10.1111/dech.12592.

Clandinin, D. J. & Connelly, M. (2000). *Narrative inquiry: Experience and story in qualitative research*. Jossey-Bass.

Conrad, S. K. (2013). Documenting local history: A case study in digital storytelling. *Library Review*, 62(8), 459–471. http://dx.doi.org/10.1108/LR-02-2013-0013.

Cooper, S. (2014). Transformative evaluation: Organisational learning through participative practice. *The Learning Organization*, 21(2), 146–157. https://doi.org/10.1108/TLO-03-2013-0003.

Costantino, T. E. & Greene, J. C. (2003). Reflections on the use of narrative in evaluation. *American Journal of Evaluation*, 24(1), 35–49. https://doi.org/10.1177%2F109821400302400104.

Dando, P. (2014). *Say it with data: A concise guide to making your case and getting results*. American Library Association.

Davies, R. (1998). An evolutionary approach to facilitating organisational learning: An experiment by the Christian Commission for Development in Bangladesh. *Impact Assessment and Project Appraisal*, 16(3), 243–250. https://dx.doi.org/10.1080/14615517.1998.10590213.

Detlor, B., Hupfer, M. E., & David, H. S. (2018). Digital storytelling: An opportunity for libraries to engage and lead their communities. *Canadian Journal of Information and Library Science*, 42(1–2), 43–68. https://muse.jhu.edu/article/717387.

Duff, W. M. & Harris, V. (2002). Stories and names: Archival description as narrating records and constructing meanings. *Archival Science*, 2(3/4), 263–285. https://doi.org/10.1007/BF02435625.

Eicher-Catt, D. & Edmondson, M. (2016). Reimaging public libraries as learning communities: What library stories can tell us. *Public Library Quarterly*, 35(3), 203–221. https://dx.doi.org/10.1080/01616846.2016.1210448.

Elliott, J. (2012). Gathering narrative data. In S. Delmont (Ed.) *Handbook of qualitative research in education* (pp. 281–298). Edward Elgar Publishing. https://dx.doi.org/10.4337/9781849807296.00029.

Fadlallah, R., El-Jardali, F., Nomier, M., Hemadi, N., Arif, K., Langlois, E. V., & Akl, E. A. (2019). Using narratives to impact health policy-making: A systematic review. *Health Research Policy and Systems*, 17(1), 26. https://doi.org/10.1186/s12961-019-0423-4.

Feng, Y. (2019). The enhanced participant-driven photo elicitation method for everyday life health information behaviour research. *Aslib Journal of Information Management*, 71(6), 720–738. http://dx.doi.org/10.1108/AJIM-02-2019-0042.

Flanagan, J. C. (1954). The critical incident technique. *Psychological Bulletin*, 51(4), 327–358. https://doi.org/10.1037/h0061470.

Fuks, H., Moura, H., Cardador, D., Vega, K., Ugulino, W., & Barbato, M. (2012). *Collaborative museums: An approach to co-design*. Proceedings of the ACM 2012 Conference on Computer Supported Cooperative Work, CSCW '12: Computer Supported Cooperative Work Seattle, 11th–15th February 2012, Washington USA, 681–684. https://dl.acm.org/doi/pdf/10.1145/2145204.2145307.

Goulding, A. (2020). The impact of evaluation: The use of evidence for decision-making and service development in public libraries. In E. Abbott-Halpin and C. Rankin. *Public library governance: International perspectives* (pp. 313–332). De Gruyter. https://doi.org/10.1515/9783110533323.

Guijt, I. M., Brouwers, J. H. A. M., Kusters, C. S. L., Prins, E., & Zeynalova, B. (2011). Evaluation revisited: Improving the quality of evaluative practice by embracing complexity: Conference report. Wageningen UR. https://library.wur.nl/WebQuery/wurpubs/fulltext/169284.

Hicks, A. & Lloyd, A. (2018). Seeing information: Visual methods as entry points to information practices. *Journal of Librarianship and Information Science*, 50(3), 229–238. http://dx.doi.org/10.1177/0961000618769973.

Hunter, O., Leeburg, E., & Harnar, M. (2020). Using PhotoVoice as an evaluation method. *Journal of MultiDisciplinary Evaluation*, 16(34), 14–20. https://journals.sfu.ca/jmde/index.php/jmde_1/article/view/603/501.

Jantti, M. & Heath, J. (2016). What role for libraries in learning analytics? *Performance Measurement and Metrics*, 17(2), 203–210. http://dx.doi.org/10.1108/PMM-04-2016-0020.

Jiang, T., Fu, S., & Song, E. (2020). Toward a description framework of information encountering experiences. *Journal of Documentation*, 76(4), 807–827. http://dx.doi.org/10.1108/JD-07-2019-0131.

Johnston, A. L. (2013). To case study or not to case study: Our experience with the Canadian government's evaluation practices and the use of case studies as an evaluation methodology for First Nations programs. *Canadian Journal of Program Evaluation*, 28(2), 21–42. https://cdm.ucalgary.ca/index.php/cjpe/article/view/30827.

Keene, K., Keating, K., & Ahonen, P. (2016). The Power of stories: Enriching program research and reporting. OPRE Report# 2016-2032a. Washington, DC: Office of Planning, Research and Evaluation, Administration for Children and Families, U.S. Department of Health and Human Services. https://www.jbassoc.com/resource/power-stories-enriching-program-research-reporting/.

Krueger, R. A. (2010). Using stories in evaluation. In J. S. Wholey, H. P. Hatry, & K. E. Newcomer (Eds.), *Handbook of practical program evaluation* (3rd edition), pp. 404–423. Jossey-Bass.

Krutt, H., Dyer, L., Arora, A., Rollman, J., & Jozkowski, A. C. (2018). PhotoVoice is a feasible method of program evaluation at a center serving adults with autism. *Evaluation and Program Planning*, 68, 74–80.

Kushner, S. (2000). *Personalizing evaluation*. Sage.

Lal, S., Donnelly, C., & Shin, J. (2015). Digital storytelling: An innovative tool for practice, education, and research. *Occupational Therapy In Health Care*, 29(1), 54–62. https://doi.org/10.3109/07380577.2014.958888.

Lanclos, D. M. (2016). Embracing an ethnographic agenda: Context, collaboration, and complexity. In A. Priestner and M. Borg (Eds.) *User experience in libraries: Applying ethnography and human-centred design* (pp. 21–37). Routledge. https://doi.org/10.4324/9781315548609.

Mansour, A. (2020). Shared information practices on Facebook. *Journal of Documentation*, 76(3), 625–646. http://dx.doi.org/10.1108/JD-10-2018-0160.

Margolis, R. (2019). May they reminisce over you: On the potential of archives as homespace. *The Journal of Community Informatics*, 15, 22–42. https://doi.org/10.15353/joci.v15i.3426.

Mathison, S. (2015). Seeing is believing. In S. Donaldson, C. Christie, & M. Mark (Eds.), *Credible and actionable evidence* (pp. 157–176). Sage. http://doi.org/10.4135/9781483385839.

Meyerson, J., Galloway, P., & Bias, R. (2012). Improving the user experience of professional researchers: Applying a user-centered design framework in archival repositories. *Proceedings of the American Society for Information Science and Technology*, 49(1), 1–7. https://doi.org/10.1002/meet.14504901208.

Mitroff, I. I. & Kilmann, R. H. (1975). Stories managers tell: A new tool for organizational problem solving. *Management Review*, 64(7), 18–28.

Mukwevho, J. & Ngoepe, M. (2019). Taking archives to the people. *Library Hi Tech*, 37(3), 374–388. http://dx.doi.org/10.1108/LHT-11-2017-0228.

Nilsson, E. M. (2016). *Prototyping collaborative (co-)archiving practices: From archival appraisal to co-archival facilitation*. 2016 22nd International Conference on Virtual System & Multimedia (VSMM), 17th–21st October 2016, Kuala Lumpur Malaysia. https://doi.org/10.1109/VSMM.2016.7863184.

Ospina, S. M. & Dodge, J. (2005). It's about time: Catching method up to meaning – the usefulness of narrative inquiry in public administration research. *Public Administration Review*, 65(2), 143–157. https://doi.org/10.1111/j.1540-6210.2005.00440.x.

Pastor, S. (2020). Decentred evaluation that empowers: Incorporating a double-storied approach to evaluation interviewing and story production. *International Journal of Narrative Therapy & Community Work*, (3), 50–57. https://dulwichcentre.com.au/wp-content/uploads/2020/10/Decentred-evaluation-that-empowers-by-Sonja-Pastor.pdf.

Poll, R. (2018). Quality in museums and libraries: A comparison of indicators. *Performance Measurement and Metrics*, 19(2), 90–100. https://doi.org/10.1108/pmm-10-2017-0049.

Public Health Agency of Canada. (2011). Reducing health disparities related to diabetes: Lessons learned through the Canadian Diabetes Strategy community-based program. Public Health Agency of Canada. https://www.phac-aspc.gc.ca/cd-mc/dia betes-diabete/rhd-rds-2011/pdf/rhd-rds-2011-eng.pdf.

Radford, M. L. (2006). The critical incident technique and the qualitative evaluation of the connecting libraries and schools project. *Library Trends*, 55(1), 46–64. https://doi.org/10.1353/lib.2006.0051.

Roughley, A. M. (2009). Developing a performance story report: User guide. Australian Government. http://www.cifor.org/wp-content/uploads/dfid/KNOWFOR%20monitoring%20tool%20kit/9.%20PSR%20guide.pdf.

Rung, M. H. (2018). Collective creativity in the art museum. In S. MacLeod, J. Hale, T. Austin, and O. Ho (Eds.) *The future of museum and gallery design* (pp. 147–159). Routledge. https://doi.org/10.4324/9781315149486-14.

Ryan, K. & Destefano, L. (2001). Dialogue as a democratizing evaluation method. *Evaluation*, 7(2), 188–203. https://doi.org/10.1177%2F13563890122209621.

Schrag, T., Mefford, C., Cottrill, J., & Paley, J. (2015). Building a public library impact data hub: A global libraries "data atlas" for storytelling, strategy development, and collaboration. *IFLA WLIC 2015*. http://library.ifla.org/id/eprint/1272.

Sherwood, G. (2018). Evaluation through story-telling! A tool for improving teaching. *Professional Development Today*, 19(3/4), 87–95. https://researchportal.port.ac.uk/portal/files/8791558/Evaluation_through_story_telling.pdf.

Sole, D. & Wilson, D. G. (2002). Storytelling in organizations: The power and traps of using stories to share knowledge in organizations. *LILA*, Harvard, Graduate School of Education, 1–12. http://www.providersedge.com/docs/km_articles/storytelling_in_organizations.pdf.

Sukop, S. (2007). Storytelling approaches to program evaluation: An introduction. The California Endowment. http://korwinconsulting.com/wp/wp-content/uploads/2015/10/StorytellingApproachestoProgramEvaluation_Final1.pdf.

Tilley E. (2016). Are you sitting comfortably …? In A. Priestner and M. Borg (Eds.) *User experience in libraries: Applying ethnography and human-centred design* (pp. 178–189). Routledge. https://doi.org/10.4324/9781315548609.

Voorbij, H. (2010). The use of web statistics in cultural heritage institutions. *Performance Measurement and Metrics*, 11(3), 266–279. https://doi.org/10.1108/14678041011098541.

Wagenaar, H. (2001). Telling tales: On evaluation and narrative. *Administrative Theory & Praxis*, 23(1), 109–115. https://doi.org/10.1080/10841806.2001.11643505.

Widdershoven, G. A. (2001). Dialogue in evaluation: A hermeneutic perspective. *Evaluation*, 7(2), 253–263. https://doi.org/10.1177%2F13563890122209676.

Yakel, E. & Tibbo, H. (2010). Standardized survey tools for assessment in archives and special collections. *Performance Measurement and Metrics*, 11(2), 211–222. https://doi.org/10.1108/14678041011064115.

4 Facilitating iteration in service design in libraries

Songphan Choemprayong

Introduction

Libraries are expected to be continuously improved, as suggested by Ranganathan's seminal fifth law of library science (1931), *"a library is a growing organism."* The continuous improvement in libraries is always driven by users' needs and behaviors, which are constantly changing and complicated. Additionally, modern libraries have also faced challenges from the accelerated advancement of information and communication technology. The amount of data and information exponentially increases every second. New business models in information industry competes with traditional library services. Libraries no longer purchase and own new materials but, instead, acquire resources through subscription. Furthermore, users are now able to access open access publications from their own devices.

The above-mentioned phenomena have changed how libraries offer their services tremendously (for instance, Aabø, 2005; Ross & Sennyey, 2008; Daigle, 2012; Leorke, Wyatt, & McQuire, 2018; Indrák & Pokorná, 2020). The roles of library services have shifted from preserving and providing access to information resources to promoting and supporting social and community activities, for instance, human library (e.g., Zhai, Zhao, & Wang, 2012; Dobreski & Huang, 2016; Groyecka et al., 2019; Bordonaro, 2020), co-working space (e.g., Bilandzic & Foth, 2013; Lumley, 2014; Schopfel, Roche, & Hubert, 2015), and learning commons (e.g., Oliveira, 2018). Libraries are now pressured to improve their current service and/or devise new ones that are innovative and add value (e.g., Poole, 2020; Smith, 2020).

While new or improved services can be exciting for library users and staff, planning for assessment of these services has become more critical in the development of library services. While evaluating an output or a short-term outcome of a service can be conducted immediately or within a short period after the service has been deployed, measuring an impact may need a longer implementation period to be able to obtain useful feedback.

Creating or upgrading a library service can be a one-and-done project. All development phases and activities are conducted in sequence, as shown in Figure 4.1. Assessment activities would normally be conducted after the new

DOI: 10.4324/9781003083993-4

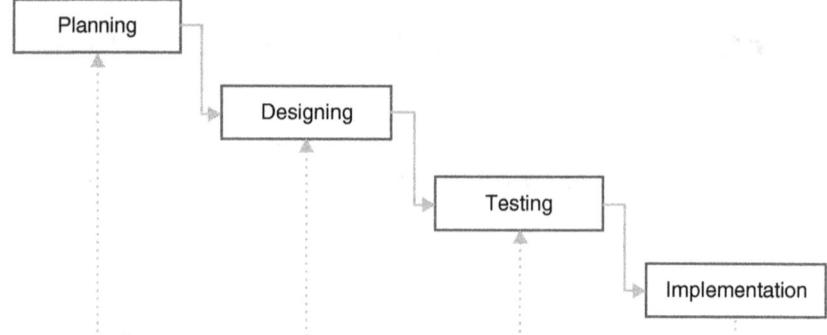

Figure 4.1 An example of the one-and-done approach in a service development project.

service has been fully developed and implemented. The one-and-done approach can be convenient and efficient in terms of managing resources (i.e., time, budget, and labor) to fit an administrative plan and schedule. Normally, the assessment in this approach would aim to obtain the most valid and reliable results to facilitate a convenient and unified decision-making process. Therefore, the assessment methods in this approach are systematic and rigid. However, the one-and-done approach can be costly in the long run, especially when assessments may be needed in the next round of service development and/or improvement (Lawson, 1972; Cross, 1982). This approach also does not support a quick evaluation within each development phase, which, in fact, could help in making a decision for the next stage.

Additionally, the one-and-done approach assumes that the results from one round of assessment can indicate whether a library service is a success or failure, which can be alarming. In general, the goal of this assessment approach is to efficiently produce a summative and conclusive answer in which an assessor tends to a rush to make a conclusion. Although such a conclusion may be easy to understand and convenient for a decision maker, the assessment process normally removes or reduces the complexity of the problems and solutions to a great extent. In addition, the conclusion based on the one-and-done approach can be sensitive to selective reporting bias, where an assessor presents the results of an assessment in favor of their preferred choices or solutions rather than giving a fair and comprehensive picture of the problems and solutions (van der Steen et al., 2019). In other words, the library practitioners may be under pressure to highlight success stories and avoid reporting failures. Therefore, it does not help in providing useful information for further improvement and it is more likely to lead to a service failure in a short period of time.

As an alternative to the one-and-done approach, an iterative process refers to the administration of development, assessment, analysis, and refinement of a product or a service for multiple cycles until the output is ready to be fully implemented (Interaction Design Foundation, 2020a). In an iterative process, an assessment is an integral part of every service development activity. An efficient iterative process, in general, can help the library practitioners improve the service accumulatively, discover and prevent any misunderstandings and errors early, obtain more reliable feedback, and indicate the progress of the project. Most importantly, an assessment in iterative process is more failure-tolerating, allowing the practitioners to be creative and experimental in their services.

Iterative processes are supported by several system development and project management approaches (e.g., Kendall & Kendall, 2019; Vacek, Puckett Rodgers, & Sitar, 2019). Service design is one of the iterative-based approaches that has increasingly gained attention in the last century among the library service community.

This chapter examines how the service design approach can promote an iterative process to improve existing services and create new services to meet ever-changing user needs and expectations. The following section introduces the principles of the service design approach and how it is implemented in libraries. The characteristics and benefits of an iterative process in service design is elaborated in the subsequent section. Guidelines on effective iterative processes are discussed at the end of this chapter, with an emphasis on assessment.

Service design in libraries

What is service design?

Service design is a design thinking-based approach aiming to guide and facilitate the design process of services. Integrating knowledge and practices from business, marketing, innovation management, and design discipline, the approach covers design frameworks, processes, methods, and tools in managing resources that are essential to service delivery, such as human resources, technology, tools and equipment, communication channels, and infrastructure. As a human-centric approach, the primary goal of service design is to improve service quality and interactions between service providers and users (Mager & King, 2009). A service provision based on this approach consists of various types of interactions, namely human–human interaction, human–machine interaction, and human–object interaction, that occur before, during, and after service delivery. The output of this approach is a value-added service that is user-friendly, usable, efficient, feasible, viable, and desirable (Mager, 2008). The product of service design can be a brand-new service, or an improved service based on an existing one. In terms of outcomes, a service developed from this approach should lead to a more pleasant user experience and a higher level of user satisfaction, increasing the loyalty of users of a service or a product.

Service design approach is a by-product of the social transformation from an industrialized product-based economy to a holistic, experience-based service economy. This transition from product-oriented to a service-oriented economy represents how users/consumers value an experience received from a service more than a tangible product (Dhaliwal, Macintyre, & Parry, 2011). In the service design approach, a product is viewed as a part of the interactions between users and providers. What users want, in fact, is an experience from using the products and interacting with service providers in related activities that serve the needs of users.

A book is normally perceived as a tangible product. However, from a service design perspective, a book is considered part of a knowledge sharing or entertaining experience. Reading can be considered as an interaction between authors/publishers and readers, while associated services can be developed around a book and reading, for example, book recommendations, readers' advisory, an author's talk, book delivery, summarization and indexing, and many other services. Another example in a library setting is an RFID tag. The tag has been developed as a product itself. However, from the service design perspective, an RFID tag attached inside a book is viewed as a means to allow library users to check out a book in a more convenient way, to expedite the inventory process, and to prevent theft and loss. Therefore, an RFID tag can be considered as one of many solutions of a library service offering desirable and pleasant experiences for different stakeholders.

Principles of service design

Service design emphasizes process improvement that is outcome-oriented and realistic in terms of the resources available. Information/communication design and prototype development play essential roles in designing and developing a service. There are five general principles of service design: 1) user-centered design, 2) co-creative, 3) sequential design, 4) evidencing, and 5) holistic design (Stickdorn & Schneider, 2011).

1   User-centered design

User involvement is the key to a successful service design project. Instead of the internal needs of the organization, services should be designed to meet the needs and expectations of users. Prioritizing the demands of the users, the designers, users, service providers, and other stakeholders should share a common language, expectations, and an understanding about the service, with an emphasis on the user's perspective. Therefore, designing and developing a service should utilize methods and tools to help gain an insight into users' expectations and understanding.

2   Co-creative

Based on the assumption that everyone has creativity, services should be co-produced by service providers, users, and other stakeholders (Polaine,

Løvlie, & Reason, 2013). Users from diverse groups covering a variety of needs and expectations should be included in the design process. At the same time, staff in different roles (e.g., professional librarians, paraprofessionals, interns, and supporting staff) and businesses in the supply chain (e.g., vendors, outsources) should also be involved as well.

3   Sequential design

Considering a service as a journey, sequencing (i.e., conceptualizing and manipulating a connection between actions, events, and contexts throughout service periods) is an important concept. All interactions between users and service providers (i.e., touchpoints) are interrelated and have an impact on one another. For example, enforcing a restriction and display information on lending rights of a particular book for a user type on the Online Public Access Catalog (OPAC) would save users time and reduce user disappointment and frustration at the checkout station.

4   Evidencing

The nature of service quality is abstract and intangible. While experience can be narrated, it can be difficult to materialize. Certain library services that have no direct interaction between users and library staff (for example, cataloging, material preparation, space and facility management, and security) tend to be overlooked by users. On the other hand, when these services fail to meet the users' expectations, they affect the overall satisfaction level. Therefore, it is important to manifest when intangible services are being served. Offering souvenirs, prizes, and merchandise are one of the most common approaches to triggering positive memory and emotions associated with the services. Strategic and efficient evidencing can also yield a higher rate of returning users and a higher degree of brand loyalty.

5   Holistic design

Service design is a well-rounded approach concerning contextual and environmental determinants of service delivery from various aspects (e.g., time, weather, season, traffic, geographical location) and the overall perceptions triggered from the basic human senses (i.e., seeing, hearing, touching, tasting, and smelling) throughout the entire service journey. Instead of designing component by component, services should be developed as a united and efficient system. For library service design, a holistic approach also includes other services provided by external organizations (for example, coffee shop, stationery store, vending machine).

Furthermore, service design is a process that requires understanding the balance between an authentic understanding of the design purposes, the requirements of a service, and the feasibility and viability of service provision. The latter includes the considerations of the ability of service providers in terms of knowledge, skills, and resources, as well as of the business model and opportunities (Interaction Design Foundation, 2020b).

Another general principle of service design should also consider any deviated situations/events or anomalies that may occur and treat them as common events. For example, users get lost on the library website and are unable to locate the information they need – the designer team should prepare how to deal with such situations/events. This would help users to recover from negative experiences in a fast manner (Wishlade, 2019).

Finally, service design is an iterative process, which is the focus of this chapter. Instead of attempting to complete the project in the first place, the design process is conducted and administered on a trial-and-error basis. Instead of avoiding mistakes as much as possible, learning from mistakes is an important part of the process to improve services. Therefore, multiple rounds of prototype development and testing prior to full implementation is an important step of service design.

Service design process: Methods and tools

While there is no conventional model on service design process (see also Designthinkers, 2009; Technology Strategy Board & Design Council, 2015), the UK's Design Council (2020) developed the Double Diamond framework, as shown in Figure 4.2, identifying the four common design phases from design thinking perspective – *discover, define, develop,* and *deliver*. The horizontal coordinate represents the progress of the design process through time. The shape of the diamond represents the amount of data, information, knowledge, and

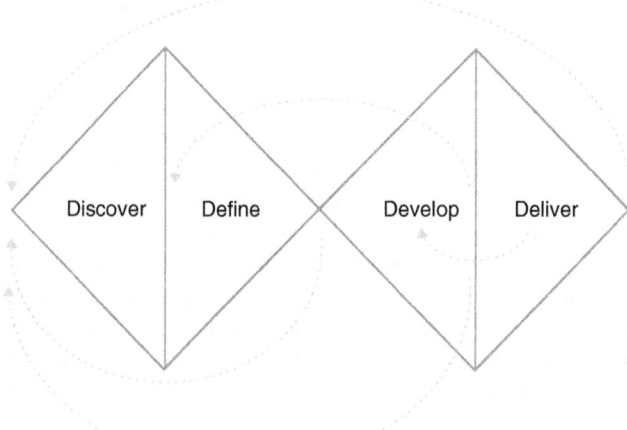

Figure 4.2 The Double Diamond framework.

outputs emerging at each phase. For instance, the left half of the first diamond (i.e., the *discover* phase) signifies it is a collection or extension phase in which the designer team should identify, look for, and explore design problems as much as possible. On the other hand, in the right half of the first diamond, the *define* phase, the designer team would try to reduce, summarize, or prioritize design problems emerging from the prior phase.

In the *discover* phase, the designer team deploys various tools to gain empathy and insights regarding problems, obstacles, and needs of both current and potential users, as well as the limitations from providers' perspectives. The *define* phase focuses on the analysis of data from the *discover* phase to identify major themes and patterns (such as problems, challenges, and opportunities). The output of this phase would be a clearly defined problem and opportunity that are understood and acknowledged by all stakeholders. The next phase, *develop*, concerns finding various possible solutions to the problem or ways to address the opportunities raised from the previous phase. In the *deliver* phase, the designer team develops prototypes and tests them with users, stakeholders, and all design members. This final phase is usually an iterative process, which continues until a feasible and practical solution that meets the needs of users is found. This phase also includes the implementation of the service as well as the monitoring of feedback for further improvement.

The Double Diamond framework has been applicable to the service design process (New Zealand Government, 2021). In a similar fashion to the Double Diamond framework but with certain variations, Stickdorn & Schneider (2011) propose their own framework for the service design process that also has four major phases, namely exploration, creation, reflection, and implementation.

Before understanding user needs, the exploration begins with environmental scanning, which includes surveying organizational culture and perceptions on changes among staff and users. Thus, co-creation is crucial in this process. The output of this phase is a product of the in-depth data analysis using both quantitative and qualitative approaches to interrelate among various themes and patterns. Similar to the *discover* phase in the Double Diamond framework, the goal of this phase is to understand the current operations and limitations of service delivery from various points of view, including users, front-line staff, the back office, the administration, suppliers and vendors, and competitors. In this phase, the design team also needs to come up with well-defined and commonly understood problems and design opportunities, just like in the *define* phase.

The creation phase is similar to the *develop* phase in the Double Diamond framework, encouraging a broad range of possible solutions for the defined challenge. This phase also covers adapting and testing ideas iteratively.

The reflection phase focuses on prototype development and testing. After getting feedback from the prototype testing, flaws and recommendations are brought to the creation phase again to revise the ideas until they are ready to be prototyped again. Once again, this is an iterative process. One of the major challenges in this phase is how to capture emotions and feelings, in addition to behaviors and outputs, which are abstract and subjective in nature. Therefore, methods and tools used in this phase should help the designer team to observe and gain insights about these abstract characteristics to inform the revision.

The last phase, implementation, mostly concerns communication among the various groups of stakeholders. Convincing different groups to recognize the same goal and their roles in service delivery become the most substantial tasks. At the same time, whenever the service provision encounters mistakes or disruptions, the solutions should be devised quickly and creatively. Therefore, in this phase, the methods and tools should help all stakeholders to see the same picture of a complete design process and service delivery specifications.

Evidently, service design pays attention to change management that would lead to exploration. The exploration then contributes to the more clearly defined problem. As discussed earlier, the entire service design process is interrelated between concepts and practice in a systematic way. Every phase may need to go back and forth with the previous phase, or even go back to the first phase. The designer team, once again, should focus more on finding mistakes, abnormalities, and appropriate solutions to improve the service in the next round.

In terms of methods and tools, service design embraces lightweight research methods (i.e., requiring a small sample size and consuming a short development cycle), instead of exhaustive and rigorous investigative protocols, facilitating and assisting a researcher/designer to obtain insights and make decisions (Polaine, Løvlie, & Reason, 2013).

There are numerous methods and tools available in each phase of the design process. One tool may be applicable to more than one phase. Some of the tools are derived from scientific and social science research, while others are developed from design (Tavangar, 2017). Design tools for service design can also be classified into major functions, including co-creation (e.g., stakeholder map, observation, shadowing, contextual interview, persona development, journey map), envisioning (e.g., ideation, storyboard, scenario model), prototyping, and implementation (e.g., storytelling, roleplay, service blueprint, and touchpoint specifications).

There are numerous resources available to learn more about different tools for service design, including how-to guidelines and examples (for instance, servicedesigntools.org, figma.com, mural.co). This chapter does not discuss each tool in detail. It is also important to note that the classification of design tools in Table 4.1 is not intended to be prescriptive. The selection of design tools has no concrete rules. Instead, the utilization of these tools depends on environment, context, and the design goal.

The adoption of service design in libraries

Service design is applicable to the development of new services and improvement of existing services in libraries in numerous ways. Today, libraries are

Table 4.1 Example of design methods and tools in different service design phases

Tools	Exploration	Ideation	Reflection	Implementation
1. Tools for exploration				
1.1 Stakeholder map	X	X		
1.2 Observation	X			
1.3 Contextual interview	X			
1.4 Persona	X	X	X	
1.5 Journey map	X	X	X	
2. Tools for ideation and reflection				
2.1 Idea development	X	X	X	
2.2 Storyboard		X	X	X
2.3 Simulate situations		X	X	
2.4 Prototyping		X	X	X
3. Tools for implementation				
3.1 Storytelling		X	X	X
3.2 Service blueprint				X
3.3 Roleplay				X

faced with ever-changing environments and contexts, with new public and commercial services (e.g., search engines, online databases, public data) that can replace or compete with what libraries have been offering emerging on a daily basis. Grounded as an iterative approach, service design accelerates processes of innovation and problem-solving.

Apparently, libraries around the world have adopted service design approach, to varying extents, in developing new services and improving existing services for several years. Based on the design thinking experience at Chicago Public Library in the United States and Aarhus Public Libraries in Denmark, as well as a few other libraries around the world (such as Romania, Brazil, China, Italy, and Portugal), IDEO, a renowned global design company, develop a design thinking toolkit for libraries to help library professionals plan and implement service design projects (IDEO, 2015).

Marquez and Downey (2015) present the service design process conducted at Reed College Library. The process was divided into four phases, including a pre-work phase (forming a design team and scheduling activities), observation phase (gaining insights through various observation and data collection methods), understanding/thinking phase (visualizing experience, creating scenarios, constructing solutions, and developing prototypes), and an implementation phase. One of the example solutions at Reed College Library is moving a reference desk to a location where users feel comfortable asking questions, by developing a prototype using a wardrobe box.

Relocating and redesigning a reference desk was also a showcase of service design output at John P. Robarts Library at the University of Toronto in Canada (Everall & Logan, 2016). After observing a downward trend of in-person interactions at the reference desk, the design team employed the service design approach to improve the visibility of reference services. In conjunction with cost analysis and other supporting data, the design team conducted focus groups with student librarians and a survey of user experience upon the exit door. Based on the insights found, the solutions created and tested included moving the reference desk, rebranding the service (i.e., changing a sign), making staff more visible by having them wearing vests/lanyard, utilizing a team collaboration platform (i.e., Slack) as an alternative to communicate among staff, and reassigning the shift. The findings show how the solutions had changed over time due to feedback obtained from users, student librarians, and staff.

Since 2016, the University of Michigan Library has been planning and implementing the transformation of its physical and online services based on the service design approach (Vacek, Puckett Rodgers, & Sitar, 2019). Beginning with the development of organizational service goals, the library has set up an interdepartmental Service Design Task Force, including recruiting in related positions to lead such an initiative. The task force was divided into six design teams that were responsible for designing and experimenting with new services in different areas, including consultation, staff innovation, digital scholarship, library as research lab, citation management, and the library lifecycle. Each team followed the four cycles of service innovation, including exploring issues, analyzing issues, generating and exploring ideas, and synthesizing and prototyping. Continuous assessment was applied throughout the entire process. The major findings include the challenges encountered, especially time pressure, scheduling issues, and commitment, and the positive impacts on team formation and dynamics, resources and capacity building, and evidence-based service design. One of the showcases at U-M Library is the library website redesign project from a few dimensions, including content organization, navigation system, and content categories refinement (Sipes, 2019).

Montana State University Library utilized a service blueprinting method iteratively to develop technology services in libraries (Young et al., 2020). This multiple-year service design project consists of three rounds of service blueprint development and revision. As a result, there are numerous areas of service improvement and development, for example, staff training and cross-training initiatives, updated user manual and scheduling platform, learning about and setting a plan for virtual reality technology, technology preservation, and physical space rearrangement. Reportedly, the service blueprint helps staff in the library to share their understanding of services as the services are evolving through time.

Another showcase of application of service design in libraries is Thailand Creative & Design Center (TCDC) Resource Center's Relocation Project (Thamtheerasathian et al., 2018). The relocation was an opportunity to create new services, and update existing services, based on user needs. The service design process of this project consists of developing empathy, ideating services, prototyping and testing, and implementation. The entire process up until the relocation took two years. Among numerous new and updated services, the library has implemented facility-based services (e.g., makerspace, co-working space, open entrance, and shelving arrangement), tool-oriented services (e.g., personalized bookmarks and brainstorming toolbox), human-oriented services (e.g., consultation), and resource-based services (e.g., new collection display, trend book acquisition and access, and local design collection building), with a plan for iterative assessment and adaptation.

The library at the Bank of Thailand Learning Center used to be a special library serving only internal users. When the library decided to open to the public, they adopted service design processes and methods to devise new services, as well as to inform the facility design (Choemprayong & Siridhara, 2021). One of the major outputs is a new classification scheme that still helps internal users navigate the collection while also helping the public understand the missions and roles of the central bank. The design team consisted of internal staff from various departments as well as representatives of public users. The prototypes were developed and evaluated in all developing stages, including classification design, shelving system design, and spine label design. Since the new classification was implemented in 2018, the scheme has been continuously reevaluated and adjusted based on users' and staff feedback.

Iteration in service design process

Iterative process

As mentioned above, a service is ongoing and ever-changing. Therefore, from the service design perspective, the iterative process (often called *rapid prototyping* or *spiral prototyping*) is one of the most critical parts of a service design project (Interaction Design Foundation, 2020a). This approach highlights the "cyclic process of prototyping, testing, analyzing, and refining a work in progress" (Zimmerman, 2003, p.176). Typically, each design phase should run in multiple cycles in order to ensure that the implemented services are actually usable, feasible, and desirable from various points of view, for instance, design, business, innovation, and marketing (Canhenha, 2019).

In each cycle, the design team would develop and test prototypes to find out how they can be amended or improved. Iteration can occur at any phase, even during a pilot study and when the services are released to the public (Interaction Design Foundation, 2020a). The primary goal of iteration is not to evaluate the quality of the prototype but to find out how the services can be improved until the services are ready to be released to the users. Therefore, it is possible that the results of an iteration could lead to a return to the previous phase to adjust the design, instead of moving on to the subsequent design phase. The dashed lines in Figure 4.1 represent iterations in the service design process.

An iterative process is the opposite to a linear design model (i.e., one-and-done approach), where there are concrete start and end points. At the same time, it is distinguished from incremental design in that the incremental design concerns only adding new design elements iteratively, while the iterative process itself is not restricted to addition, but also includes reworking and refining. Canhenha (2019) points out that iterations are not interchangeable to repetition. Instead, iterations include adjustments, augmentations, and clarification of design aspects. It is important to note that the methods and tools can be different in each iteration depending on the objective of the prototype and testing.

Rengifo (2018) addresses three key elements of the iterative design process, including understanding, exploration, and validation. Understanding is an initial point to be familiar with user personae (including needs and habits), situations, and context that are fundamental to the design problems. Lack of understanding could lead to poor solutions and additional problems. Exploration concerns how to come up with solutions and prototypes from low fidelity to higher fidelity while still sticking to the original efforts addressed in the understanding phase. For validation, the solutions are assessed to make sure that they are still in line with assumptions of the designer team. The validation process itself can be conducted in three cycles with different groups of users. The first cycle would only need the design team's input. The second cycle deals with more people, members of other areas, and stakeholders, including technical staff. The last cycle concerns the usability testing by non-design team members and potential users.

One of the great examples of iterative design in related contexts is Wikipedia. An article is developed and revised repeatedly, with no expectation that it would cease to update the content. Users can continuously edit the article at any time with no pressure to develop an absolute final version.

Benefits of an iterative process

There are numerous benefits of the iterative design process. Some of the major benefits are given below.

Improving incrementally

From a user interface design perspective, Nielsen (1993) argues iteration can save users time in completing a task, and improve task efficiency and effectiveness. He reports that an average improvement from the first to the last iteration, based on numerous usability measures, is 165%. The first few iterations in particular would help avoid design "catastrophes". Later iterations would result in a more refined and polished version of the solutions. However, Nielsen cautions that the improvements from the iterative process are not expected to be in an exponential pattern across the project. While there is still no consensus on the upper and lower thresholds of iterative cycles, the first two or three are considered the initial iterations. Nevertheless, multiple iterations may require an abundance of resources, labor, and time. Nielsen (2011) recommended conducting a parallel design process where multiple competing design solutions are developed and tested at the same time. Only one solution with the best outcome will be chosen for iterative design process subsequently.

Avoiding major mistakes later in the process

Another feature of iterative design is discovering design issues early on, rather than later in the process, which can pose a greater risk to the project (Zimmerman, 2003; Ramsay, 2009). The iterative process can be applied to a very early phase of service design process. Even during the exploration phase, the design team can iterate the data collection process until they are confident that they really understand the users' needs and expectations. This would ensure that the service requirements and design problems are well grounded. While the iterative process may take time from the designer's side, an effective iterative design would save users time and energy, and avoid major mistakes in the long run.

Obtaining reliable feedback from users

Iterative prototyping would also help the design team obtain more valid and reliable feedback. Since the iterative process is based on prototype development, even with a low level of fidelity, feedback providers (e.g., users, staff, and other stakeholders) have an opportunity to sense and imagine the prototyping services. With a low fidelity prototype, participants can focus on the issues or activities that are highlighted in each iteration.

Demonstrating progress regularly

The iterative process can also demonstrate progress of the project at each iteration to all stakeholders (Interaction Design Foundation, 2020a). The process itself helps an organization and the design team to communicate with users and other stakeholders on the upcoming changes. This would also promote a trustworthy relationship among the design team, users, and stakeholders.

Less documentation, more actual design

Instead of spending too much time on documentation, Ramsay (2009) argues that the iterative process can help the design team focus more on the actual design. Since service design is less concerned about hypothesis and assumptions, the prototypes from each iteration become documents and archives themselves. On the other hand, since the strategy in obtaining feedback is much more focused, the documentation requires less time and resources.

Allowing failures

The iterative process is an approach that promotes creativity by allowing failures, instead of coercing perfect solutions in one cycle. As mentioned earlier, the primary objective of the iterative process is to find problems rather than summarize the user performance. The design process, according to this approach, allows the design team to try and develop ideas that might not be supported by traditional approaches.

Avoiding misunderstanding among team members

Since the iterative process requires rapid prototyping, this would help the design team and all stakeholders to resolve any misunderstandings and ambiguities, especially during the early iterations (Interaction Design Foundation, 2020a). Discovering any misunderstandings and ambiguities later in the design process can cause a lot of problems in the project.

Focusing on users

In each iteration, the design team must obtain feedback from representatives of actual and potential users prior to making any changes or even redesigning. This helps the design team and developers to stay focused on the users' needs as well as ensuring the design solutions are valuable to users (Interaction Design Foundation, 2020a).

Easy to develop framework for performance evaluation

The iterative process can help the design team to observe various measures and evaluation methods. After several iterations, the team should be able to choose applicable and meaningful measures and evaluation methods. At the same time, the developers in the later phases can focus on enhancing the performance of services and products based on selected measures and methods (Interaction Design Foundation, 2020a). This would also avoid misunderstandings between the design team and developers if they are separated.

Easy to integrate with agile approach and lean process

The iterative process can be applicable with other management approaches, such as agile approach and lean management. In each iteration, the design team can focus on certain parts of services and eliminate unnecessary parts or details.

Assessment in the iterative process

Assessment plays an essential role in the iterative process. In each cycle, the prototypes must be evaluated based on the purpose of the design. Vacek,

Puckett Rodgers, and Sitar (2019) argue that an assessment is blended into the service design process through different methods and tools. In general, from a design perspective, assessment can be classified into two categories: formative and summative assessment (Hewett, 1986; Drew, 2017). Formative assessment concerns iteratively monitoring, learning, and refining outputs of the design process, either as a product or a service. Summative (or evaluative) assessment pays attention to impact, usability, and performance. The primary goal of summative assessment is "to prove something works" (Drew, 2017, p.23). These two approaches lead to different goals, measures, and methods.

Based on the design and development of an automated personalized instruction and an interactive search performance feedback for a bibliographic information system, Hewett (1986) points out that both approaches play important but different roles in each iteration. Therefore, both approaches should be considered in each iterative process to some extent. The selection of approaches should be based on the goals of the design process, the expected outputs and outcomes, and the nature of the assessment process. However, Drew (2017) argues that formative assessment is more important to the iterative process than the summative approach, since the user feedback can be responsive and any changes can be made in a short period of time.

Moreover, Drew (2017) points out that traditional assessment approaches are heavily based on scientific ground with rigorous methodological foundations. Such an approach tends to pay a great deal of attention to stringent study design and sampling methods, while the activities in a service are normally chaotic, with numerous social challenges. Therefore, traditional approaches may not be appropriate for the iterative service design process.

Chen (2015, p.1) characterizes how assessments in the service design approach differ from those in conventional approaches, as follows.

1 In contrast to a completed form, most assessments in service design process are conducted on the intermediate basis (e.g., concept plans, mock-ups, or prototypes).
2 In service design, a new service should be, if possible, compared against the previous or existing services, rather than services of others (such as competitors).
3 As an iterative process, sending feedback from an assessment to the subsequent process in each iteration would help the design process be effective.
4 Assessment of the service design approach should be done in a short timeframe.

According to Chen (2015), assessment can be applied to three phases of service design: studying solutions, designing, and development. In the study of solutions phase (i.e., exploration, developing empathy), the goal of assessment is to verify the proposed solutions with user needs and resources. In the design phase, low-fidelity prototypes (such as wireframes, mock-ups, paper prototypes) are developed and evaluated in terms of feasibility, functionality, information architecture, and usability. For high-fidelity prototypes, more details are added into the prototypes. The assessment in this phase would also include appearance and subjective acceptability. In the development phase, the assessment should focus on the performance (such as effectiveness) as well as usability of services in real or virtual environments.

Considerations for an iterative service design process

While the iterative process seems to be simple in nature, there are certain considerations to pay attention to when implementing such an approach. In general, Canhenha (2019) recommended that the iterative process should be done in a short cycle and continuous manner. Below are some specific guidelines for the iterative service design process that can be implemented in a library setting.

Prototype development and testing

Rapid prototyping is a key component of the iterative design process. There are numerous tools available, both online and offline, to create and test prototypes in a short period of time. The development of a prototype can be roughly divided into two types: a low-fidelity and high-fidelity prototype. Designed to provoke ideas among the design team, a low-fidelity prototype is an early sketch of the alternative solution in a paper form, which can be created in a short timeframe. Developing a low fidelity prototype can cost nothing, except pen and paper. In contrast, a high-fidelity prototype embraces major detailed representations of the design solution. The objective of a high-fidelity prototype is to fine-tune details of the design and discover errors and mistakes after testing with the potential users. Attention needs to be paid to details when creating a high-fidelity prototype. The development of a high-fidelity prototype can follow several refinements of a low-fidelity prototype, as shown in Figure 4.3. However, it is important to keep in mind that prototyping should be done rapidly and purposefully to make the design process efficient.

Beginning iteration earlier in the cycle

While the iterative process can be applied in any design phases, applying the iterative design approach early in a service design process may be more cost-effective. Prototypes in the early stages are normally cheaper and easier than developing and refining a high-fidelity prototype or a full system. Iterations can be strategically planned earlier in the design process. However, of course, iterations should also be strategically placed after the implementation phase, as shown in Figure 4.4. It can also be done as an ongoing monitoring system or a dashboard (Thamtheerasathian et al., 2018). However, when designing

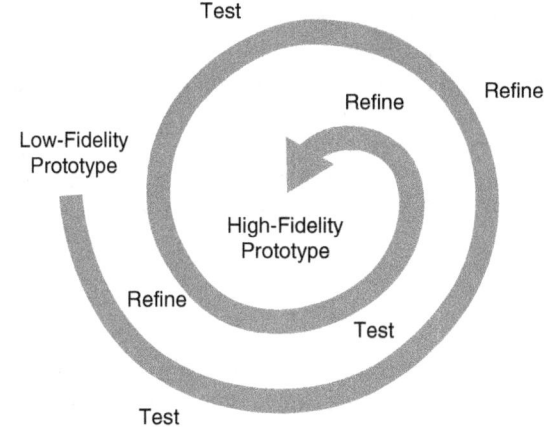

Figure 4.3 Prototyping and testing process.

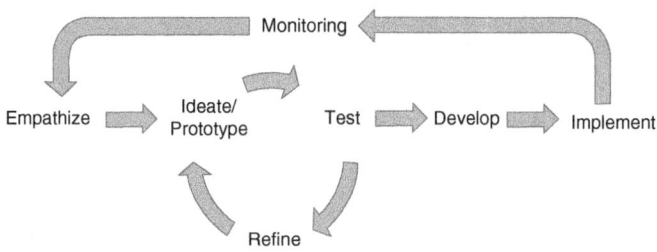

Figure 4.4 Iterative process for rapid prototyping.

such a system, the designer team should discuss and pinpoint thresholds for crisis alert (e.g., when a serious error occurs or when the maximum capacity of service is reached).

Well-structured framework

The iterative process is a broad approach covering a variety of interrelated methods and tools. The connection between these elements affects the efficiency and effectiveness of the design process. Therefore, Rengifo (2018) suggests that a framework addressing the scope and relationship between these technical aspects is needed, and it should be flexible and solid enough to support the scalability.

Minimum viable service (MVS)

To improve efficiency of the iterative process as well as facilitating user feedback, the service should be developed as a minimum viable service (MVS) before the deployment (Millward, 2019; Interaction Design Foundation, 2020b). MVS is a concept derived from an integrated product management approach, so called minimum viable products (MVP), emphasizing the creation of a product model just to obtain feedback for future development. Adopting the major characteristics, the service in an MVS concept can be developed with basic features and functions, providing enough opportunity for users to provide feedback. Waiting for a full load service might take up too much time and resources, which could potentially be wasted.

Being prepared

Thorough preparation is one of the common recommendations when using an iterative process. Prior to an assessment in each iteration, details about prototype, evaluation tasks and sequences, design goals and phases, and user environment, as well as the characteristics of testing users, should be confirmed. To facilitate efficient communication among the design team members and developers, appropriate documentations should also be well-prepared (Chen, 2015). In addition, it is important to check the availability of tools and resources to be used for assessment (Canhenha, 2019).

Providing enough time

While each iteration should be in a short cycle, there are many activities, people, and resources involved in each round of development, assessment, and refinement. To be thorough, it takes some time to work on certain tasks, for instance, communicating among team members, reaching out to potential participants, developing tasks and questions, scheduling, analyzing data, and making decisions (Canhenha, 2019). According to Chen (2015), rushing and being careless about the process might cause major issues, including missing essential information or elements that should be tested, and obtaining inaccurate data.

Appropriate participants

Selecting the participants in each round of assessment is a crucial task. The participants should have similar characteristics, motivations, and interests in the designed services with potential users. Chen (2015) argues that those who share the same motivations to use the service are likely to have a similar level of acceptance of and satisfaction with the service.

Having the same group of participants is not necessary in all iterations. In designing certain services and products (such as games), the first few cycles can be tested internally among the design team members. Subsequent iterations can assess with major stakeholders, a few potential users, and a large group of users, respectively (Zimmerman, 2003). Expanding testing groups outward from the design team to a large group of users can be an efficient strategy for an iterative process.

Empowering frontline staff

Frontline staff are usually the ones who interact with and receive the most feedback directly from users. They are the gatekeepers of service delivery. In fact, they largely take part in controlling the outcomes of a service design project (Drew, 2017). In addition to feedback from users, the tacit knowledge and opinion from this group of staff may contribute to the development and improvement of services. Therefore, it is important to keep them in the design cycle. In a more progressive manner, empowering the frontline staff to lead the iterative design can accelerate the design process, since they are responsive to user feedback, particularly in a critical moment.

Listen

Positive feedback is normally desirable when assessing the success of the service (i.e., summative assessment). However, receiving negative feedback in formative assessments can be valuable in helping the services improve and be successful, although it can be painful and hard to experience sometimes as a design team member or a developer. Therefore, learning how to listen and be open-minded is one of the recommendations to improve the iterative process (Zimmerman, 2003). The development or improvement of a service can lead to nowhere if the design team fails to obtain insights about the actual needs of users (Travis, 2017).

Conclusion

The objective of this chapter is to encourage the use of the iterative process in the development and design of library services. A library as a living organism should not be static. Instead, it should be constantly changing to meet the ever-changing user needs and expectations. Service design is an appealing approach to help libraries adapt to the fast-changing environment. Various types of libraries around the world have adopted service design principles in continuously transforming their physical and online services.

Service design is a management approach integrating perspectives from innovation, business, marketing, and design. As a holistic, user-centric approach, service design offers methods and tools facilitating various design processes, including developing empathy, defining design problems, ideating solutions, prototyping and testing, and implementation. Iterative design, administering multiple cycles of the design process, is central to service improvement and development. Assessment plays an essential role in iterative design, especially in the form of formative assessment.

Essentially, each iteration should take a short period of time to maintain cost-effectiveness. One of the major challenges is that the iterative process can be time consuming (ranging from a few months to many years) and exhaust a great amount of investment (including human resources, budget, and space).

This aspect is a major challenge for many libraries and other organizations, especially those with limited resources. Strategic planning and thorough preparation of assessment is highly recommended.

While scientific rigor is not a major concern in service design, the design team still needs to control certain aspects of assessment to meet the development and design goals. For example, participants should represent anticipated users as well as show an interest in using the service. Frontline staff are key resources to hasten the iteration process and make the designed services successful.

One should be mindful that all processes and iterations are conducted to solve the design problems and address user needs and expectations. The outputs of the service design process are a usable, feasible, and desirable service and product. Careless planning and operation of assessment and other steps in the iterative process (i.e., development, analysis, and refinement) could lead to a common pitfall, in which each iteration does not give rise to a better solution than the previous version (Nielsen, 1993).

Bibliography

Aabø, S. (2005). The role and value of public libraries in the age of digital technologies. *Journal of Librarianship and Information Science*, 37(4), 205–211.

Bilandzic, M. & Foth, M. (2013). Libraries as coworking spaces: Understanding user motivations and perceived barriers to social learning. *Library Hi Tech*, 31(2), 254–273.

Bordonaro, K. (2020). The Human Library: Reframing library work with international students. *Journal of Library Administration*, 60(1), 97–108.

Canhenha, P. (2019). Assessing iteration and testing in design. Retrieved from https://uxplanet.org/assessing-iteration-and-testing-in-design-f1d2a623038c.

Chen, X. (2015). Evaluation methods for service design. *NTT Technical Review*. Retrieved from https://www.ntt-review.jp/archive/ntttechnical.php?contents=ntr201512fa8.html.

Choemprayong, S. & Siridhara, C. (2021). Work centered classification as communication: Representing a central bank's mission with the library classification. *Knowledge Organization*, 48(1), 42–54.

Cross, N. (1982). Designerly ways of knowing. *Design Studies*, 3(4), 221–227.

Daigle, B. J. (2012). The digital transformation of special collections. *Journal of Library Administration*, 52(3–4), 244–264.

Design Council. (2020). What is the framework for innovation? Design Council's evolved Double Diamond. Retrieved from https://www.designcouncil.org.uk/news-opinion/what-framework-innovation-design-councils-evolved-double-diamond.

Designthinkers. (2009). DT 5 steps service innovation method. Retrieved from http://www.designthinkers.nl.

Dhaliwal, J. S., Macintyre, M., & Parry, G. (2011). Understanding services and the customer response. In M. Macintyre, G. Parry, & G. Angelis, *Service Design and Delivery* (pp. 1–18). Boston, MA: Springer.

Dobreski, B. & Huang, Y. (2016). The joy of being a book: Benefits of participation in the human library. *Proceedings of the Association for Information Science and Technology*, 53(1), 1–3.

Drew, C. (2017). An iterative, experience and practice-led approach to measuring impact. *Touchpoint: Journal of Service Design*, 9(2), 22–25.

Everall, K. & Logan, J. (2016). A mixed methods approach to iterative service design of an in-person reference service point. *Evidence Based Library and Information Practice*, 12(4), 178–185.

Groyecka, A., Witkowska, M., Wróbel, M., Klamut, O., & Skrodzka, M. (2019). Challenge your stereotypes! Human Library and its impact on prejudice in Poland. *Journal of Community & Applied Social Psychology*, 29(4), 311–322.

Hewett, T. T. (1986). The role of iterative evaluation in designing systems for usability. In M. D. Harrison & A. F. Monk, *People and Computers II: Designing for Usability* (pp. 196–214). Cambridge: Cambridge University Press.

IDEO. (2015). Design thinking for libraries. Retrieved from www.designthinkingforlibraries.com.

Indrák, M. & Pokorná, L. (2020). Analysis of digital transformation of services in a research library. *Global Knowledge, Memory and Communication*, 70(1/2), 154–172.

Interaction Design Foundation. (2020a). Design iteration brings powerful results. So, do it again designer! Retrieved from https://www.interaction-design.org/literature/article/design-iteration-brings-powerful-results-so-do-it-again-designer.

Interaction Design Foundation. (2020b). The principles of service design thinking – Building better services. Retrieved from https://www.interaction-design.org/literature/article/the-principles-of-service-design-thinking-building-better-services.

Kendall, K. E. & Kendall, J. E. (2019). *System analysis and design*. 10th ed. Camden, NJ: Pearson.

Lawson, B. R. (1972). Problem solving in architectural design (Doctoral dissertation, University of Aston in Birmingham). Retrieved from http://publications.aston.ac.uk/id/eprint/40597/.

Leorke, D., Wyatt, D., & McQuire, S. (2018). "More than just a library": Public libraries in the 'smart city'. *City, Culture and Society*, 15, 37–44.

Lumley, R. M. (2014). A coworking project in the campus library: Supporting and modeling entrepreneurial activity in the academic library. *New Review of Academic Librarianship*, 20(1), 49–65.

Mager, B. & King, O. (2009). Methods and processes of service design. *Touchpoint: Journal of Service Design*, 1(1), 20–29.

Mager, B. (2008). Service design. In M. Erlhoff & T. Marshall. *Design dictionary: Perspectives on design terminology* (pp. 354–357). Basel, Switzerland: Birhauser.

Marquez, J., & Downey, A. (2015). Service design: An introduction to a holistic assessment methodology of library services. *Weave: Journal of Library User Experience*, 1(2). https://doi.org/10.3998/weave.12535642.0001.201.

Millward, P. (2019). Deliver a minimum viable service before you invest in a minimum viable product. Retrieved from https://medium.com/@ArtofTheStartup/deliver-a-minimal-viable-service-before-you-invest-in-a-minumum-viable-product-1ff0cd7be80d.

New Zealand Government. (2021). Service design – overview. Retrieved from https://www.digital.govt.nz/standards-and-guidance/design-and-ux/service-design/service-design-overview/.

Nielsen, J. (1993). Iterative user-interface design. *Computer*, 26(11), 32–41.

Nielsen, J. (2011). Parallel & iterative design + competitive testing = high usability. Retrieved from https://www.nngroup.com/articles/parallel-and-iterative-design/.

Oliveira, S. M. (2018). Trends in academic library space: From book boxes to learning commons. *Open Information Science*, 2(1), 59–74.

Ranganathan, S. R. (1931). *The five laws of library science*. Madras: The Madras Library Association.

Polaine, A., Løvlie, L., & Reason, B. (2013). *Service design: From insight to inspiration.* Brooklyn, NY: Rosenfeld media.

Poole, N. (2020, March 19). The future of library and information services [Keynote address]. *OpenAthens Access Lab 2020.* Retrieved from https://openathens.org/access-lab-2020/.

Ramsay, A. (2009). Three reasons to start designing iteratively. Retrieved from http://coderchronicles.org/2009/03/01/three-reasons-to-start-designing-iteratively/.

Rengifo, E. (2018). Iterations in the design process. Retrieved from https://blog.prototypr.io/iterations-in-the-design-process-41bd8d01f244.

Ross, L. & Sennyey, P. (2008). The library is dead, long live the library! The practice of academic librarianship and the digital revolution. *The Journal of Academic Librarianship*, 34(2), 145–152.

Schopfel, J., Roche, J., & Hubert, G. (2015). Co-working and innovation: New concepts for academic libraries and learning centres. *New Library World*, 116(1/2), 67–78.

Sipes, J. (2019). Cookies, user research, and an iterative design process. Retrieved from https://sites.temple.edu/assessment/2019/05/08/cookies-user-research-and-an-iterative-design-process/.

Smith, C. (2020, June). What the future holds: Library thinkers on the most exciting technology and noteworthy trends. *American Libraries.* Retrieved from https://americanlibrariesmagazine.org/2020/06/01/library-technology-what-future-holds/.

Stickdorn, M. & Schneider, J. (2011). *This is service design thinking.* Hoboken, NJ: John Wiley & Sons.

Tavangar, N. (2017). Measurement beyond surveys. *Touchpoint: Journal of Service Design*, 9(2), 66–69.

Technology Strategy Board & Design Council. (2015). Design methods for developing services. Retrieved from https://www.designcouncil.org.uk/sites/default/files/asset/document/Design%20methods%20for%20developing%20services.pdf.

Thamtheerasathian, L., Choemprayong, S., Teerathammonkol, P., & Srisatriyanon, S. (2018). Service design for the design community: TCDC Resource Center's relocation experience. *Arts Libraries Journal*, 43(4), 175–184.

Travis, D. (2017). Why iterative design isn't enough to create innovative products. Retrieved from https://www.userfocus.co.uk/articles/why_iterative_design_isnt_enough.html.

Vacek, R., Puckett Rodgers, E., & Sitar, M. (2019). Diffusing organizational change through service design and iterative assessment. *Library Assessment Conference: 2018 Conference Proceedings.* Retrieved from https://deepblue.lib.umich.edu/handle/2027.42/151766.

van der Steen, J. T., Ter Riet, G., van den Bogert, C. A., & Bouter, L. M. (2019). Causes of reporting bias: A theoretical framework. [Version 2; peer review: 2 approved]. *F1000Research*, 8. Retrieved from https://www.doi.org/10.12688/f1000research.18310.2.

Wishlade, K. (2019). Service design heuristics. Retrieved from https://clearleft.com/posts/service-design-heuristics.

Xie, I. & Matusiak, K. (2016). Interface design and evaluation. In I. Xie & K. Matusiak, *Discover Digital Libraries: Theory and Practice* (pp. 205–230). Amsterdam: Elsevier.

Young, S. W. H., Mannheimer, S., Rossmann, D., Swedman, D., & Shanks, J. D. (2020). Service blueprinting: A method for assessing library technologies within an interconnected service ecosystem. *Public Library Quarterly*, 39(3), 190–211.

Zhai, Y. H., Zhao, Y., & Wang, R. M. (2012). Human Library: A new way of tacit knowledge sharing. In M. Zhu, *Business, Economics, Financial Sciences, and Management* (pp. 335–338). Berlin, Heidelberg: Springer.

Zimmerman, E. (2003). Play as research: The iterative design process. Retrieved from http://www.ericzimmerman.com/s/Iterative_Design.pdf.

5 The assessment and analysis of materials availability

A mixed-methods approach

David Wells

Introduction

The question of the availability of library materials is central to the effective running of a library. Does the library have what its clients want? Can they find or access it? And if not, why not? The analysis of materials availability can thus provide a fundamental measure of performance. It can also deliver valuable information to determine strategies for improvement to library services, for example to collection development practice, discovery system design or information literacy programmes.

This chapter provides a brief historical overview of materials availability surveys, describes the work that has been done in this area at Curtin University Library, and proposes a model that can be applied elsewhere and which reflects the dynamic nature of today's libraries. The increasingly rapid development of technology and the changing and widening expectations of library clients mean that it is now, more than ever, important for library collections and discovery services to be able to respond intelligently to the needs of library users. The systematic monitoring of materials availability is one way to ensure this is achieved. Although the model described was developed in the context of a university library, it can equally be applied to libraries of any size and from any sector.

The main theoretical work in the area of materials availability was done in the 1970s and focused on print resources and on searches by library clients for known items in the card catalogue (Mansbridge, 1986; Nisonger, 2007). Within a physical library, data could quite easily be collected from clients about whether they found what they were looking for and the reasons why they might not have done so. There have, however, been relatively few attempts to transfer the principles of this early work to the far more complex electronic information universe and to the new styles of information searching that have come into being with the development of 'web-style' library discovery systems (Wells, 2020).

Of course, library catalogues and discovery systems are no longer the only tools that clients use to discover information sources or indeed to access them. Google Scholar, ResearchGate, ArXiv, and a myriad of other services

DOI: 10.4324/9781003083993-5

all offer alternative discovery pathways. Clients may also access subscribed databases directly, to a greater or lesser extent bypassing library-provided technical infrastructure. Nevertheless, library systems and holdings continue to play a major role in providing the information needed for study and research, particularly in academic and research institutions. A robust measure of their effectiveness remains an important management tool, and, perhaps more importantly (Town, 1998, p. 81), the monitoring and improvement of performance is an enduring concern.

Work done at Curtin University Library in the last few years has suggested that the current discovery and access environment is too complex to be captured within a single survey instrument (Wells, 2018, p. 16). This chapter presents a mixed-methods approach to collecting data on materials availability from multiple sources, addressing different aspects of the question. These include qualitative data collected from surveys and focus groups, alongside analysis of quantitative data from discovery system logs, document delivery requests and catalogue problem reports. These can be combined to create a holistic view of interactions between clients and library collections, and to provide a basis both for a sustainable performance measure and for ongoing control of service quality. There is no single formula that will serve the requirements of all libraries, but practitioners are invited to choose and adapt those measures which are appropriate to local circumstances.

A short history of materials availability assessment

The beginnings of the systematic study of library availability can be traced back to at least the 1930s (Gaskill et al., 1934). The numerous availability studies conducted since then have been documented in some detail by Mansbridge (1986) and Nisonger (2007). Up to the mid-1980s there had been considerable variation in availability studies in respect of data sources, methodology and analytical framework (Mansbridge 1986, p. 311), but the method developed by Kantor (1976) and Saracevic et al. (1977) was rapidly becoming a standard performance measure, both within individual libraries and for benchmarking against other institutions. It was, for example, promoted in a handbook for performance measures for academic and research libraries that was issued by the US Association of Research Libraries in the mid-1980s (Kantor, 1984).

The Kantor methodology has several distinctive features. First, it differs from other types of availability studies (for example, those based on shelf-lists, bibliographies, items cited in publications by the library's clients or lists specially prepared by subject specialists) by taking actual user search experience as its source of data, collected through a simple user survey. This ensures that a reliable assessment of client satisfaction with the collection can be reached and that an accurate estimate of both client skills and library performance can be made. Secondly, unlike some other approaches that also rely on data collected directly from client requests (e.g. Van House et al., 1990, pp. 60–71), the Kantor method advocates the checking of responses by library staff as soon as possible after the survey is completed to confirm the reported experience. Thirdly, Kantor, building on the probability-based approach outlined by De Prospo et al. (1973), identified a hierarchical series of non-availability categories, or 'branches', following the logic taken in the search process. A 'failure' might occur at any point, and would be sufficient to prevent the library user from proceeding to the next step. In the method's original form (Kantor, 1976), there were four branches:

1 Acquisition – the library does not hold the title.
2 Circulation – all available copies are on loan.
3 Library error – e.g. the item is missing or misshelved.
4 User error – e.g. the client misread the catalogue or looked at the wrong place on the shelf.

It was then possible to calculate a percentage availability figure for each branch, as well as an overall availability figure, and to target remedial action to improve performance at each stage.

Kantor (1984) later introduced a fifth branch between Acquisition and Circulation to accommodate the case where the client noted down the call number from the catalogue incorrectly. Subsequent studies continued to develop the original model (Nisonger, 2007, pp. 31–32). Ciliberti et al. (1987), for example, added a 'Bibliographic' failure to capture the possibility that clients were starting from incorrect citations, and also extended the model to cater for subject searches rather than searches for known items by including branches for 'Matched Query' errors, resulting from a client failing to find the appropriate catalogue thesaurus term for the search they had in mind, and 'Appropriate Title' errors, which occur when users find items matching their search but they have already read them, or the items are in the wrong language, at the wrong audience level or otherwise unsuitable. Other studies, including Harris and Garner (1992), extended the Kantor method to explore the availability of serials as well as books.

The formal materials availability study, whether using the Kantor method or not, was developed in the context of print library collections. Later iterations, such as Poll and te Boekhorst (2007, pp. 64–70), acknowledged that the availability of electronic resources is governed by a distinct set of factors but remained predominantly print focused. The increasingly wide accessibility of the Internet from the mid-1990s, however, meant that ongoing applicability of existing methods began to be questioned. Kaske (1994, p. 317) was already looking for an availability measure that would take into account the newly improved ability of patrons to easily search across multiple libraries to whose holdings they might have access through a distributed collection model. As electronic resources began to form a significant part of library collections, the question of measuring the practical availability of these, alongside the availability of print materials, also began to be raised (Nisonger, 2007, p. 36).

Notwithstanding these reflections at a theoretical level, however, the rapid development of the electronic or digital library, and the systems for managing it, has, in practice, meant there is little consensus about how overall materials availability in the new hybrid print-electronic world might be effectively and consistently measured. Instead, studies have focused on specific aspects of the problem and/or specific technologies facilitating access to electronic materials. One established method, which has its roots in catalogue success surveys (Gouke & Pease, 1982), has been to examine the transaction logs of online catalogues for search failures (that is, searches which produce zero results), often in conjunction with a broader range of measures of catalogue use behaviour (Peters, 1989; Peters, 1993; Thorne & Whitlach, 1994). Ciliberti et al. (1998) used OPAC transaction log analysis to cross check the results of a Kantor-style survey in those cases where searches were reported as unsuccessful. As catalogue technology developed, transaction log analysis has been extended to openURL link resolvers (Crum, 2011). Investigation of link resolver performance has also been combined with survey or sampling methods (Mann, 2015; Mann & Sutton 2015; Stuart et al., 2015). Other studies that have focused on a single aspect of the materials availability question include a citation sampling technique to test the electronic availability of journal articles (Nisonger, 2009) and an analysis of the availability of bibliographic references from graduate dissertations (Rosenberg, 2015).

Building on early work by Michael Buckland (1975) into the practical problem of making books available to library users, some studies have also tried to distinguish between 'immediate' availability, as measured by conventional availability studies, and 'later' availability, which takes into account the operation of recall systems and, especially, inter-library loan (Chaudhry & Ashoor, 1994, pp. 300–301; Gregory & Pedersen, 2003, pp. 286). While many researchers have been happy to confine themselves to a single data source, others have begun to explore questions of materials availability using both quantitative and qualitative data. Nancy Kress et al. (2011), for example, have explored the failure of users to locate known items in the context of the placement of unnecessary inter-library loan requests using a cognitive workflow technique combined with usability testing.

Materials availability at Curtin University Library

Curtin University is a large public teaching and research institution based in Perth in Western Australia, delivering teaching programmes in Perth, in regional Western Australia, and at campuses in Malaysia, Singapore, Mauritius and Dubai. In 2019 the total student headcount was approximately 58,000 (Curtin University, Office of Strategy and Planning, 2019). The University Library maintains physical collections for the use of staff and students in Australia as well as electronic resources available to all Curtin clients regardless of location. At the end of 2019 the library's collection comprised some 340,000 physical monographs, 580,000 ebooks and 165,000 electronic journal titles (Council of Australian University Librarians, 2020). Ensuring that the collection is relevant to the needs of clients, easily discoverable and accessible when required is an essential task of the Library's Collections Team.

The University Library has used materials availability surveys as one element of its quality programme for a number of years, and a summary of the approaches used can be found in Table 5.1.

In 1995, The Council of Australian University Librarians (CAUL) published a materials availability indicator for internal evaluation and benchmarking purposes based, essentially, on the Kantor model (Taylor, 1995; Poll & te Boekhorst, 2007, p. 68). Curtin University Library ran this on several occasions between 2005 and 2010. While the CAUL instrument produced valuable results and facilitated clear improvements to library services, it remained focused on print, and by the end of this period it was clear that the relevance of the survey to actual client use of the library and its collections had sharply diminished (Tang, 2014, pp. 706–707). This realisation led to two attempts at Curtin in following years to develop a methodology that would adapt the earlier process to the increasingly electronic library by investigating the availability of electronic resources as well as print resources. The emphasis remained on the actual practical experience of library clients, rather than proxy measures such as sampling or list checking. At the same time, the data collection itself was moved into an online environment to reduce the amount of staff time required to conduct the survey and facilitate the processing of data.

First, a revised methodology was developed (Tang, 2014, pp. 707–708). This involved a locally written script, embedded into Curtin's Primo discovery system, which randomly intercepted client searches and invited clients through a pop-up window to take part in a survey. If they agreed to participate and indicated they were looking for a specific item, they were subsequently sent a survey form to complete. The methodology then allowed for the reasons given by responders for not finding items to be later verified by

Table 5.1 Summary of materials availability surveys run at Curtin University Library

Year	Survey Method
2005 2008 2010	The Council of Australian University Librarians (CAUL) Materials Availability Survey for known physical items only, using forms handed out in the library.
2013	Pilot survey by random invitation in library catalogue, covering both physical and electronic items.
2017	Full revised survey by random invitation in library catalogue, covering both physical and electronic items.
2018 2019	Simplified survey offered from catalogue and library website, allowing for all formats, and for subject searching as well as known item searching.

library staff. In the pilot survey, which was run over a 3-day period in 2013, however, this step was omitted. Although the number of responders was relatively small, the survey reported an availability rate of 67 per cent (Tang, 2014, p. 708), which is broadly comparable to earlier studies (Nisonger, 2007, p. 40). Running the 2013 pilot survey brought to light several practical problems. Most significantly, it depended on custom programming that was not easily transferrable from one catalogue system to another; the invitation pop-up behaved inconsistently across different browsers and did not work well on mobile devices; and the delay between when responders searched for their item and when they completed the survey was likely to reduce the response rate and to make subsequent library verification unreliable.

In 2017, Curtin ran a follow-up to the 2013 pilot (Wells, 2018). This again relied on an in-house script, encoded into the catalogue search box on the Library home page, to invite participants on a randomised basis. This time the invitation appeared in a new browser tab or window, with a link through to a survey in Qualtrics. The survey asked respondents for some contextual information about their physical location and enrolment, what they were looking for and whether they found it. If they answered 'No' they were asked to select one of the following reasons:

- The Library does not have it.
- It was not clear to me whether the Library has it or not.
- It is available electronically but I cannot access it.
- It is only available in print but I want an electronic copy.
- None of the above [respondents were asked to provide further details].

Responses were then verified by Library staff and coded accordingly. The survey achieved a disappointingly low response rate, and failed to reach the threshold of 400 respondents recommended by Kantor (1984, p. 44). This was partly perhaps because of 'survey fatigue' in the online environment, and partly because the survey delivery method was, in practice, quite cumbersome. The browser tab or window with the invitation and survey often appears to have obscured the catalogue results screen from view, causing some confusion among participants. Because the survey was constructed as part of a research project, ethics approval from participants was required to indicate consent to the data collection and this made the survey itself quite wordy. Moreover, paradoxically, the decision to provide an incentive for people to participate by inviting them to enter a draw for a small prize may also have added a further discouraging level of complexity. Nevertheless, the 2017 survey reported that 66 per cent of clients had found what they were looking for (Wells, 2018, p. 14), in line with the 2013 pilot. Some acquisitions failures were identified and corrected, while the number of errors related to poor information literacy was relatively small.

Although the 2017 survey only invited responses from people who were looking for a specific known item and who wanted it in electronic format, the results suggested that, in fact, many respondents were conducting more general searches for works on a given subject or by a given author. Restricting materials availability to known items was thus confirmed as only a very partial guide to client satisfaction with the library's collection. Another shortcoming was the need for searchers to re-identify the item they were looking for after already searching for it in the catalogue. The data provided was not always complete, and it was hard to proceed to verification of the survey response without being sure whether the search as recorded actually corresponded to the search as conducted by the client in the catalogue.

The overall experience of the 2013 pilot and the 2017 Curtin Materials Availability Survey (CMAS 2017) suggested that the survey-based approach to data collection, advocated by Kantor and others and used successfully in earlier investigations at Curtin, was no longer effective. Response rates had also fallen in other library surveys. The increased complexity of library materials and access in a hybrid print–electronic library had made it difficult to construct a simple survey instrument that would capture the detail of either clients' interactions with library systems or their experience with the discovery and location of the materials they were looking for. Nevertheless, there remain clear advantages to attempting to analyse materials availability on the basis of actual client data.

In September 2018 Curtin ran a considerably simplified survey (CMAS 2018) embedded into the library catalogue search page. This asked a single question, 'Did you find what you were looking for?', allowing for a yes/no response, and also providing a box for feedback. No personal data was collected and no attempt was made to collect information about possible reasons for failing to find desired items. The survey response, however, did contain a referrer URL, which replicated the search which had been made in the library catalogue. In recognition that not all clients use the library catalogue as the starting point for searching for information the survey was also placed on a website providing links to the library's most important full-text and indexing databases.

CMAS 2018 was more successful than CMAS 2017 in attracting client responses (and did reach the threshold of 400), and the referrer URLs allowed library staff to verify the availability of items that were reported as not found in a relatively straightforward way, even though they did include reasons for 'failure' as identified by the clients. The 'Yes' response rate was 56.6 per cent. A similar simplified survey (CMAS 2019) was run in April 2019 and achieved a 'Yes' response rate of 59 per cent.

A framework for a mixed-methods approach

The survey used for CMAS 2018 and CMAS 2019 was designed ultimately to form part of a mixed-methods approach to the materials availability question. Rather than relying on a single and intricate survey instrument, the project team identified a series of approaches, each of which addresses separate, though sometimes overlapping, parts of the problem, to create a rich and complex overall set of findings (Fidel, 2008, p. 266). Some of these depend on data collected directly from clients; others, in line with the principle of Killick and Wilson (2017, p. 1) that, whenever possible, assessments should be made from information already held, make use of data already collected by systems in use in the library. At the time of writing none of the identified techniques apart from the simplified survey have been put into practice, and development of the full methodology is a work in progress. Nevertheless, it is hoped that the framework will provide libraries wishing to pursue the concept of materials availability as an assessment measure with a useful starting point.

The framework makes use of a revised categorisation of availability errors based on the Kantor model, and amendments to it by Ciliberti, but it is further adapted to allow for both electronic information resources and for subject searching. (The more neutral term 'error' is preferred here to the 'failure' used by earlier studies.) The types of error are listed hierarchically below, though because of the increased complexity of the search and fulfilment process it may not be possible within the mixed-methods framework to provide a meaningful analysis in terms of Kantor's conception of branching. Investigation of the different types of error has implications for different aspects of library service provision, as summarised in Table 5.2.

A. Bibliographic Error. Caused by searching from an incorrect citation, either manually or by following an incorrectly constructed link from an external source, such as Google or from an online reading list. Libraries can potentially reduce the incidence of bibliographic errors by improving information literacy if citations have been poorly constructed by clients, or by alerting those responsible for presenting incorrect citations.

Table 5.2 Error types and areas of remediation

	Acquisition	Information Literacy	Catalogue Design	Workflow	Other
A. Bibliographic		X			X
B. Acquisition	X				X
C. Inappropriate Search		X	X		
D. Catalogue Use		X	X		
E. Fulfilment	X			X	
F. Library Process				X	
G. System				X	
H. Retrieval		X	X		
I. Inappropriate Result	X				

B. Acquisition Error. Caused by the item(s) required not being held in the library's collection, and by extension, not being available through the library's systems, which might include links to freely available items on the web and the library's document delivery networks. Libraries can correct this type of error by acquiring missing resources or by improving alternative access paths for clients.

C. Inappropriate Search Error. Caused by the client using search terms or strategies which are not best aligned to the desired outcome. For a subject search this might involve inappropriate choice of thesaurus terms. For known-item searches, depending on the search functionality of the library's discovery system, poor results might be caused by including too much information, for example, by cutting and pasting whole citations from external sources. Libraries can provide mitigation through information literacy training and/or by improving catalogue indexing and retrieval algorithms.

D. Catalogue Use Error. Caused by the client misinterpreting information presented in the library catalogue or other library systems, for example, searching in an inappropriate discovery scope or index. Libraries can reduce this type of error by optimising catalogue design and ensuring that suitable help and training is available on catalogue use.

E. Fulfilment Error. Caused by a desired item being unavailable because it is in use by another client, for example, for a physical item because it is on loan; for an electronic item because licence limits have been reached. Options available for libraries to improve in this area include purchase or licensing of additional copies for high-use items, and refinement of library processes to predict usage and to share limited access equitably.

F. Library Process Error. Caused when an item is missing or in process, or when a link to an electronic item is incorrect. Libraries can potentially limit this type of error by making changes to workflows, for example, to improve through-put times, implement closer inventory control and ensure systematic checking of broken links.

G. System Error. Caused by a technical problem with access or authentication. This type of error is likely to be temporary and unpredictable, but libraries can minimise the risk of it occurring by paying close attention to information technology protocols.

H. Retrieval Error. Caused when the client misreads the shelf for physical items or misunderstands access instructions for electronic material. Libraries may be able to address this through information literacy training and/or through improvements to catalogue design.

I. Inappropriate Result Error. Caused, for example, when the client wants an electronic version but only print is available, or the client wants print but only electronic is available. For a subject search, this error may be caused when the client retrieves items but these do not satisfy the client's information requirement because, for example, they have already been read or because they are pitched at the wrong readership level. The primary remediation available here is for libraries to expand the materials they hold or to which they provide access.

Assessment of materials availability 85

The different data sources in the framework are intended to collect different sorts of information, as indicated below. The availability error types that are illuminated by each data source are summarised in Table 5.3. The discussion which follows refers primarily to the information management context at Curtin but is intended also to inform thinking at other libraries.

1 **Survey.** The 'Did you find it?' survey used in CMAS 2018 and CMAS 2019 was primarily intended to establish a simple overall measure of client satisfaction. However, the fact that the response from the catalogue includes a referring URL provides a secondary tool for analysing the reasons behind non-availability. Analysis of the search terms used by clients who recorded they did not find what they were looking for allows the library to investigate most, if not all, of the identified error types. However, care needs to be taken with interpretation, as it cannot always be certain that the reason for error identified by the researcher is the same as that actually experienced by the client. Acquisition, Inappropriate Term, Circulation and Library Process errors may be fairly easy to establish, but other types of error may not be evident unless the client takes advantage of the opportunity to leave an explanatory note. Bibliographic errors, in particular, may be difficult to spot if clients, as is not uncommon, choose to search for specific items using keywords from the title or author. For the same reason, it may not always be easy to distinguish between a specific item search and a search for items on a subject.

Table 5.3 Availability errors and assessment methods (notations in brackets indicate partial coverage)

	1. Survey	2. Catalogue Transaction Analysis	3. Catalogue Problem Reporting	4. Document Delivery Requests	5. Focus Groups
A. Bibliographic	(X)	X			
B. Acquisition	X	X		X	X
C. Inappropriate Search	X	X			X
D. Catalogue Use	(X)	X	X	X	X
E. Fulfilment	X		X		
F. Library Process	X		X	X	
G. System	(X)		X		
H. Retrieval	(X)		X		X
I. Inappropriate Result	(X)				X

2   **Catalogue Transaction Analysis.** The log files from Curtin's Primo discovery system provide a huge volume of data about search behaviour. Most relevant to the materials availability question are searches with no results. Since there may be multiple ways to formulate a search in order to retrieve the desired results, and since in the discovery system environment it is relatively unusual for a search to produce zero results, this type of report cannot be considered to provide a comprehensive measure of availability. However, transaction analysis does provide an indicative measure relating to certain types of search error, and may be useful to suggest improvements to library processes, catalogue design or information literacy. Specifically, it can identify Bibliographic errors, where the user proceeds from an incorrect citation, Acquisition errors, Inappropriate Term errors and Catalogue Use errors, which might arise, for example, from inadvertently searching in the wrong catalogue scope. Preliminary investigations at Curtin have shown the presence of a type of Catalogue Use error that results from including too much metadata in a search or including punctuation or characters that prevented a direct match. A specific type of Bibliographic error also results from following incorrectly formed links into the catalogue from an external source, such as a student reading list. When identified, library staff can trace these back to the originating location and arrange for them to be corrected. The actual number of searches with zero results may be less significant than the causes. Many appear to result from mistyping and are presumably immediately corrected by the user.

3   **Catalogue Problem Reporting.** Authenticated users of the Curtin Library Catalogue (that is, Curtin staff and students) have access to a help facility within the Availability section of all records for electronic resources. Alongside links which resolve to the full text of journal articles, for example, they see a link labelled 'Report a problem with this resource'. This connects to a web form that allows users to report any problems that they have encountered. The form is imported into the Library's LibAnswers instance together with referring information from the relevant catalogue page and the clients contact details. This enables a member of library staff to investigate the problem reported, take appropriate action and contact the client to provide assistance or ask for clarification. In closing the case within LibAnswers it is possible to add a category code to indicate what type of problem was encountered and thus, to some extent, reflect the 'failure types' referenced in the Kantor materials availability methodology. (This approach, of course, is not specific to the use of the LibAnswers software, but libraries can adapt it for any customer relationship management tool.) In practice the majority of issues picked up through this process are linking errors within the Primo Central database. Since the 'report a problem' link is only available from within the catalogue and for electronic information resources, its ability to pick up Bibliographic or Acquisition failures is somewhat limited. On the other hand, because the link requires users to authenticate to library systems, it would be possible to correlate reported problem types to

demographic data, such as year level and enrolment data for students, and academic department for staff.

4 **Document Delivery Requests.** Eligible clients who are unable to obtain access to items they require may choose to place requests through the library's document delivery service. The number of requests thus forms a measure of Acquisition errors from the point of view of the library's immediate collection. Document delivery requests may also be placed erroneously for items that are in fact held by the library. In this case, further investigation by library staff may reveal Catalogue Use errors or Library Process errors – either the user will have read the catalogue incorrectly (or perhaps failed to consult it altogether), or will have been blocked at an access level, perhaps by an incorrect link. In many cases, this component will not provide a comprehensive view of the library's performance because the document delivery service may be restricted to some client groups only (e.g. staff and research students, as at Curtin). If, with Chaudhry and Ashoor (1994), and in line with Lorcan Dempsey's conception of the 'facilitated collection' (Dempsey, 2016), we take the document delivery service to form part of the library's fulfilment suite, then document delivery supply times and success rates can also be used as a measure of materials availability.

5 **Focus Groups.** Focus groups are less suitable for generating a performance measure than the four approaches listed above, but can be designed to elicit qualitative data about library clients' experience in discovering information and gaining access to resources. Specifically, libraries can use them to establish clients' perception of gaps in the collection and identify any difficulties that clients find in formulating searches, interpreting results and making the best use of catalogue functionality. Focus groups are thus able to provide data to allow library staff to address, on the one hand, Acquisition and Inappropriate Result errors and, on the other hand, Inappropriate Search, Catalogue Use and Retrieval errors. Moreover, unlike the four primarily quantitative approaches, focus groups are also able to take into account demographic data, and thus provide a more targeted analysis in respect of specific client segments. Focus groups are relatively costly to run in terms of staff time – in practical terms it may be more valuable to use them to explore areas of concern that have been identified through other measures rather than as a completely independent instrument.

Conclusion and implications for practice

The mixed-methods approach outlined above offers an adaptable, practical and sustainable methodology for libraries to assess materials availability geared to the complexities of today's hybrid library services and discovery systems. Compared with the earlier survey-centred approach, it loses some ability to gather potentially useful data about client demographics, for example, the location of the clients and whether they are staff, undergraduates or postgraduates. Moreover, because of its explicitly multifaceted nature, this framework does not allow for clear analysis of the 'failure branches' identified by Kantor. On the other hand, it gains much in simplicity and consistency. It is neither intrusive for clients nor a huge burden in staff time to administer. The methodology is inherently flexible, as it no longer relies on a single instrument but involves a series of analyses that can easily be run on different schedules. Libraries can add new instruments as and when they are identified, and can easily adjust the data collection to cater for different and evolving library systems technology.

In line with the original aims of materials availability analysis, the framework allows library staff to collect quantitative data that can be used for performance measurement and benchmarking. The basic survey provides a simple overall measure of availability. Data derived from catalogue transaction logs, catalogue problem reporting and document delivery requests can also be used as partial and indicative measures of availability. It would further be possible for a library to combine the measures derived from different inputs, with suitable weighting of each corresponding to local priorities, to form a single generalised metric for performance monitoring. At the same time, the approach collects qualitative data that can be used to inform collection development, system design and information literacy, and facilitate specific service improvements.

Libraries of all sizes and types can easily adapt the suggested framework to meet their needs. In practical terms, and depending on which measures were chosen for implementation, a library would require the following roles:

1   A coordinator, or coordinating group, to determine which measures were to be undertaken, to establish scheduling, and to analyse outcomes with a view to identifying possible improvements to library services.
2   A technical lead and/or systems librarian to create and embed a simple survey form into the library's catalogue or web page, to extract systems data relating to catalogue transactions and document delivery requests, and to configure the library's catalogue problem reporting system as required.
3   A librarian to verify non-availability of items as reported from the survey instrument and from catalogue problem reporting.
4   Expertise in convening and running focus groups and in collating and analysing the feedback received.

Bibliography

Buckland M.K. (1975). *Book availability and the library user*. Pergamon.
Chaudhry, A.S., & Ashoor, S. (1994). Comprehensive materials availability studies in academic libraries. *Journal of Academic Librarianship*, 20(5), 300–305.
Ciliberti, A., Casserly, M., Hegg, J., & Mitchell, E. (1987). Material availability: A study of academic library performance. *College and Research Libraries*, 48(6), 513–527.

Ciliberti, A., Radford, M.L., Radford, G.P., & Ballard, T. (1998). Empty handed? A material availability study and transaction log analysis verification. *Journal of Academic Librarianship*, 24(4), 282–289.

Council of Australian University Librarians. (2020). [Institutional Data page]. https://statistics.caul.edu.au/inst_data.php [accessed 10 October 2020].

Crum J. (2011). An availability study of electronic articles in an academic health sciences library. *Journal of the Medical Library Association*, 99(4), 290–296.

Curtin University, Office of Strategy and Planning. (2019). Curtin University student statistics 2015–2019. https://planning.curtin.edu.au/stats/students2015-2019.cfm [accessed 10 October 2020].

De Prospo, E.R., Altman, E., & Beasley, K.E. (1973). *Performance measures for public libraries*. Public Library Association.

Dempsey, L. (2016). The facilitated collection. http://orweblog.oclc.org/towards-the-facilitated-collection/ [accessed 7 July 2020].

Fidel, R. (2008). Are we there yet? Mixed methods research in library and information science. *Library and Information Science Research*, 30(4), 265–272.

Gaskill, H.V., Dunbar, R.M., & Brown, C.H. (1934). An analytical study of the use of a college library. *Library Quarterly*, 4(4), 564–587.

Gouke, M.N., & Pease, S. (1982). Title searches in an online catalog and a card catalog: A comparative study of patron success in two libraries. *Journal of Academic Librarianship*, 8(3), 137–143.

Gregory, D.J., & Pedersen, W.A. (2003). Book availability revisited: Turnaround time for recalls versus interlibrary loans. *College and Research Libraries*, 64(4), 283–299.

Harris, M., & Garner, I. (1992). Using an availability survey to improve service at a university library. *Australian Academic and Research Libraries*, 23(1), 25–34.

Kantor, P.B. (1976). Availability analysis. *Journal of the American Society for Information Science*, 22(5), 311–319.

Kantor, P.B. (1984). *Objective performance measures for academic and research libraries*. Association of Research Libraries.

Kaske, N.K. (1994). Materials availability model and the internet. *Journal of Academic Librarianship*, 20(5–6), 317–318.

Killick, S., & Wilson, F. (eds.) (2017). *Putting library assessment data to work*. Facet.

Kress, N., Del Bosque, D., & Ipri, T. (2011). User failure to find known library items. *New Library World*, 112(3/4), 150–170.

Mann, S. (2015). Electronic resource availability studies: An effective way to discover access errors. *Evidence Based Library and Information Practice*, 10(3), 30–49.

Mann, S., & Sutton, S. (2015). Why can't students get the sources they need? Results from a real electronic resources availability study. *Serials Librarian*, 68(1–4), 180–190.

Mansbridge, J. (1986). Availability studies in libraries. *Library and Information Science Research*, 8(4), 299–314.

Nisonger, T.E. (2007). A review and analysis of library availability studies. *Library Resources and Technical Services*, 51(1), 30–49.

Nisonger, T.E. (2009). A simulated electronic availability study of serial articles through a university library web page. *College and Research Libraries*, 70(5), 422–445.

Peters, T.A. (1989). Why smart people fail: An analysis of the transaction log of an online public access catalog. *Journal of Academic Librarianship*, 15(5), 276–273.

Peters, T.A. (1993). The history and development of transaction log analysis. *Library Hi Tech*, 11(2), 41–66.

Poll, R., & te Boekhorst, P. (2007). *Measuring quality: Performance measurement in libraries* (2nd rev. ed.). Saur.

Rosenberg, Z. (2015). Citation analysis of M.A. theses and Ph.D. dissertations in sociology and anthropology: An assessment of library resource usage. *Journal of Academic Librarianship*, 41(5), 680–688.

Saracevic, T., Shaw, W.W., & Kantor, P.B. (1977). Causes and dynamics of user frustration in an academic library. *College and Research Libraries*, 38(1), 7–18.

Stuart, K., Varnum, K., & Ahronheim, J. (2015). Measuring journal linking success from a discovery service. *Information Technology and Libraries*, 34(1), 52–76.

Tang, K. (2014). Did they find it? Developing a revised materials availability survey. In S. Durso, S. Hiller, M. Kyrillidou, & A. Pappalardo (Eds.), *Proceedings of the 2014 Library Assessment Conference: Building effective, sustainable, practical assessment, 4–6 August* (pp. 706–709). Association of Research Libraries.

Taylor, C. (1995). *Materials availability*. Council of Australian University Librarians.

Thorne, R., & Whitlach, J.B. (1994). Patron online catalog success. *College and Research Libraries*, 55(6), 479–497.

Town, J.S. (1998). Performance or measurement? In Department of Information and Library Management, University of Northumbria at Newcastle, *Proceedings of the 2nd Northumbria International Conference on Performance Measurement in Libraries and Information Services, 7 to 11 September 1997*. Information North.

Van House, N.A., Weil, B.T., & McClure, C.R. (1990). *Measuring academic library performance: A practical approach*. American Library Association.

Wells, D. (2018). The Curtin Materials Availability Survey 2017. *Performance Measurement and Metrics*, 19(1), 12–17.

Wells, D. (2020). Online public access catalogues and library discovery systems. In B. Hjørland & C. Gnoli (Eds), *Encyclopedia of Knowledge Organization*. International Society for Knowledge Organization. https://www.isko.org/cyclo/opac [accessed 6 October 2020].

6 Data visualisations for library collections

Applying an inquiry-based approach

Susan Payne, David Dudek, Bonnie Wittstadt, Mark Cyzyk and Tom Edwards

Introduction

Libraries at research intensive institutions build collections that are the accumulation of hundreds of years of individual faculty and librarian choices and the varying changes in the institution's research agenda. This approach to collections can often lead to gaps, building areas that are no longer as crucial to the institution while leaving potential gaps in the collection. As libraries seek to figure out how their collections fit into the context of the institution's research, assessment and data visualisations can help illuminate a collection's strengths and gaps. Describing collections with data attributes has been happening for decades. This additional information—such as numbers of checkouts or how many items exist in a call number range—provides little help in telling the story of a library collection that has been built over years. Data visualisations, on the other hand, can quickly reveal a pattern that may have failed to emerge from thousands of lines on a spreadsheet. This paper will explore how an assessment team (the authors of this chapter) at the Sheridan Libraries at Johns Hopkins University employed new techniques to make visualisations that overcome the limitations of simply knowing numbers of volumes and assorted collection metadata. These visualisations help librarians perceive the story of how that collection fits together within a larger context of collections across the Johns Hopkins libraries, both in print and online materials.

The library has considerable data and analysis that has been collected or created over the years either for reporting or collection development. Key pieces of information were often spread over multiple spreadsheets, which made advanced computational analysis on the data difficult. Most importantly, the data from the Integrated Library System (ILS) failed to answer how scholars were using the collection beyond raw circulation numbers and, more importantly, why. Because this data often existed in separate spreadsheets, it often failed to yield answers to questions that librarians asked about a collection. Articulating these questions and grouping them into themes helped frame and develop the assessment and visualisations. Inquiry-based assessment enabled librarians to examine their understanding of the collection

DOI: 10.4324/9781003083993-6

as well as identify pain-points that existed for them when trying to make sense of thousands of rows of collection data on one spreadsheet. Focusing on creating better ways to visualise collection data helped the assessment team build a culture of inquiry and continuous learning around collection assessment projects. The goal of this assessment began with the questions raised by librarians around what content scholars would need in the collection on-site, off-site, online, and through other libraries via resource sharing. Other considerations included the following:

- What easy decisions could be made to move materials out based on low local usage patterns?
- Could the library leverage resource sharing and e-book data and relate it to physical circulation usage data to understand overall usage patterns that would make managing the print collection easier?

By starting with existing circulation data, this assessment helped us understand what data was missing and what approaches proved successful.

Literature review

Collection assessment has become increasingly important to libraries as budgets shrink and library staff are increasingly called on to articulate the value of their services and collections. Over the past four years, the library staff at the Sheridan Libraries have encouraged and fostered a culture of assessment by employing formulas to predict shelf density and measurement on library floor plans and through other visualisations. Collection assessment can appear quite different for each library and employ many different strategies, methodologies, and approaches (Horava 2010). Well-thought-out studies have included evaluating physical collections by publisher, publication year (Adams & Noel 2008), density of use (Altmann & Gorman 2000), and through employing formulas to predict growth (Kohl, Benaud, & Bordeianu 2017, Castro 2011, and Sapp & Suttle 1994).

The Sheridan Libraries, like many peer libraries, have extensive electronic holdings as well as print holdings. Developing methodologies helped the team understand how to correlate different formats and data, such as how usage and resource sharing data (Knievel, Wicht, & Connaway 2006) might overlay and relate to physical usage data from the circulating collection. In the literature review, Geographic Information Systems (GIS) came up as a potential option for overlaying collections data in layers (Xia 2004) and other space usage measures (Bishop & Mandel 2010). The team ultimately pursued both a formulaic and mapping approach simultaneously in an effort to determine which resulting visualisations would best support librarians in their decision making and collection evaluations (Borin & Yi 2011). This enabled the team to think about how to employ GIS, as well as other tools such as Tableau and Excel, to display and compare data on the collection.

Inquiry-based collection assessment and evaluation

The literature review helped inspire the idea of asking questions around the collection in order to pinpoint where existing data needed to be connected or new data needed to be created. To begin, librarians and other library staff engaged in a series of conversations around collection assessment to raise any existing concerns or issues with the current collection evaluation workflow. Librarian responses were documented on white boards and then later organised by theme and ranked by level of difficulty. This, in turn, informed the next steps of developing overall collection assessment priorities by seeking answers to the following:

- Who is using the collection in terms of academic departments and groups of users, such as undergraduate students, graduate students, and faculty, and what are they using?
- How much and what type of material is requested, renewed, or recalled? Can this drive decisions on what is moved off-site and kept in the building?
- What is the relationship between circulating books from print and online? This includes attempting to correlate information from different sources, such as resource sharing statistics and online book downloads.
- Where are collections being used physically and how can this be visualised differently?
- A more challenging question: Why are these users using the collection?

Of the questions above, how much and what type of material that is used, requested, or recalled can be determined through the ILS directly? Correlating the collection usage to user data requires changing how data for both circulation activities and user transactions are saved and stored to comply with legal and privacy requirements. Due to privacy concerns, the library had saved only the last check-out date and aggregated all other dates. This practice of retaining cumulative circulation data makes answering some of the questions about who is using the collection, normally the most accessible user-based question in terms of collection assessment, more difficult. The assessment team began to ask whether periodic exports of circulation data could be connected to aggregated user information to protect patron privacy. Also, could circulation data then be mapped to high-level user information like academic major or school division to understand who is using the collection in terms of aggregated groups of users? The assessment team also began to think about how the library could leverage existing resource sharing and vendor-supplied data, which might then allow them to paint a fuller picture of usage across formats of print and online usage.

Asking who is using the collection is different from trying to understand why they are using that collection. Although this is a worthy question, the assessment team decided the first step was to focus on who and what, before the why. To safeguard patron privacy, Library of Congress call numbers, as well as any patron data, would be aggregated at the highest possible level. Plenty informed the team's thinking at the time, including well-timed National Information Standards Organization (NISO) webinars on patron privacy, such as "Understanding Privacy, Part One: What Data is Being Collected and By Whom?" and "Two Part Webinar: Understanding Privacy." In addition, the assessment librarian for the Sheridan Libraries had support for this approach from both library IT staff and the library's Chief Privacy Officer. Later, best practices would be codified into best practices through a newly created Library Assessment and Data Analytics committee, and this is still true as of the printing of this book chapter.

Methodology

In 2017, a large-scale collection evaluation project focused on curating the library collection and provided the catalyst for subject-specialist librarians (hereafter referred to as librarians) desiring new ways and easier methods for making decisions around the collection. At the time, the Sheridan Libraries (hereafter referred to as Library) created a new department focused on assessment. One of the early projects assigned to this new team involved a large-scale evaluation of the collection in order to recommend what should stay on-site before, during, and after the planned renovation of the library. When the project began, expertise and experience of the assessment team varied and spanned a wide range of library operations, collection assessment, data analytics and visualisations, and computer programming. The literature review helped the assessment team decide to pursue different strategies for data visualisation in parallel. Even though the methods varied, the underlying intent was the same across all of the efforts—a desire to develop visualisations that would inform what should remain on-site in the Library and what should move to a nearby high-density storage facility.

The team chose a dual approach to save time evaluating which method might work better for evaluating the collections. The first method focused on formulas, while the other used data from the ILS, which was imported into a Geographic Information Systems software. The underlying commonality between each approach was an intent to be able to layer different types of datasets together to illustrate a story. In this effort, the team undertook the task of standardising data definitions and sought to display assessment data at the highest possible call number or shelf range. While this work can be implemented at other libraries, the ongoing assessment is a continual effort, with lessons learned from both successes and failures. Employing multiple approaches has, ultimately, helped refine the approach and the resulting techniques and visualisation. This assessment work took place over the course of several years in the Milton S. Eisenhower Library, a collection of over one million volumes on the university campus, with an additional three million volumes in off-site storage.

Library rings and space heat maps

At this point, library staff began to consider how this usage data might be displayed effectively on library maps and charts. The underlying goal still revolved around helping library staff better manage retention, acquisitions, using off-site storage, and efficiently utilising limited stack space in advance of future Milton S. Eisenhower Library renovation plans. Data has been compiled over a number of years on various aspects of the print collection at Eisenhower Library, indicating its strengths, weaknesses, use, and overcrowding. This data, along with usage data, seemed like information that would translate well to the library floor plan.

One way to determine the size of a library's collection is to measure open space on each shelf. In this case, size is defined by the number of physical shelves, the length of shelves, and the total length of empty space on each shelf. Library staff experimented with different ways to measure shelf space before settling on a standard approach. As measuring empty shelf space in the library requires time and attention to detail, often one staff member measured and documented all the empty space using a laser distance measuring tool, available from a local hardware store for less than $30 USD. This tool provided an accurate measure of space and was used in determining numbers of books on the shelves. The empty space measurement has proven to be more accurate, and more time-saving, than measuring the space filled. Space filled is easily calculated by subtracting empty space from the length of the shelf.

In 2017 and 2019 library interns added additional collection size data in linear feet to the library's traditional library spreadsheets. Including the space data allowed library staff to create library ringed-data visualisations comparing collection size to circulation usage and in-house collection usage (see Figure 6.1). This allowed, for example, for the comparison of American literature collection size against the usage of the item both within the library (internal usage) and through circulation data, specifically the number of checkouts. At this time, library interns helped by documenting the process with step-by-step instructions so others could recreate this data later on or in different libraries. The process is as follows:

1   Start by entering the shelf range and call number into a paper form or spreadsheet (using paper if you prefer to enter the data into a spreadsheet later). In situations in which there are multiple two-character call numbers in one range, split the data up by call number. In situations in which a two-character call number spans multiple ranges, split the data up by range.
2   Count the number of used, usable shelves. Note: Do not include unused shelves and folio shelves consisting of large art books that lie flat on the shelf instead of upright. These were counted with a separate formula.
3   Count the number of used folio shelves, again, not measuring this shelf as all of our folio shelves had books lying flat on them so they were treated as full shelves.

4 Count the number of unused, usable shelves.

   a   Do not include unusable shelves, which include the top and bottom rows when they are too close to the ceiling or rows that are in front of a maintenance panel.
   b   Count top and bottom rows that are consistently empty in the unused, usable shelves.
   c   When there are a set of empty usable shelves between two call numbers, count them as usable shelves at the end of the last call number (not the beginning of the next call number).

5 Use the laser pointer to calculate the total amount of empty space.

The measurement data was then entered into a form for later input into an Excel spreadsheet:
Team Member_____
Date _____
Two-character Call Number Section _____
Range # _____
# of used, usable 36" shelves _____
# of used, usable 30" shelves _____
# of used, usable 18" shelves _____
# of unused, usable 36" shelves _____
# of unused, usable 30" shelves _____
# of unused, usable 18" shelves _____
Total empty space as measured by the laser pointer _____

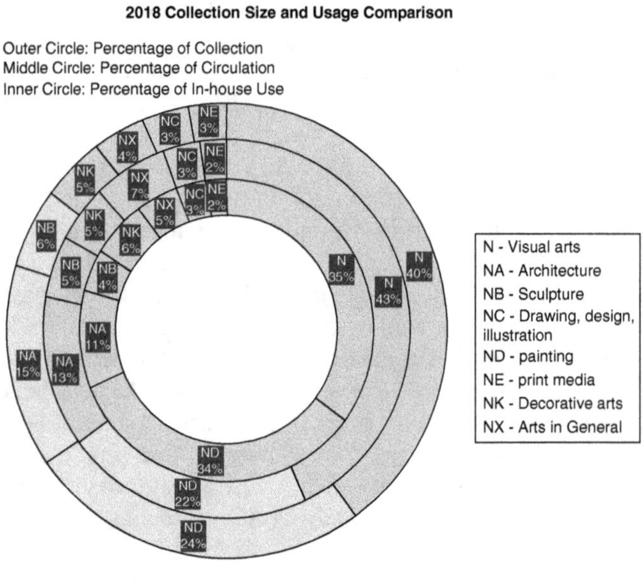

Figure 6.1 2018 collection size and usage comparison.

This data was also later entered into a spreadsheet through the use of a google form to make data entry easier for library staff, although the above information could also be entered on a sheet of paper and tallied in an Excel spreadsheet if that would be an easier approach. This space data was then presented on a graphic representation of the library floor plan. The types of data include usage, space crowding, and growth areas of the collection (available through acquisition data).

The floor plan, created in an Excel spreadsheet, illustrated space issues for various subjects, such as art history and literature monographs. Each range of bookshelves is represented by a range of cells, and each section is represented by an individual cell. When displaying the floor plan, it is important to include landmarks like tables, carrels, restrooms, elevators, stairs etc. This use of visual cues by way of familiar landmarks helps orient staff curating the collection represented on the spreadsheet. Labeled landmarks and numbered ranges also reinforce physical associations between the collection and informed data queries.

The library rings compared collection size, circulation data, and in-house usage by all top call numbers, and then later by specific two-letter call numbers. The data gathered in the measurement of shelves was also used in a simple table set up in Excel that compared these measures (see Figure 6.1).

Resource sharing and circulation data comparisons

In 2018 the team began comparing usage between circulation data, resource usage data for borrowing and lending, and online book vendor-supplied statistics. Library of Congress call numbers (LCCN) joined these different datasets, although this effort required extensive data clean-up. This represented the first successful effort by MSEL library staff to relate print, electronic, and resource sharing data. After some internal discussion about user privacy, library staff then compiled the data by call number, specifically to two-letter Library of Congress call numbers. The team referred to the resulting efforts as a crosswalk because usage data from different sources and formats were related to the same two-letter LCCN.

Starting with the fiscal year (FY) of 2017–2018, library staff exported the circulation reports from Horizon, the integrated library software (ILS). In order to export these reports, staff worked with technical services staff to identify what data would need to be extracted from the system. IT staff used this data request to export that data from the ILS. Sometimes clarification would be needed to make sure the resulting spreadsheets would be useful.

Ivy Plus Libraries Confederation's (IPLC) borrowing consortium includes Johns Hopkins University, Columbia University, Cornell University, Princeton University, Harvard University, Stanford University, Massachusetts Institute of Technology, Yale University, University of Chicago, Brown University, University of Pennsylvania, Duke University, and Dartmouth College in a book resource sharing endeavour.

Table 6.1 2018 collection size and usage comparison

LCCN	In-house Use	Circulation	Collection Size
PQ	613	3,961	25,611
PS	650	5,523	19,227
PN	452	7,822	17,946
PR	553	4,618	17,334
PT	246	1,648	14,571
PA	448	1,695	9,891
P	154	3,728	7,371
PJ	941	1,167	4,644
PL	94	647	3,228
PG	62	726	3,174
PC	104	392	3,042
PE	253	256	1,857
PF	31	107	1,263
PB	6	14	585
PM	3	25	492
PK	6	96	429
PD	8	4	165
PH	5	24	165
PZ	0	37	105

The IPLC's data, compiled on the Penn Library Data Farm at the University of Pennsylvania and downloaded as Excel files, included usage data based on the borrowing and lending activities of each institution by lender/borrower—such as request number, request date, shipped/received date, pick-up location, OCLC accession number, LCCN or Dewey call number, ISBN, publisher information, and final status (received/unfilled).

The raw data had many incomplete fields, based on the cataloguing supplied by the ultimate lending library for each transaction. This necessitated using searches to normalise the data to the LCCN. Efforts were made to use a script later on, but initially, this work involved extensive manual searching and evaluation. OCLC Worldcat database was chosen as a starting point for likely matches, with the following order of priority:

- OCLC accession number—many numbers were outdated or incorrect
- LCCN often not in record
- ISBN
- JHU Catalyst public catalogue
- Catalogue of lending library
- Conversion of Dewey numbers to LCCN

- Other—included searches in Google of "Title + OCLC" (which often produced new results not initially found in OCLC database); OCLC searches of author output with similar subject matter, based on common keywords.

Diacritics complicated searching in OCLC. When present in Romance languages, searches were often successful, but in other languages (Turkish and Arabic, most notably), title fields were rife with block characters, question marks, and other punctuations. These characters were deleted from title fields, which made the searches easier.

For this assessment, 10,800 call number fields needed to be manually searched, representing over 18% of over 60,000. Despite rigorous searching, some call numbers were not found: 12 titles in FY 2017, 9 in FY 2018. These books were usually single copies of titles not listed in OCLC Worldcat, or were designated as "non-circulating" and without a call number in the lender's library catalogue. For both years analysed, Sheridan Libraries borrowed and lent equally 30,000 books and videos through one of our significant resource sharing programmes.

ProQuest Ebook Central (formerly called EBL), is a web-based online library containing academic electronic books. This was the first choice for analysis of database-supplied e-books as vendor-supplied usage data include LCCN. While vendor-supplied statistics indicated that downloads of e-books were easily quantifiable, views were harder to interpret. Page views, included in the data, showed what triggered e-book purchases through a demand driven acquisition model.

Library staff compiled barcode scans, performed daily on books pulled from book stacks by patrons, into a yearly total that reflected interest in serial or monograph titles. This usage occurs in the library and does not require checking out the book, i.e., if a title did not circulate, if only a view of an image was needed, if a quick view of a citation or reference was needed, or if the size of the book was inconvenient for carrying. These scans were particularly helpful in assessing interest in art history titles, as many patrons use these over-size titles for quick reference before placing them on tables to be scanned and reshelved. These in-house totals, by LCCN, were added to a spreadsheet that compared the print and e-book usage. Next the team decided that space data for the collection would help create more useful visualisations using all or elements of this data crosswalk, ultimately displayed in heat maps or other comparative visualisations.

Compiling data using Excel

Shelves are visualised on the spreadsheet, with one cell representing each stack of shelves. So, if the range contained ten sections, they were allocated ten cells. The ranges on the spreadsheet correspond to the actual floorplan, which includes familiar reference points, which are also labelled cells. Each shelf range on the spreadsheet is assigned the appropriate call number range, corresponding to the ranges on the actual shelves. Space is left between columns to represent aisles. The spreadsheet represents the physical layout of the library floor and is recognisable for library staff.

When the replication of the floor was complete on the spreadsheet, colour coding of the cells was first applied to represent data. For publishing this work, the team converted colours in our example (see Figure 6.2) to a pattern fill feature to indicate the free space availability of the collection within a range. Our measurements were now represented by patterns that were assigned the following values: Overcrowded, Full, Caution, Critical, and Growth Space. These values, contained on a legend, were defined by percentages of open space relative to either the rest of the collection or the floor, depending on the question being asked of the data. Notably, these percentages differed by floor or area depending on the size of the books and the density of the books and how much desired growth space needed to be achieved. Newly acquired volumes and monographs can also be depicted by adding their counts to existing data and assigning new cell patterns, if necessary, based on their ranges' subsequent densities.

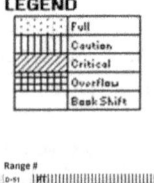

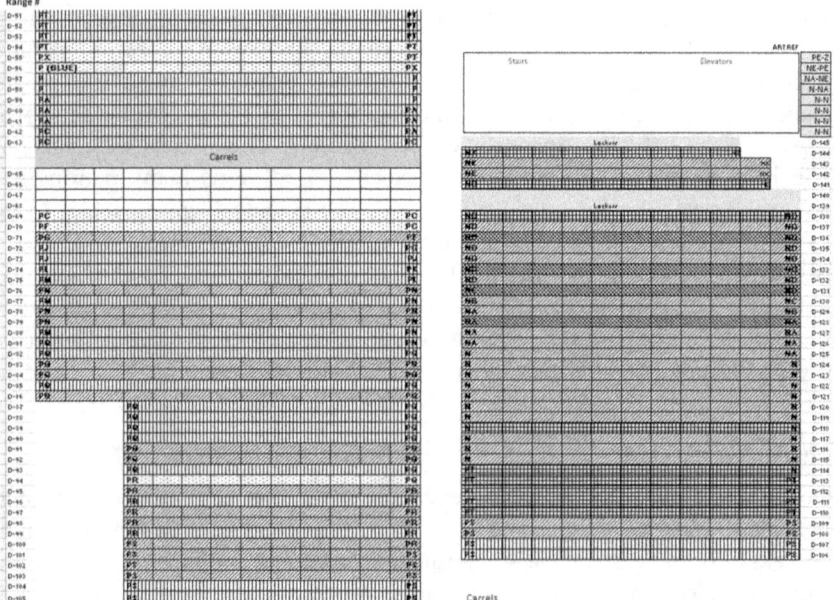

Figure 6.2 D-level heat map.

The completed spreadsheets, one for each Library level, graphically represent the library space and shelving needs of the physical collection. A collection development librarian can locate their section of the stacks easily and have an immediate picture of space trends in this section. When using patterns or colours to represent space, librarians will be presented with data that indicates where the collection requires weeding, for instance, or where there is little growth, and can then compare this to curricular and discipline data. The most important aspect of this visual is that it will raise questions about areas of the collection, allowing librarians to make deeper inquiries of further data. Combining usage data will also prompt questions of whether a subject area should be a) developed, b) an area for de-acquisition, or c) an area with likely transfers to our off-site Libraries Service Center storage facility.

In addition to the spreadsheet as a tool to make collection development decisions, librarians will have usage visualisations that will inform their respective disciplines. Academic departments require this data during external reviews and when making curricular decisions. The spreadsheets will answer broad questions immediately and inform the reader on what specific questions to ask and what data to apply in the future.

Once library staff grow accustomed to using the heat map tool to gauge the collection's strengths and weaknesses, the spreadsheet images of the library stacks will be used to reveal additional aspects of the collection and assist in creating a finely curated collection. Acquisitions data can be applied to the same spreadsheet with values assigned to colours that represent growth or atrophy. Since the floor designs on the spreadsheets are images that are familiar and bear meaning to library staff, the spreadsheets then lend themselves to present other types of data.

GIS library collection assessment project

ArcGIS, from Esri, is a program designed to capture, store, manipulate, and present spatial and geographic data. While library circulation rates, gate counts, and reference statistics give administrators a view of library usage, this project was designed to explore if ArcGIS might help fill in details from other sources for a more nuanced view of usage data within the physical footprint of the Library. Historically, the Library's circulation data has limitations due to how the data was collected and retained. As a result, spreadsheets generated from the Library's integrated library system tended to be text-heavy, long, and difficult to finesse. With its innate ability to overlay different data, ArcGIS seemed like an intriguing option for illustrating areas of heavy library usage. In addition, this project hoped to provide a common location-based uniform identifier for library space-related projects. In the ArcGIS visualisations, call numbers act as addresses on shelves; if a call number is an address, then a shelf range becomes a street. This made visualisation by location possible. Although this sort of analysis can be done with spreadsheets, using a

GIS rendition provides immediate visual feedback, which often has more impact than looking at and interpreting raw data in tabular form.

If a call number is an address, then a shelf range is a street. Due to ever shifting physical volumes, call numbers, addresses, and on-shelf ranges, streets do not have a precise location; but relatively stable demarcations of the shelf ranges do exist. The Sheridan Libraries at Johns Hopkins subscribe to a commercial product, StackMap, which is integrated into the public interface of our catalogue and shows patrons the shelf range for a particular call number. The Library supply the StackMap service with our shelf ranges, and they then provide an Application Programming Interface (API) that locates a single call number on a shelf range, which is then highlighted on a patron-facing floor map of our building. The initial thought for this project was to use the existing StackMap API to locate a call number on a shelf range. While this approach worked well for 10 call numbers, it did not work for 100+, insofar as each call number look-up required a slow, web-based API call. Using this approach for a 5+ million volume collection did not scale beyond proof of concept.

The next step involved translating this process into something that could run locally against a feed of millions of call numbers if needed. The first step involved exporting shelf range data out of StackMap and into a spreadsheet. The second step included exporting collection usage data, complete with call numbers, out of the integrated library management system and saving it in a spreadsheet. With these two sets of data exported in structured format, the team then wrote a Ruby script as follows:

- Create an in-memory database ("LookupAndResults").
- Create a table in that database for the shelf range look-up data ("tblLookup").
- Create another table in that database in which to store the results of our processing ("tblResults").
- Open the look-up spreadsheet ("lookup.xls") and loop over it, inserting each row into the tblLookup table.
- Open the call number spreadsheet ("callnumbers.xls").
- The goal at this point is to loop over each row in the call number spreadsheet and perform a look-up against the tblLookup table to determine the shelf range for that call number. A few notes about this: First, for the sake of speed and efficiency, the only rows looped over in tblLookup are ranges that either begin and/or end with the first letter of the call number we are attempting to look up. Second, the team needed a way to parse and normalise call numbers so they can be compared against our look-up begin- and end-range call numbers. Luckily there is a handy Ruby "gem" for this: lcsort (https://github.com/pulibrary/lcsort).
- Once the begin-shelf-range call number, the end-shelf-range call number, and the call number in question have been parsed and normalised, the

call number fits between two end points. To do this we made an algorithm that created a three-item list out of these data, then sorted the list. If the call number in question is the middle/second item in this sorted list, then it's between the two range end points and in that specific range.
- As the loop proceeds, these results are logged into the tblResults table in our database.
- Once all call numbers have been processed, and shelf ranges determined for each, the contents of the tblResults table export to the local filesystem in CSV format, suitable for importing into ArcGIS.

In Ruby, this was accomplished with the help of the following utility libraries: rubygems, roo, lcsort, sequel, sqlite3, and csv. At the time of this writing, the team is translating the Ruby script into Python, one of the native languages of ArcGIS, in the hope that we can then integrate these processes directly into our GIS application.

Any stacks that held only non-circulating volumes were removed from the analysis, as to not skew the classification breaks with null values, but these stacks were noted as non-circulating in the final map visualisations. The initial framework for the model was created in ArcGIS Desktop ArcMap using CAD (computer-aided design) drawings of each floor. A line feature class, i.e., a rectangle representing each stack in the building, showed where circulating items were shelved, ultimately presenting the usage statistics of each stack. With a "From_" call number and a "To_" call number listed in the associated attribute table, the Ruby script could use this bounding call number information as an index that would determine in which stack a book should be located. Assuming this process would be repeated on a regular basis to show trends and changes in where the circulating hotspots were, it made sense to create a model in ArcGIS' ModelBuilder.

The initial model was created in ArcGIS Desktop ArcMap and then migrated into ArcGIS Pro, which allows for more capability for multi-floor overlays and eventually better integration with Johns Hopkins Organizational ArcGIS Online account. This model looped together as follows:

- Created a scratch geodatabase (to hold necessary temporary outputs).
- Put tabular.csv file in scratch geodatabase, GIS-ready format by adding an object ID (Table to Table). Note: it is a parameter of the model, and needs to be filled in @ run.
- Computed frequency of checkouts per each stack (Frequency).
- Determined on which floor each stack is located (i.e., Query[Left](StackNum, 1]).
  a Initially used in ArcMap because each floor was mapped separately.
  b SQL expression used because the first character of a stack number (StackNum) is floor designation.
- Divided table into subsequent floors (Table Select).

- Joined each table to correct floor map stack feature layer (Add Join).
- Symbolised stacks (Apply Symbology by Layer), so that all five floor maps were symbolised in a similar breakdown by frequency; the classifications were calculated using the initial frequency table prior to separating by floors.

Because of the ability to view multiple maps simultaneously, and with the future option to use improved indoor capabilities, the model was updated to be used in ArcGIS Pro. This updated model is constructed as follows:

- Created a scratch geodatabase (to hold necessary temporary outputs).
- Tabular.csv file was put into scratch geodatabase, with GIS-ready format by adding an object ID (Table to Table). Note: it is a parameter of the model, and needs to be filled in @ run.
- Computed frequency of checkouts per each stack (Frequency).
- Joined full table to correct stack feature layer (Add Join).
- Symbolised each stack based on full data set (Apply Symbology by Layer).

All floors will be viewed in a single map frame, using the Range tool to take advantage of the slider functionality to view only one floor at a time within the same frame, i.e., the maps are stacked on top of one another. The Range tool allows you to then interactively cycle through the levels of the stack via the slider bar.

Conclusion and lessons learned

Over the past few years, we have learned a great deal about our library usage data, as well as limitations within datasets and various tools. Librarians and library staff want easy-to-use tools that they can manipulate and interact with to access both visualisations and the data behind them. An initial pilot project designed to test this concept included extracting data from the Johns Hopkins ID card system to count patron entries to Eisenhower Library and Brody Learning Commons. This includes setting up the library data warehouse by central IT, loading J-card data successfully, as well as data from library services like circulation and reserves. By gradually hosting more library services and operational data in the Johns Hopkins University Data Warehouse, library staff will have a better process for data extraction, transformation, and visualisation that can be displayed through Tableau dashboards. Exporting circulation data monthly solves a long-standing problem presented by data that could only previously be extracted cumulatively, except for the last checkout date.

Additional challenges involve pulling in data from different sources and connecting them together, where clear connectors or common identifiers do not exist in the original data. For example, Interlibrary Loan or other vendor-provided statistics often do not include LCCN or subject information. In order to compare data from different sources without a unifying subject or call number, a common element must be added. Depending on the size of the data sets, this could take a significant amount of time and expertise. While librarians still use Excel spreadsheets to help make collection decisions, these visualisation efforts have given librarians a new way to undertake targeted reviews of usage data, connected to user information by call numbers, as well as visuals that illustrate overcrowding, growth, and usage in a dynamic collection that is constantly adjusted to curate the most useful on-site scholarly collection possible. The authors recommend that the development of consistent metadata standards across e-book publishers would help make this usage data easier to incorporate in future assessments.

Visualising the collection by floor plan in Excel or through rings proved accessible, as the resulting images were easily sharable and understood. Long term, Library staff will be able to filter data as needed to make these visualisations. A standard data structure and consistent data dictionary will save time by not having to create or correlate the data from scratch, as initially. While GIS has been proven to be successful as a concept and an approach, in practicality it has not been implemented into the collection evaluation workflow; however, the assessment team remains hopeful that more applications and use cases may be developed in the future. The various approaches the assessment team have employed leverage existing data to answer questions about the Library collection. These efforts have helped librarians engage with collection data visually—first manually, but long-term through data stored in the data warehouse. The most significant benefit has been to tell a better story about print and electronic resources usage while aiding with collection maintenance by predicting where the collection will need to be shifted based on growth. While the exercises of creating meaningful visualisations proved time intensive initially, overall, the assessment team has succeeded by helping librarians engage with complex and rich datasets through an inquiry-guided approach.

Bibliography

Adams, B., & Noel, B. (2008). Circulation statistics in the evaluation of collection development. *Collection Building*, (2), 71. https://doi.org/10.1108/01604950810870227.

Altmann, K. G., & Gorman, G. E. (2000). Density of use as a criterion in the deselection and relegation of serials. *New Library World*, (3), 112. https://doi.org/10.1108/03074800010324567.

Bishop, B. & Mandel, L. (2010). Utilizing geographic information systems (GIS) in library research. *Library Hi Tech*, 28(4), 536–547. https://doi.org/10.1108/07378831011096213.

Borin, J., & Yi, H. (2011). Assessing an academic library collection through capacity and usage indicators: Testing a multi-dimensional model. *Collection Building*, 30(3), 120–125. https://doi.org/10.1108/01604951111146956.

Bradley, W. B., & Mandel, L. H. (2010). Utilizing geographic information systems (GIS) in library research. *Library Hi Tech*, 28(4), 536–547. http://dx.doi.org/10.1108/07378831011096213.

Castro, R. C. (2011). Developing tools to calculate space availability, establish collection distribution, and determine growth rates: A case study. *Technical Services Quarterly*, 28(4), 406–418. https://doi.org/10.1080/07317131.2011.597691.

Hendley, M. (2019). Discovering data discrepancies during deselection: A study of GreenGlass, Aleph, and due date slips circulation data. *Technical Services Quarterly*, 36(3), 233–248. https://doi.org/10.1080/07317131.2019.1621558.

Horava, T. (2010). Challenges and possibilities for collection management in a digital age. *Library Resources & Technical Services*, 54(3), 142–152. http://dx.doi.org/10.5860/lrts.54n3.142.

Knievel, J. E., Wicht, H., & Connaway, L. S. (2006). Use of circulation statistics and interlibrary loan data in collection management. *College & Research Libraries*, 67(1), 35–49. https://doi.org/10.5860/crl.67.1.35.

Kohl, L., Bénaud, C.-L., & Bordeianu, S. (2017). Finding shelf space in an academic library: A multifaceted approach. *Technical Services Quarterly*, 34(3), 268–282. https://doi.org/10.1080/07317131.2017.1321378.

Sapp, G., & Suttle, G. (1994). A method of measuring collection expansion rates and shelf space capacities. *Journal of Academic Librarianship*, 20(3), 156–161. https://doi.org/10.1016/0099-1333(94)90009-4.

Weare, W. H., Moffett, P., & Cooper, J. P. (2016). Preparing for renovation: Estimating shelf occupancy to inform decision making regarding the redevelopment of library space. *Collection Management*, 41(3), 168–181. https://doi.org/10.1080/01462679.2016.1212755.

Xia, J. (2004). Using GIS to measure in-library book-use behavior. *Information Technology and Libraries*, 23(4), 184–191.

7 Moving beyond downloads and views when assessing digital repositories

Hollie White

Introduction

The digital repository creation story has been repeated many times by practitioners and researchers (Rodgers & Sugarman, 2013; Wang, 2011). The story is as follows. An institution or organisation decides to invest time and money into building a repository. Staff members, working within their own budgetary and permission-based constraints, pull together a beginning collection of relevant digital objects. Downloads begin to escalate, and at times skyrocket. Overjoyed at its success, the staff turn to other collections and concerns, leaving the original collection to its own devices, to be occasionally updated but rarely analysed or studied. Sometimes this repository is rarely analysed due to time constraints, while in other instances it is due to a lack of knowledge as to what would be the best approaches for studying the repository.

This chapter discusses how to assess the impact and use of repositories by developing an holistic assessment programme. This work elaborates on content presented in White, Aiken, and Shapiro (2012), White and Le (2015), Buckland, White, and Szydlowski (2016), and White (2017), which explored building repository metrics programmes specifically for the American law library community. The chapter begins by introducing the various types of repositories. Next, the literature surrounding institutional repository history related to development and assessment is presented by methodology type. The chapter then looks at the difference between repository downloads, views, and use. It concludes with a section on how to develop a systematic repository assessment programme that incorporates both stakeholder input and repository statistics. The systematic repository assessment programme presented is meant to be used by individuals who manage their own repository system and does not cover the evaluation of external repositories, such as how to evaluate the best external repository for data deposit or open sharing.

Types of repositories

Repositories sit in a unique space encompassing both collections and services. Functions of repositories include collecting, organising and preserving objects, enhancing the visibility of scholarship or data, and demonstrating an institution's commitment to Open Access (Baughman, Roebuck & Arlitsch 2018, p. 68). They can support publications, data, and other intellectual outputs not typically managed by 'traditional' publishing. Repositories serve institutions and organisations at different stakeholder levels, ranging from students to faculty members to researchers in the field (Schatz, 2012; White, 2014). For that reason, different types of repositories have been developed and are in current use.

Two main repository types are institutional and subject repositories. Institutional repositories are, "a library of digital objects and associated metadata from a single institution" (Clobridge, 2010, p. 7). These repositories respond to the individual goals of the institution and can be multidisciplinary in nature when operating in an academic/university environment. Much of the academic and professional literature around repositories focuses on this type of repository.

Subject repositories are similar to institutional repositories in that they are digital archives for research outputs, but instead of having an institutional connection as the uniting collecting criterion, it is the domain or subject area that is central to these repositories. Subject repositories are also known as domain repositories, centralised repositories, or disciplinary repositories. Other forms of repositories include national repositories, which focus on collecting content produced within a certain country, and potentially funded by national-level funding, and data repositories, which collect and make available data underlying research and/or publication, such as Dryad or the CEDA repository.

Repository history: Development and assessment

A large part of the academic and professional literature around repositories focuses on institutional repositories. In July 2002, the Scholarly Publishing and Academic Coalition (SPARC) released a position paper that introduced the concept of the academic institutional repository (Crow, 2002). Lynch (2003), though, is commonly attributed as beginning the repository movement and defined an institutional repository as, "a set of services that a university offers to the members of its community for the management and dissemination of digital materials created by the institution and its community members". Many of the papers written between 2002 and 2005 focus on encouraging buy-in to the repository movement (Crow, 2002; Dill & Palmer, 2005; Lynch, 2003) or explore individual repository creation experiences (Graham, Skaggs, & Stevens, 2005).

The thoughts of information scientists and library administrators involved in repository development during these early years was, "if you build it, they will come". This sentiment emphasised the belief that by simply providing repositories to user communities, the collections within them will develop naturally without intervention from information professionals. Yet, van Westrienen and

Lynch (2005) examined academic institutional repository deployment in 13 countries (in North American and Europe) and found that when submission was cumbersome, multiple submissions by an individual was less likely.

By 2007, more institutions concluded that just building a repository was not enough to engage people in using it (Davis & Connolly, 2007; Markey et al., 2007; Xia, 2007). From this point in time, many repository creators had to rethink recruitment strategies and deposition guidelines (Davis & Connolly, 2007). While in the 2000s researchers (as opposed to librarians) may not have been active participants, there was still documented need within certain communities to have open access to information, especially research data (Scherle et al., 2008). In addition, the extent to how embedded and invested library and information professionals should be in repository development (especially data repositories) was unclear (Big Data, 2008; Heidorn, 2008; Salo, 2010; Scaramozzino, Ramirez, & McGaughey, 2012). The data repository movement gained more momentum around this time, particularly in relation to subject-based data.

Assessment became more important within the various repository communities as repository creators began to examine the purpose, impact, and use of repositories in more detail to understand the unique role that repositories have within different environments. Repository assessment has been conducted to demonstrate 'impact and value' and often manifests in the form of reports (Baughman, Roebuck, & Arlitsch 2018, p. 66). In addition to surveys being used to investigate repository implementation and use, other methods include basic statistical frequency reporting (Council of Australian University Libraries, 2013; Gieseke, 2011), interviews (Cullen & Chawner, 2010), and usability studies (Hee Kim & Ho Kim, 2008).

From December 2015 to March 2016, an Institute of Museum and Library Service (IMLS)-funded project used a survey to assess how institutional repositories report use and impact (Baughman, Roebuck, & Arlitsch, 2018, p. 65). This research impacted the development of the Repository Analytics and Metrics Portal (RAMP) (https://www.montana.edu/disc/projects/ramp/), which is designed to help improve repository metrics. Researchers, such as Price and Fleming-May (2011) and White, Chen, and Liu (2018), point out that descriptive and inferential statistical approaches to assessment can be helpful in explaining a repository's use and potential impact.

Overall, the literature indicates a variety of approaches have been taken to assess repository impact and use. This suggests that there is no single method for assessing repository usage that is sufficient for creating a comprehensive understanding of the impact and use of a repository. What is needed instead is a systematic repository assessment programme that can be used in any repository setting and will continuously and holistically transform easily accessible downloads and views data into understandable narratives.

Downloads, views and use

> Understanding the intent and use of institutional repositories (IR) is essential to justifying their expense and maximizing their value.
>
> (Baughman, Roebuck, & Arlitsch, 2018, p. 66)

Terms such as downloads, views, and use are often vague despite their almost ubiquitous application within the repository community and literature. As the repository literature emphasises, the study of use is a central part of trying to determine repository success. But what does 'use' mean in a repository context and how should it be measured? According to Price and Fleming-May (2011), the term 'use', as utilised by library scientists, is often vague, general, and can mean any interaction involving a library. The same can be said for the term 'repository use', which is contextualised by repository visits to and downloads of repository content to individual item level. Usage and download statistics are considered a "simple way" to evaluate interest in repository content (Neylon & Wu, 2009, p. 3). To interpret and assess the value of this use, "current [in 2009] institutional repository software provides few tools for metadata librarians to understand and analyze their collections" (Nichols et al., 2009, p. 230). However, downloads themselves are frequently called into question about being an accurate academic measure of scholarly impact, while citations are seen as a measurement of the impact or influence of a paper or research. Haddow explores using bibliometrics for collection assessment in a later chapter. Earlier research has shown that downloads and citations influenced each other (Brody, Carr, & Harnad, 2002) including a correlation between items that were downloaded leading to citation (O'Leary, 2009) and increased downloads after citation (Moed, 2005). Yet, a download is not the same as a citation. In fact, Moed (2005) found that within two years of publication it took, on average, 100 downloads to equal one citation. This research suggests that downloads may not be equivalent to academic citations, but downloads, especially from open access sources, can indicate the use of works in non-academic or more practical ways.

External software, apps, badges, plug-ins, and widgets integrated into repositories have also been used to assist in understanding use beyond citations. There are two main types of external software/applications: those that track website activity and altmetrics. Tools that track website activity include Google products like Google Analytics products and Google Search console data. Google Marketing Platform and Google Analytics products, download reports, and search logs are tools that provide insight into how repository collections are used by the community (White, Chen, & Liu, 2018, p. 14). Downloads are one type of usage-based metric that can be supplemented by using altmetrics (i.e. alternative metrics), a type of crowd-sourced peer-review or practice (NISO, 2016; Priem & Hemminger, 2010; Priem et al., 2010). Alternative metrics standards like those implemented in Altmetric (https://www.altmetric.com/products/free-tools/) and Plum Analytics (https://plumana

lytics.com/integrate/embed-metrics/) examine downloads and other online interactions at the article level and can be included in repository badges or widgets. Information professionals have used altmetrics to add value to existing repository content by:

- encouraging further content deposition;
- emphasising scholar outputs, increasing research awareness;
- assisting with collection development based on researcher publication patterns;
- supporting academic promotion; and
- suggesting ways to promote public attention. (NISO, 2016, p. 3)

Instead of taking downloads at face value, Altmetric emphasises how downloads need to be qualitatively analysed and examined in order to understand how and why they occur, in addition to expanding on quantitative approaches to thinking about downloads. Similarly, Impactstory (https://profiles.impactstory.org/), which evolved into Our Research (https://our-research.org/), is the researcher version of Altmetric that focused on the overall qualitative story and context of research outputs and its dissemination in order to understand use and impact. Taken as a whole, the interest in altmetrics, traditional citations, downloads, and views of researcher outputs shows an evolving understanding of the impact and use of scholarly output. The development of a systematic repository assessment programme can achieve this from a repository perspective.

Developing a systematic repository assessment programme

The following section presents information on how to develop a systematic repository assessment programme. This programme is the repository equivalent to periodic health evaluations. In medicine, the periodic health evaluation (PHE)

> consists of one or more visits with a health care provider to assess patients' overall health and risk factors for preventable disease, and it is distinguished from the annual physical exam by its incorporation of tailored clinical preventive services and laboratory testing as part of health risk assessment.
>
> (Boulware et al., 2007)

PHE examinations differ in that they look at history and risk assessments. Instead of only responding to obvious problems, the examinations are meant to help prevent future illness and improve overall quality of life. By relying on downloads and view reports alone, a repository's impact is not fully represented. Developing a systematic repository assessment programme is a more holistic approach to understanding repository impact and use.

Methodological overview

The recommendations that follow use a nested mixed methods approach to evaluating repository content and impact. Nested mixed methods designs collect both quantitative and qualitative data with one approach embedded in the other (Castro et al., 2010; Creswell et al., 2003). In this type of research design, quantitative data collection is embedded within the qualitative methodology and analysis in order to produce narratives. Both descriptive statistics and basic qualitative analysis is used to understand repository impact. The descriptive statistics include basic frequencies (counts), as would be used in a download or views-only analysis, combined with analysis revolving around themes that examine repository interactions to construct a story of repository impact. This approach is ongoing and cyclical in nature as data will be collected, analysed, documented, and continuously communicated over a repository's lifetime.

Repository assessment programme development steps

While every repository instance and institution or organisation responsible for a repository is unique, the process of creating a systematic repository assessment programme can be applied in most settings. The four steps outlined in Figure 7.1 are a consolidation of the steps presented in White (2017).

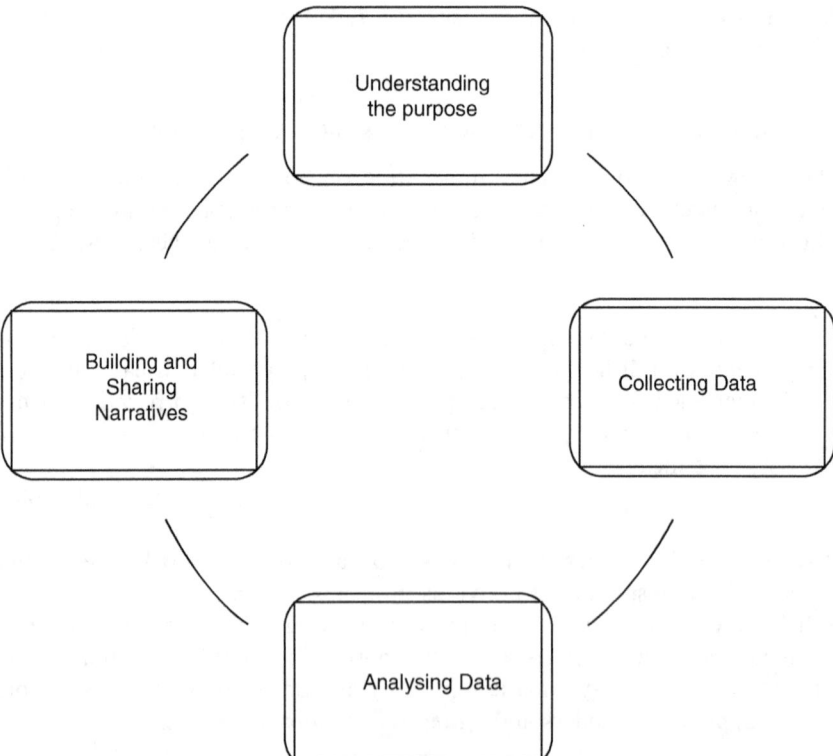

Figure 7.1 Repository assessment programme development steps.

Step 1: Understanding the repository purpose

Before commencing data collection, it is important to get a sense of the repository purpose. The purpose should be understood in the following ways:

- When was the repository created?
- Why was it created?
- In what ways has the repository changed over time? Why and when did it happen (e.g. provider or software changes; interface updates etc.)?
- Who is the main user community? What other stakeholders care about repository content?
- What is collected in the repository?
- How is repository content added?

Understanding the story of how the repository was created and grew over time will create a base narrative to build analysis upon. If the purpose and history of the repository are not already documented, then this is a good time to write a narrative explaining the answers to all of the questions above and to collocate supporting documents (e.g. annual reports, notes discussing repository development, and any press releases etc.). Once the questions above have been answered, a final preliminary question needs to be considered:

- How does the repository support institutional or organisational goals and objectives?

To demonstrate impact to funding bodies and administrators, the purpose of the repository ultimately needs to clearly link to higher level priorities. If this cannot be clearly articulated, the overall purpose and scope of the repository will need to be re-examined and drafted prior to starting any data collection. Since the goal of the assessment programme is to understand impact and use, having a solid understanding about the bigger picture of why the repository matters at an institution or organisational level will help in driving data collection and building the repository narrative.

Step 2: Collecting quantitative data

The systematic collection of data is another aspect of a repository assessment programme. Prior to starting the data collection, a plan should be set in place about what type(s) of data will be collected and at what frequency this data collection will occur. Data collection should begin by focusing on areas that are most important to the purpose of the repository and assist in promoting how the repository supports institutional goals, as articulated in Step 1. As a minimum, quantitative data about the number of items and depositors, in addition to views and downloads, can be discovered at the individual item and collection levels.

Ideally, this data will be collected both retrospectively and into the future, based on the criteria established in the plan. While it may seem easier and more time efficient to collect present and future data only, the absence of retrospective data will affect the construction of a complete narrative of the repository. The purpose of knowing the entirety of the data history of the repository is to understand the 'baseline' of repository use so that anomalies and issues can be investigated when necessary. To extend the health analogy into the repository space, collecting predetermined repository data at regular and planned intervals will allow a holistic picture about the repository 'health' to emerge.

Step 3: Analysing data

Once a critical mass of data has been collected, analysis about what that data means and how it can support the purpose of the repository can begin. Analysis, like data collection, should be planned and scheduled in a systematic way, as opposed to being spontaneous. Analysis can occur in both quantitative and qualitative ways.

In relation to quantitative data analysis, beyond basic frequencies (counts or adding), mathematical means and median may be helpful to calculate at the month and year level for views and downloads. Another approach is to create quartiles to understand which items are high and low use (White & Haddow, 2018). Extending the descriptive statistics into inferential statistics, like correlations or significance testing, may allow further use of data-focused analysis (White, Chen, & Liu, 2018).

Qualitative analysis is less number-focused and more interpretative. Kim (2015, p. 189) identifies four basic elements of qualitative data analysis: codes, categories, themes, and patterns. These four elements can be used to examine what the data are indicating about repository use. To start, try to identify patterns by asking questions, such as what times of the year experience the most or least use? High or low levels of use can then be compared with certain annual events, such as academic finals or conferences, or seen in alignment with repository history, for example software migration or interface redesign. Data analysis pulls together the data you have collected and contextualises it within the history and overall environment of the repository.

Step 4: Building narratives to share with stakeholders

Many different narratives can be built around repository data, but not all narratives are correct for different user communities and stakeholders. Reviewing written explanations, documents, and notes collected in Step 1 helps connect the data collected in Step 2 and analysed in Step 3 to be shared with the true audience of a certain narrative. Communicating with stakeholders about assessment results can take the form of one-on-one conversations, emails, or newsletters, written reports or articles, or presentations at conferences or board meetings.

Sharing narratives is a key part of any assessment activity that has an impact both inside and outside an institution or organisation. Within an organisation, narratives are kept as documentation to support the evolving purpose and history of the repository. Outside of an organisation, sharing helps connect with other repository managers who may be experiencing the same situations.

Conclusion

This chapter explains how to create a systematic repository assessment programme in order to explain repository impact and use. First, the different types of repositories are defined and explained. Next, a short literature review presents the history of repository development and assessment. This is followed by an explanation of downloads, view, and use. The last section presents a step-by-step guide on how to begin developing a systematic repository assessment programme.

Central to a systematic repository assessment programme is the planned and scheduled nature of data collection and analysis. These scheduled instances of assessment connect solidly with the purpose and history of the repository to form narratives that can be shared with the main user communities and stakeholders of the repository. By creating a systematic repository assessment programme, clear links between the repository and the overall institutional or organisational goals can be articulated in meaningful ways.

Bibliography

Baughman, S., Roebuck, G., & Arlitsch, K. (2018). Reporting practices of institutional repositories: Analysis of responses from two surveys, *Journal of Library Administration*, 58(1), 65–80.

Big Data. (2008). *Nature*, 455(7209), 1–136.

Boulware, L.E., Barnes, G.J. II, Wilson, R.F., et al. (2007, April). Value of the periodic health evaluation. Rockville, Maryland: Agency for Healthcare Research and Quality. *Evidence Reports/Technology Assessments*, 136, 1–134.

Brody, T., Carr, L., & Harnad, S. (2002). Evidence of hypertext in the scholarly archive. *Proceedings of Hypertext 2002, presented at 13th ACM Conference on Hypertext*. June 11–15, 2002, College Park, Maryland, USA, 74–75. https://doi.acm.org/10.1145/513338.513359.

Buckland, A., White, H., & Szydlowski, N. (2016). *Sustainable planning for a digital repository.* Panel Presentation at American Association of Law Libraries. July 16–19, 2016, Chicago, Illinois, USA.

Castro, F.G., Kellison, J.G., Boyd, S.J., & Kopak, A. (2010). A methodology for conducting integrative mixed methods research and data analyses. *Journal of Mixed Methods Research*, 4(4), 342–360.

Clobridge, A. (2010). *Building a digital repository program with limited resources.* Chandos Publishing.

Council of Australian University Librarians. (2013). *Research publications repository survey report.* Council of Australian University Librarians.

Creswell, J.W., Plano Clark, V.L., Gutmann, M.L., & Hanson, W.E. (2003). Advances in mixed methods research design. In A. Tashakkori & C. Teddlie (Eds.), *Handbook of mixed methods in social and behavioral research* (pp. 209–240). Sage Publishing.

Crow, R. (2002,August). The case for institutional repositories: A SPARC position paper. *ARL Bimonthly Report,* 223, 1–37.

Cullen, R. & Chawner, B. (2010). Institutional repositories: Assessing their value to the academic community. *Performance Measurement and Metrics,* 11(2), 131–147.

Davis, P. & Connolly, M. (2007). Evaluating the reasons for non-use of Cornell University's installation of Dspace. *D-Lib Magazine,* 13(3/4).

Dill, E. & Palmer, K. (2005). What's the big IDeA?: Considerations for implementing an institutional repository. *Library Hi Tech News,* 22(6), 11–14.

Giesecke, J. (2011). Institutional repositories: Keys to success. *Journal of Library Administration,* 51(5–6), 529–542.

Graham, J.B., Skaggs, B.L., & Stevens, K.W. (2005). Digitizing a gap: A state-wide institutional repository project. *Reference Services Review,* 33(3), 337–345.

Hee Kim, H. & Ho Kim, Y. (2008). Usability study of digital institutional repositories. *The Electronic Library,* 26(6), 863–881.

Heidorn, P.B. (2008). Shedding light on the dark data in the long tail of science. *Library Trends,* 57(2), 280–299.

Kim, J. (2015). *Understanding narrative inquiry: The crafting and analysis of stories as research.* Sage Publishing.

Lynch, C.A. (2003). Institutional repositories: Essential infrastructure for scholarship in the digital age. *ARL Bimonthly Report,* 22, 1–7.

Markey, K., Rieh, S.Y., St. Jean, B., Kim, J., & Yakel, E. (2007). *Census of institutional repositories in the United States: MIRACLE Project Research Findings.* Council on Library and Information Resources.

Moed, H.F. (2005). Statistical relationships between downloads and citations at the level of individual documents within a single journal. *Journal of the American Society for Information Science and Technology,* 56(10), 1088–1097.

National Information Standards Organization (NISO). (2016). *NISO RP-25–2016 Outputs of the Alternative Assessment Metrics Project.* National Information Standards Organization.

Neylon, C. & Wu, S. (2009). Article-level metrics and the evolution of scientific impact. *PloS Biology,* 7(11), 1–6.

Nichols, D.M., Payntner, G.M., Chan, C., Bainbridge, D., McKay, D., Twidale, M.B., & Blandford, A. (2009). Experiences in deploying metadata analysis tools for institutional repositories. *Cataloging and Classification Quarterly,* 47(3–4), 229–248.

O Brien, P., Arlitsch, K., Mixter, J., Wheeler, J., & Sterman, J. (2017). RAMP – The Repository Analytics and Metrics Portal: A prototype web service that accurately counts item downloads from institutional repositories. *Library Hi Tech,* 35(1), 144–158.

O Brien, P., Kenning, A., Sterman, L., Mixter, J., Wheeler, J., & Borda, S. (2016). Undercounting file downloads from institutional repositories. *Journal of Library Administration,* 56(7), 854–874.

O Leary, D. (2009). Downloads and citations. *Intelligent Systems in Accounting, Finance and Management,* 16(1–2), 21–31.

Price, A. & Fleming-May, R. (2011). Downloads or outcomes?: Measuring and communicating the contributions of library resources to faculty and student success. *The Serials Librarian,* 61, 196–199.

Priem, J. & Hemminger, B. (2010, July 5). Scientometrics 2.0: Towards new metrics of scholarly impact on the social web. *First Monday*, 15(7).

Priem, J., Taraborelli, D., Groth, P., & Neylon, C. (2010, October 26) Altmetrics: a manifesto. http://altmetrics.org/manifesto/.

Rodgers, J.R. & Sugarman, T. (2013). Library technical services: Key ingredients in the recipe for a successful institutional repository. *The Serials Librarian*, 65, 80–86.

Salo, D. (2010). Retooling libraries for the data challenge. *Ariadne*, 64.

Scaramozzino, J.M, Ramirez, M., & McGaughey, K.J. (2012). A study of faculty data curation behaviors and attitudes at a teaching-centered university. *College & Research Libraries*, 73(4), 349–365.

Schatz, B (2012, June). A brief primer on institutional repositories. *Against the Grain*, 24(3), 26–27.

Scherle, R., Carrier, S., Greenberg, J., Lapp, H., Thompson, A., Vision, T., & White, H. (2008, April). *Building support for a discipline-based data Repository*. Poster session presented at the 2008 International Conference on Open Repositories. Southampton, United Kingdom, April 1–4, 2008.

van Westrienen, G. & Lynch, C.A. (2005). Academic institutional repositories: Deployment status in 13 nations as of mid 2005. *D-Lib Magazine*, 11(9).

Wallis, J.C., Mayernik, M.S., Borgman, C.L., & Pepe, A. (2010). *Digital libraries for scientific data discovery and reuse: From vision to practical reality*. Joint Conference on Digital Libraries'10, June 21–25, 2010, Gold Coast, Queensland, Australia.

Wang, F. (2011). Building an open source institutional repository at a small law school library: Is it realistic or unattainable? *Information Technology and Libraries*, 30(2), 81–84.

White, H. (2014). Descriptive metadata for scientific data repositories: A comparison of information scientist and scientist organizing behaviors. *Journal of Library Metadata*, 14(1), 41–68. doi:10.1080/19386389.2014.891896.

White, H. (2017, July/August). Building a repository metrics program to enhance the value of library services. *AALL Spectrum*, 26–29.

White, H. & Haddow, G. (2018). *User-focused mixed methods approaches to assess collections*. IFLA 2018: 84th IFLA General Conference and Assembly, August 24–30, 2018, Kuala Lumpur, Malaysia.

White, H. & Le, A. (2015). *Using metrics to make repository decisions*. Panel Presentation at Law Repositories 2015: Shaping the Future, March 2015, Williamsburg, VA.

White, H., Aiken, J., & Shapiro, F. (2012). *Duke and Yale present: Institutional repositories and law reviews*. Panel Presentation at American Association of Law Libraries, July 21–24, 2012, Boston, MA.

White, H., Chen, S., & Liu, G. (2018). Relationships between metadata application and downloads in an institutional repository of an American law school. *LIBRES ejournal*, 28(1), 13–24.

Xia, J. (2007, December). Assessment of self-archiving in institutional repositories: Across disciplines. *The Journal of Academic Librarianship*, 33(6), 647–654.

8 Taking a quantitative approach to collection assessment
An introduction to bibliometrics in practice

Gaby Haddow

Introduction

Quantitative approaches to collection assessment are amongst the oldest forms of evaluating collections (Johnson, 2018). Typically, these methods included counting the number of items in a collection against a list, the number of borrowers and of borrowed items, the number of requests, the number of acquisitions and the amount of money expended on those acquisitions. Although qualitative approaches have gained momentum, quantitative data collection remains an important component of collection assessment.

Bibliometric methods are a particular form of quantitative assessment most suited to academic and research libraries. That is because they generally rely on the publications used and produced by researchers as a data source. In the application of bibliometrics an assumption is made that an author's citation to a work is evidence of use of that work. Journals and journal articles are the primary source of data, although books, websites, conference papers and other communication forms can also be analysed using bibliometric methods.

A bibliometric study can answer the following questions to inform retention, selection and deselection in a collection assessment:

1   What materials are important to research fields at the institution?
2   What materials are important to teaching at the institution?
3   What are the core journals in a field?
4   What backfiles are needed to meet demand?
5   How cost-effective is the collection in a field?
6   Does the collection support the research and/or teaching priorities of the institution?

Collection assessment by bibliometric methods is usually limited in scope due to the vast amount of materials available to academic and research libraries, and the many different fields studied in their institutions. However, as the sophistication of tools and techniques for undertaking bibliometric analysis has developed, so too has the feasibility of conducting a collection assessment based on bibliometric methods. All that is required is a clear aim, a defined

DOI: 10.4324/9781003083993-8

sample of publications, attention to detail, and an understanding of what the quantitative data is revealing.

The discussion below aims to provide this grounding by firstly introducing bibliometrics as a research method that has particular applications. It goes on to describe some of the key tools required to conduct a bibliometric analysis and the measures that assist in making judgements when assessing a collection. The core of the chapter is designed as a guide to using bibliometric analysis in practice, by setting out the steps and considerations that will achieve meaningful outcomes for an assessment team. A case study illustrates these steps. The chapter concludes with a discussion about the assumptions and limitations that accompany bibliometric analysis.

The development of bibliometrics as a collection assessment method

With its foundation in the 19th century positivist movement, bibliometrics is a quantitative research method that focuses on forms of communication, such as journal articles, conference papers and books. Pritchard, who coined the term 'bibliometrics' in 1969, defined its intent as "to shed light on the process of written communications and of the nature and course of a discipline" (cited by Nicholas & Ritchie, 1978, p. 9). Forty years later, after new and digital formats had emerged, De Bellis (2009, p. 3) provided an update to the aim of bibliometrics: "to analyze, quantify, and measure communication phenomena to build accurate formal representations of their behavior for explanatory, evaluative, and administrative purposes". Together these descriptions of bibliometrics illustrate the relevance of the approach in collection assessment. That is, the method is appropriate for discipline-based analysis of publications and its outcomes can inform evaluation decisions.

Bibliometrics was first used in collection assessment almost a century ago, in a study to determine the most useful journals for chemistry students at an American college (Gross & Gross, 1927). The method used by the researchers differs little from an approach that could be applied today. A volume of a single journal judged as representative of chemistry in the United States was selected as the primary data source. All references to journal articles in the volume were extracted and sorted by frequency of journal cited and by the year the cited article was published. References to the sample journal (journal self-citations) were excluded, as this journal was considered core to the collection. By examining the frequency and the publication age of cited journals, the authors made several important points in their discussion, including the following:

- citation frequencies can indicate core journals in a field;
- the age of a journal, that is years since first published, may influence citation numbers; and
- the year of cited publications can inform the need for backfiles.

In 1934, Bradford developed his law of scattering (Haddow, 2018), which is linked to the first point above. Bradford's work found that, in any field, a small core group of journals are highly 'productive', that is they are responsible for about a third of the field's most relevant articles. A larger group of journals are responsible for another third of the articles and an even larger set of journals are responsible for the remaining articles.

The notion of core journals is an important consideration in collection assessment. Sets of core journals can be identified in different ways but are clearly evident in bibliometric indicators, such as the impact factor and the *SCImago Journal Rank*. The "patriarch of citation indexing" (Cronin & Barsky Atkins, 2000, p. 1), Eugene Garfield, suggested that citation frequencies and the impact factor could be "helpful in determining the optimum makeup of both special and general collections" (1972, p. 477). The impact factor, or at least the calculation that is required to arrive at an impact factor, was noted as essential by Line and Sandison (1975) a few years later in their critique of library use studies.

Early bibliometric analyses were based on data drawn from printed sources, either individual journals or Garfield's citation indexes, and required extensive manual data collection and analysis. Major advances in the application of bibliometrics occurred in the late 20th century with the availability of CD ROMs and online databases. These studies are numerous and varied. A few examples are analyses of:

- The references in polymer science dissertations by students of an American university. The purpose was to identify journal titles in the collection that had lower use in order to cease subscriptions (Edwards, 1999).
- The references in works produced by researchers at an astrophysics institute. The study aimed to determine the cost-effectiveness of journals in the collection to inform subscription decisions (Gomez, 2002).
- The references in works by researchers at an oceanic and atmospheric science institute. The authors aimed to produce data that would provide justification for retaining subscriptions (Belter & Kaske, 2016).
- The references in patents and clinical trials by staff of an American university. The study's purpose was to assess the extent to which the collection met research priorities of the institution (Pastva et al., 2020).

For additional information about how bibliometrics has been used in collection assessment activities, a review by Gureev and Mazov (2015) provides an overview of developments since Gross and Gross first devised their study of chemistry journals.

Tools and techniques for bibliometric approaches to collection assessment

Information technologies have made both data gathering and data analysis for bibliometric studies achievable for all large research collections. Citations, specifically citations to journals, are the primary data required for the bibliometric approaches discussed in this chapter and these data are available from sources such as *Web of Science, Scopus* and *Microsoft Academic*. For large-scale studies, the vendors can provide a dataset based on inclusion and exclusion criteria for a fee. However, for the purposes of collection assessment at a single library, manual extraction of data from these sources is not difficult. In fact, manual extraction of citation data from original sources, that is examining a list of references in a researcher's article and noting journals cited, is also not difficult, but it is time consuming.

It is worth noting that citation sources are not critical for a collection assessment activity of the kind being discussed here. Many databases will provide publications data including the references listed at the end of a publication. This is the critical aspect. The functions of a database are likely to influence decisions about which source(s) to use because ideally the extraction of data for the assessment is not too time consuming and the transfer of data into analysis tools, such as spreadsheets, is uncomplicated. There may be a trade-off between ease of use and extent of coverage. In this case, additional sources should be consulted to gather the remaining data required for the analysis.

Alongside the citation and publication sources are the bibliometric indicators that can inform how a journal performs relative to others in the same field. These indicators can be useful as a secondary analysis tool. For example, a bibliometric analysis of researchers' cited references may result in a set of journals with the same characteristics of use, such as frequency and age. If the library is unable to subscribe to the full set of journals, indicators can be used to create benchmarks for the final decision. It is worth noting that bibliometric indicators come with qualifications and contexts relating to citation behaviour in different fields and the coverage of citation sources. For example, in a collection assessment exercise that includes ranking of journals to determine benchmarks, the indicators are useful only if journals in the same field are being compared. In addition, journals with shorter publication ages or in languages other than English may not be indexed by the citation source, and therefore no indicator will be available.

The impact factor is the oldest and best known of these indicators (Haddow, 2018). Developed by Eugene Garfield and a colleague, the impact factor shows the average citations per article in a journal over a two-year period. The impact factor is available through the *Journal Citation Reports* (*JCR*) section of the *Web of Science* database, and is updated in the middle of each year. Impact factors vary widely across different fields and a journal's impact factor can increase or decrease over time due to special issues, numbers of review articles and numbers of articles published in the journal over a two-year period. There is, however, no calculation of impact factors for journals classified as arts and humanities by *Web of Science*.

JCR also publishes an Eigenfactor score for journals. This indicator was developed by researchers at the University of Washington to illustrate a journal's importance, which is achieved by weighting citations to the journal from highly ranked journals over a five-year period (http://www.eigenfactor.org/). Although subject to influence from the number of citations received, the Eigenfactor score has been reviewed positively (Franceschet, 2010) and is available freely online through the Eigenfactor.org site.

Scopus data is the source of another journal indicator, the *SCImago Journal Rank (SJR)*, which is available freely online (SCImago, n.d.). The *SJR* is calculated for a three-year publishing period and uses a formula similar to the impact factor but with an additional algorithm (based on Google PageRank) that weights citations according to prestige. While the impact factor is presented as a number only, SCImago presents the *SJR* along with a quartile, so that the top 25% of journals in a field are in quartile 1, the next 25% in quartile 2, etc. Like the impact factor, an *SJR* is affected by variations in citation behaviour in different fields.

SCImago includes an *h*-index for journals. The *h*-index was initially devised by Hirsch (2005) as a measure of an author's productivity and impact. It is calculated by listing the works produced by an author against the citations to those works, ordered by least to most number of citations. Where the numbers correspond, for example 10 citations are given to the 10th publication, the *h*-index is 10. This indicator is heavily influenced by time, both for authors and journals, and although the *h*-index has become well-known by researchers, it is not without its critics (Bornmann & Daniel, 2007).

Understanding how bibliometric indicators are calculated will assist in determining how much weight to place on them when making decisions about a journal's importance in a field. The indicators have the potential to inform as a secondary tool, but it would be inadvisable to rely solely on an indicator in the selection and deselection of journals.

As noted above, the extent to which a journal is indexed, and a library's subscriptions to those indexes, will affect access and use. This is a consideration when determining usage, such as number of citations, and also when identifying titles to select or deselect for subscription. *Ulrichsweb* is the best source of information about indexing coverage.

Preparing for a bibliometric analysis

The bibliometric approach to collection assessment discussed in this chapter involves gathering citations in staff publications on the assumption that they are using the materials they reference in their work. This requires several important steps guided by clear aims and parameters, as is the case for any workplace project. In the case of bibliometrics, an assessment team must decide how they will define the subject area or field that they are assessing, and what set of literature will be assessed. These are not difficult activities, but it is important they occur before any data is collected and, like many activities in the workplace, should be documented.

What field(s) will be assessed?

As noted above, bibliometric approaches to collection assessment are ideally limited to a discrete field. This is to ensure clarity of purpose and defined data collection activities. If the usage of journals in several fields are of interest, then separate analyses for each field should take place. The decision about field is likely to relate to the introduction of a teaching programme or changes in research focus at an institution. In some cases, it may relate to the recruitment of a single academic or a team charged with a specific purpose. Alternatively, a field may be shifting its objectives and approaches.

How will a field be defined?

Defining discrete fields is not easy and every institution is likely to organise its teaching and research areas in slightly different ways. Organisational units are a useful starting point and can provide the 'sample', that is the publications by staff of that organisational unit. However, care should be taken that outliers are identified. Outliers in this context are staff whose teaching or research activities are in fields other than the field 'defined' by their organisational unit. Outliers may also exist as staff who contribute to the field from outside the organisational unit.

When defining the field for collection assessment a list of inclusions and exclusions is useful. For example: will teaching-only staff publications be included in an assessment of a research collection? In large organisational units, such as a school of education, there may be several sub-fields. How will delineation between sub-fields be made? Some of these decisions will be assisted by consulting with key staff in the field selected for the collection assessment.

If the collection assessment intends to use bibliometric indicators, the field(s) defined for analysis will need to be mapped to subject headings and discipline categories used by the indicator's source or sources. That is, the assessment may be focusing on research in the field of K-12 curricula, but *SJR* uses the main term 'education' and *JCR* includes two categories under which to list journals.

How will citing publications be identified?

At this stage the assessment exercise will have a list of staff who are central to the field. For an analysis of teaching resources, the best sources of data are the reading lists and recommended readings provided to students. Some academic libraries collect these data through tools embedded in learning management systems. In others, the assessment team will need to request the information directly from teaching staff.

An assessment of research materials may not require the involvement of research staff. With their full names and field of research, as well as their affiliation with the institution, an effective search of relevant database sources should produce a list of the publications by staff and the references that have been made in those publications. Institutional repositories may also provide a starting point for identifying publications. Alternatively, the assessment team can request publication lists directly from the researchers.

The selection decisions made about publications for bibliometric analysis will influence the results, so it is important that the selection is justifiable and aligns with the assessment aims. Establishing criteria for inclusion is vital in that it will not only define what is included but also determine what is not. Some questions that can be posed are:

- Will all publications by identified staff in the field be included, regardless of their potentially varied research foci?
- Will all publications by identified staff be included regardless of year of publication? In most cases a bibliometric analysis for collection assessment purposes will include only recent publications. How will 'recent' be defined?
- Will Doctoral student publications be included?
- How will the publications by staff who collaborate primarily with authors at different institutions be treated? Are these outliers?

What publications' data source will be used?

The first consideration in relation to selecting a source of publications data is what access/subscriptions are available to the assessment team. The source must include the references listed at the end of a publication and ideally the source has a function that allows these data to be downloaded in a format that is easily transferred into spreadsheet software. As noted above, the assessment team may need to use several sources to gather all data required. They may also need to contact researchers directly for the full publication if it cannot be located in a source.

When the assessment team has access to a range of sources, the decision about which source(s) to use will depend on the field that is being assessed (Andrés, 2009). Preparatory work to determine the best possible sources will enable the assessment team to follow a logical series of steps and save time in the collection of data.

What data should be collected and what will be counted?

A bibliometric analysis requires data about the citations given by publications in the field being assessed. These are the references at the end of publications by staff in the field. At face value this is a relatively straightforward process. The references are downloaded and different aspects, such as journal title and publication year, are analysed for frequency. Before this occurs, however, several important questions should be addressed.

The first question links directly to the purpose of the assessment exercise and relates to time. Some fields tend to use older materials and, in these cases, it is possible that backfiles are important resources. Is this an aspect of the collection that the assessment aims to explore? If so, all references should be collected. If the assessment is focused on current and future subscriptions, the data required are citations to recent works. What parameters will be established for age of cited publication?

A second consideration is how self-citations will be treated. These are the references the author makes to their own work and, as a general rule, the assessment team would assume the author has access to that work. On the other hand, if other authors in the field being assessed are citing the same journal, then these data are useful. It is probably better to collect the data with a note to indicate self-citations.

Adding notes to clarify data, such as a self-citation, will reduce the amount of double-checking that can occur in a bibliometric analysis. It raises the question of what data should be collected overall. A cited reference's year of publication and journal title is essential. Further than that, the data might include the citing author, so that sub-fields can be identified among the staff whose publications are being analysed. The reference may or may not indicate use of a print or digital version of a work. Because publishers have different formatting requirements for references, these data are likely to be inconsistent across a body of publications. The decision about how much data to collect for each cited work will relate to the ease with which data can be downloaded from sources and a judgement about the usefulness of the additional data.

Finally, while this chapter is focusing on a journal collection assessment exercise, the use of other publication forms can be instructive. Whether citations to these other publications are collected should be discussed by the assessment team, and there are arguments for both approaches. Including other publication forms will add to the time required to conduct the analysis, but collecting data about these publications may inform, for example, the acquisition of ebook packages or indicate high use of material in languages other than the language used in the institution.

As this discussion shows, there are numerous decisions that need to be made prior to conducting a bibliometric analysis for collection management. In the next section, a case study is presented to illustrate how a bibliometric analysis might be conducted and how some of the various questions posed above can be tackled.

Case study

The field chosen as the case is archaeology. Archaeology is usually associated with the social sciences and its literature ranges from quantitative and science-based to qualitative and humanities-based work. This spectrum of academic endeavour means that citations to journal articles are likely to play an important role for the more science-related work. However, archaeology is a field that will include citations to books and reports also. This variety of literature use creates a useful set of factors to consider when conducting a bibliometric analysis and is therefore applicable across most fields.

The publication lists of five 'real' archaeology scholars were consulted to inform the case study. All stages in the process described below can be achieved through manual use of relevant databases and software for sorting data, however the time required will be significantly reduced if coding expertise is available to the assessment team.

Aim

To identify the journals cited by the archaeologists to determine if the collection was meeting their needs, both with current subscriptions and backfiles.

Publication sources

In total the five staff had published 248 works, published over the years 2000 to 2020.

The first six works published between 2018 and 2020 (30) in the archaeologists' publication lists were extracted and entered into a table. Non-journal publications were excluded, leaving 20 publications. There were no duplicates. If duplicate publications exist these should be removed.

Note: The archaeologists were identified from their staff profile and a decision was made to focus on those working in a specific region. No distinction was made between teaching and research staff; however PhD students were not included. All staff published with co-authors outside of their institutional unit. Their publications were available on the webpage. Recent publications were included because the focus of the analysis was to identify current needs. Journal articles were strongly represented in the publication lists and, therefore, the analysis was limited to cited references in articles.

Data gathering

To gather a list of cited works by the archaeologists' publications, the database *Web of Science* was searched. Using a combination of title and author search, and refined by year of publication and institutional affiliation, the search located 19 of the archaeologists' works.

The works were added to the 'marked list' function and then downloaded as a text file to ensure the 'cited references' are included. A second download was useful to capture the details for the archaeologists' publications in a spreadsheet file. This database function does not allow the export of cited references however, so the text file is required.

Scopus, on the other hand, does allow the download of publication details and cited references to a spreadsheet file. Although both datasets require additional formatting to arrive at a clean list of cited references.

Note: Both of the main citation databases were pilot tested to gauge their coverage and functions. There was no difference in coverage, so the source that provided the better functions and data formats was selected. Data for the age of cited references were important to collect in order to determine if backfiles and current subscriptions were adequate for the archaeologists. Self-citations were included in the data collected for analysis.

Data sorting

Citation data in the text file and the csv file are easier to manipulate if copied into a word file and sorted later in a spreadsheet. The aim is to identify just the citations given by the archaeologists' publications, but ideally these should retain a link to the citing author. The example in Table 8.1 illustrates the format that will provide the best possible opportunity for analysing the data.

Table 8.1 Citation data required for analysis

Citing publication	Cited publication year	Cited journal (and/or other publication form)
Pub1 – year, title, journal	2009	Journal of ABC
Pub1 – year, title, journal	2011	Journal of XYZ
Pub1 – year, title, journal	2003	International Journal of ABC
Pub1 – year, title, journal	2007	International Journal of XYZ
Pub2 – year, title, journal	2010	Journal of ABC
Pub2 – year, title, journal	2007	International Journal of XYZ
Pub2 – year, title, journal	2011	International Journal of XYZ

To create this table in a word file, the cited publications will need to be separated by a return. This can be done using the 'find (semicolon) and replace' (return) function. The cited publications' data can then be converted into a table using a comma as the separator for columns. The data from *Web of Science* will look like the example in Figure 8.1.

Bentley RA 2009 ASIAN PERSPECT V48 P79 DOI 10.1353/ASI.0.0017

Bishop P 2004 J ARCHAEOL SCI V31 P319 DOI 10.1016/j.jas.2003.09.002

Figure 8.1 *Web of Science* data.

The data from *Scopus* includes all authors of a cited publication, creating more work in the conversion to a table.

At this stage in the process the list of archaeologists' publications should be combined with the table of cited publications in a spreadsheet file. This allows the assessment team to sort the rows by journal name to identify frequencies of use and age of cited references.

Note: Extracts of the dataset were tested in different software to identify the best way to convert the data into a usable format.

Data analysis

Sorting the data for analysis is now very simple. Using the example presented in Table 8.1, the analysis involves sorting the columns 'Cited journal' and 'Cited publication year'. Alternatively, a filter function or the 'Group' and 'Sub-total' functions can be used. Each approach will provide the data required, but the format of its presentation will differ.

Data analysis will also benefit from understanding the extent of a journal's use in terms of proportion. Again, the spreadsheet functions will enable a calculation of percentage.

This case study illustrates that a bibliometric analysis for collection assessment is not a complicated process. It does require time and testing, however. It also comes with considerations that relate to, and go beyond, those discussed in the earlier section, *Preparing for a bibliometric analysis*.

Provisos and considerations

As noted earlier in this chapter, citation analysis involves an important assumption – that the works that are cited by an author are used by them. In assessing a collection this is an important assumption to explore further. As Fleming-May (2011) makes clear, the way our field understands library use is manifold. In the case of citations, use of that work aligns with an 'instance' based on an activity by the citing author. It suggests the cited work has been located, read and cited to support or compare an argument, theory, method or findings presented by the citing author. In collection assessment it also assumes that if the library provides access to the cited work, then the citing author is likely to have accessed it through the library. Clearly, there are alternatives to these assumptions. For example, cited works:

- may be selected on the basis of availability to the author;
- may be given to bolster a colleague's citations, or alternatively;
- may exclude publications by competitors; and
- may be added to enhance the perception of scholarliness.

The first point could have a direct influence on the reliability of the results from a bibliometric analysis for collection assessment. An author may have a personal subscription to a journal or own a book (if other publication forms are being examined). In a co-authored publication, the cited work may have been accessed elsewhere.

A large body of literature (see, for example, Cronin, 1984; Kaplan, 1965; Smith, 1981) exists around the motivations for citing, and an assessment team should be aware of the discussion and accept that these considerations have the potential to affect results to some extent. While the team would not be expected to explore these motivations in detail, there are ways of testing some of them (discussed below).

All bibliometric analysis is faced with the limitations of indexing services' coverage and scholarly communication behaviour differences. Coverage can and will influence what sources of publications data are selected, and this selection should be made on the best possible evidence. That is, a good understanding of coverage across several potential sources and pilot testing with random samples of the publications being used to identify cited works (Brittain & Line, 1973). As noted above, the preparatory work may reveal the need to use more than one source to collect data. The challenge of coverage increases for works in languages other than English, a place of publication outside Northern America and Europe, and non-journal forms of publications.

Scholarly communication behaviour, that is the publication forms produced and the publication forms cited, vary across, and even within, disciplines. The extent of citations given and self-citations are a component of these differences. Awareness of the scholarly communication behaviour of a field subject to a collection assessment team can be gained by examining the literature of the field and should be carried out during the planning stage.

Addressing the limitations of bibliometric analysis

As Gureev and Mazov (2015, p. 37) state, "the best bibliometric methods for use in the acquisition process of a library will be those in which data sets will be obtained from several sources". It is a message that has been communicated in the collection assessment literature for many years (see, for example, Brittain & Line, 1973). 'Several sources' may involve using several databases for publications data, but it also refers to the use of different methods to gather supporting or supplementary data.

In a bibliometric analysis of journals in a field, the download and access statistics available from journal publishers and database vendors will provide additional evidence for decision-making. These data are particularly important if an assessment activity is aimed at identifying journals for deselection. Download and access data may contradict the bibliometric analysis findings, such as indicating high numbers of downloads for a journal with low levels of citation frequency. Disparate data of this nature suggests that further exploration of the journal's use is required.

Further exploration can occur through user surveys. As noted above, the motivations for citing works are diverse and citing a work doesn't necessarily mean that access to that work is required from the library. A survey can investigate personal subscriptions of staff in a field, personal libraries of back issues, and the opinions of relevant staff about key resources for the field. These qualitative data will not only enhance the assessment team's understanding of the field and use of the collection, it will also engage users in the decision-making. This is an important consideration at all times, but more so if deselection decisions are being made.

Conclusion

Bibliometric analysis is a tested method for assessing collections and is most useful for assessment of journal collections. Bibliometrics provides an alternative to how libraries understand use of their collection and draws on skills that information professionals are experienced in. This is the search and information organisation expertise that is unique to the profession.

As Baker and Lancaster (1991, p. 39) point out, "there is no one best technique to use for collection evaluation in all libraries". A range of qualitative and quantitative methods are useful and should be selected on the basis of their appropriateness to meet the objectives of the collection assessment activity. Qualitative approaches can include learned knowledge of a collection and judgements made on the underlying value of works, such as key authors and publishers. However, as library budgets tighten the need for strong and compelling evidence of use becomes more important, and this is where a quantitative approach such as bibliometrics contributes. It is not a recent phenomenon, as a quote from 1982 suggests: "traditional skills are insufficient without a quantitative context in which to exercise them" (Betts & Hargrave, 1982, p. 4).

Bibliometric approaches deliver quantitative data to support collection management decisions in that "local cited reference statistics can be used to identify titles of high value to local faculty" (Belter & Kaske, 2016, p. 412). While bibliometrics will not answer all collection assessment questions, the data gathered in a bibliometric analysis will enhance a library's knowledge of the fields of study in their institution and the scholarly communication behaviour characteristic to those fields. It will also challenge library staff to think beyond more 'comfortable' approaches to collection assessment and develop their expertise as information professionals.

Bibliography

Andrés, A. (2009). *Measuring academic research: How to undertake a bibliometric study*. Oxford: Chandos Publishing.

Baker, S. L. & Lancaster, F. W. (1991). *The measurement and evaluation of library services*. 2nd Ed. Arlington, VA: Information Resources Press.

Belter, C. W. & Kaske, N. K. (2016). Using bibliometrics to demonstrate the value of library journal collections. *College & Research Libraries*, 77 (4), 410–422. doi:10.5860/crl.77.4.410.

Betts, D. A. & Hargrave, R. (1982). How many books? *Library Management*, 3 (4), 3–31.

Bornmann, L. & Daniel, H-D. (2007). What do we know about the h index? *Journal of the American Society for Information Science and Technology*, 58 (9), 1381–1385. doi:10.1002/asi.20609.

Brittain, J. M. & Line, M. B. (1973). Sources of citations and references for analysis purposes: A comparative assessment. *Journal of Documentation*, 29 (1), 72–80.

Cronin, B. (1984). *The citation process: The role and significance of citations in scientific communication*. London: Taylor Graham.

Cronin, B. & Barsky Atkins, H. (2000). The scholar's spoor. In B. Cronin & H. Barsky Atkins (Eds), *The Web of Knowledge: A festschrift in honor of Eugene Garfield* (pp. 1–7). Medford, NJ: Information Today.

De Bellis, N. (2009). *Bibliometrics and citation analysis: From the Science citation Index to cybermetrics.* Lanham, MD: The Scarecrow Press.

Edwards, S. (1999). Citation analysis as a collection development tool: A bibliometric study of polymer science theses and dissertations. *Serials Review,* 25 (1), 11–20. doi:10.1080/00987913.1999.10764479.

Fleming-May, R. A. (2011). What is library use: Facets of concept and a typology of its application in the literature of library and information science. *The Library Quarterly: Information, Community, Policy,* 81 (3), 297–320.

Franceschet, M. (2010). Ten good reasons to use the Eigenfactor^{TM} metrics. *Information Processing & Management,* 46 (5), 555–558. doi:10.1016/j.ipm.2010.01.001.

Garfield, E. (1972). Citation analysis as a tool in journal evaluation. *Science,* 178 (4060), 471–479.

Gomez, M. (2002). A bibliometric study to manage a journal collection in an astronomical library: Some results. In B. G. Corbin, E. P. Bryson, & M. Wolf (Eds), *Library and Information Services in Astronomy IV (LISA IV), Emerging and Preserving: Providing Astronomical Information in the Digital Age* (pp. 214–222). Proceedings of a conference held at Charles University, Prague, Czech Republic, 2–5 July 2002. Washington, DC: U.S. Naval Observatory.

Gross, P. L. K. & Gross, E. M. (1927). College libraries and chemical education. *Science,* 66 (1713), 385–389.

Gureev, V. N. & Mazov, N. A. (2015). Assessment of the relevance of journals in research libraries using bibliometrics (a review). *Scientific and Technical Information Processing,* 42 (1), 30–40. doi:10.3103/S0147688215010050.

Haddow, G. (2018). Bibliometric research. In K. Williamson & G. Johanson (Eds), *Research Methods: Information, Systems, and Contexts* (2nd Ed.) (pp. 241–266). Cambridge, MA: Chandos/Elsevier.

Hirsch, J. E. (2005). An index to quantify an individual's scientific research output. *Proceedings of the National Academy of Sciences,* 102, 16569–16572.

Johnson, P. (2018). *Fundamentals of collection development and management.* 4th Ed. Chicago: ALA Editions.

Kaplan, N. (1965). The norms of citation behavior: Prolegomena to the footnote. *American Documentation,* 16 (3), 179–184.

Line, M. B. & Sandison, A. (1975). Practical interpretation of citation and library use studies. *College & Research Libraries,* 36 (5), 393–396.

Nicholas, D. & Ritchie, M. (1978). *Literature and bibliometrics.* London: Clive Bingley.

Pastva, J., Davis, B., Gutzman, K., Kubilius, R., & Sorensen, A. (2020). Compelling evidence: New tools and methods for aligning collections with the research mission. *The Serials Librarian,* 78 (1–4), 219–227. doi:10.1080/0361526X.2020.1701393.

SCImago. (n.d.). SJR — SCImago Journal & Country Rank [Portal]. Retrieved 17 July 2020, from http://www.scimagojr.com.

Smith, L. C. (1981). Citation analyses. *Library Trends,* 30, 83–106.

9 Assessment in practice

Effectiveness and impact

Gaby Haddow and Hollie White

Introduction

The contributing authors to this book have discussed assessment experiences unique to their organisation or their research expertise with the aim of providing readers with ideas that they can adopt and adjust for their specific environment. The goal of this final chapter is to show how the assessments in this book relate to other approaches found in the literature. Firstly, the chapter discusses key points raised by contributing authors and these are combined with examples in practice to illustrate how information professionals can develop their own effective assessment programmes. The second part of this chapter focuses on the increasingly important approaches to assess impact.

The chapters in this book explore a range of assessment possibilities, from highly qualitative storytelling approaches to purely quantitative bibliometric methods; design thinking to visualisations. All of what is explored in these chapters focuses on common information categories, like users, collections and services, but beyond that the chapters include topics, such as:

- planning an assessment;
- examining issues systematically;
- implementing iterative processes in an assessment; and
- using multiple methods in assessment.

These topics are not unique to *Assessment as Information Practice*. They are also covered in other resources that should be reviewed by any information professional interested in working more with assessment. The first three topics listed above are included in Dahler-Larsen's definitions of *evaluation* and *evaluation machines* (2012, p. 7; p. 177), referring to evaluation activities being "planned in advance", "systematic" and "repetitive". Baker and Lancaster (1991, p. 17) discuss the use of multiple methods in relation to macroevaluation and microevaluation, noting the importance of "quality" measures and user feedback alongside quantitative data. These components of effective and sustainable assessment are also common in the wider literature about assessment in the GLAM sector.

DOI: 10.4324/9781003083993-9

Effective assessment

Planning and taking a systematic approach

Assessment planning and taking a systematic approach go hand in hand. In fact, the act of creating an assessment plan is in itself systematic. A plan will state the purpose of the assessment, or as Johnson (2014, p. 304) states, "begins with an unambiguous question to be answered". In turn, the approach taken in an assessment activity aligns with the primary question or purpose.

A guide to designing evaluations by the US Government Accountability Office (GAO) (2012, p. 18) lists five key elements in assessment design, as follows:

- the evaluation questions, objectives and scope;
- information sources and measures, or what information is needed;
- data collection methods, including any sampling procedures, or how information or evidence will be obtained;
- an analysis plan, including evaluative criteria or comparisons, or how or on what basis programme performance will be judged or evaluated; and
- an assessment of study limitations.

The first and last points listed by the GAO are discussed by Hoffman (Chapter 2), when she writes that clarity, context and constraints must be considered alongside the purpose of an assessment. Choemprayong (Chapter 4) also notes the importance of a clearly defined question in the *Design* phase of the service design process. The GAO indicates that an assessment plan can include a number of questions, something that Payne et al. (Chapter 6) implemented to ensure that clear guiding questions were established for each of the components of their assessment. In an example from the literature, Burrows with others (2020) included 26 questions in their evaluation of a portal developed for the Mapping Manuscript Migrations project. While that number of questions seems high, many of them involved the collection of quantitative data that tested the portal's capacity for retrieving information. Deciding on the question or questions to be asked in an assessment is highly dependent on the context in which it is taking place. Both the nature and number of questions will differ according to the purpose of the assessment and they will be influenced by parent organisations' strategic plans, stakeholders and the collecting institution's wider environment (Holden & Zimmerman, 2009; Zaugg, 2020).

The question(s) asked in an assessment will also impact on the resourcing required, such as time, expertise and supporting technologies. These are factors that must be considered prior to an assessment commencing. By establishing the purpose of an assessment, that is the questions it will address, an assessment plan will also establish the limitations or constraints of the activity. Careful development of an assessment plan should highlight if the scope is too ambitious or if the resourcing requirements are likely to exceed an organisation's ability to support the activity. As Covey (2002, p. 4) points out, if the data gathered in an assessment become out-of-date or the results are not implemented, "morale takes a hit and human and financial resources are wasted".

An important component of an assessment plan is how it will be carried out. In the GAO's guide (2012), this includes:

- what data is needed and what sources are available to gather that data;
- what methods will be used to collect data; and
- how the data will be analysed and measured against the assessment question(s).

Combined, these points equate to one of Dahler-Larsen's (2012, p. 9) four components of evaluation: "a systematic approach or methodology to collect information about how the evaluand performs on these [evaluation] criteria". Covey (2002, p. 3) goes into more detail, noting the "need to know what sampling and research methods are available to recruit research subjects [...], which methods are best suited for which purposes, and how to analyze, interpret, present, and use the quantitative and qualitative data they gather to make effective decisions and strategic plans."

Establishing these kinds of details can make the difference between success and failure. Like a research project, as Hoffman's discussion (Chapter 2) illustrates, an assessment activity must incorporate a systematic approach. The need for a systematic approach is particularly emphasised in the steps required for a bibliometric analysis (Chapter 8). However, the importance of being systematic is not limited to the 'doing' of an assessment, it also relates to the recording of processes, such as those outlined by Payne and others (Chapter 6). A record of decisions and processes, both at the time of developing an assessment plan and throughout the assessment activities, enables the same assessment to be performed at a later date, thereby contributing to the next point: *implementing iterative processes* in assessment.

Implementing iterative processes in an assessment

Several authors in this book have raised the important matter of building in iterative processes in assessment activities. For some, such as Choemprayong (Chapter 4), it is a key element of the service design approach. Others, like Wells' experience (Chapter 5), use iteration to refine processes over time. The importance of repeating assessment activities or assessment being implemented *routinely* (Covey, 2002, p. 4) is widely acknowledged in the literature and should be "an integral part of the planning cycle" (Baker & Lancaster, 1991, p. 5; Zaugg, 2020).

Implementing iterative processes and a repeating cycle of assessment renders the activity more manageable for busy information professionals. It is beneficial for two main reasons:

- it reduces the need to reinvent the wheel every time an assessment is planned; and
- the resulting data can be used to compare performance over time.

The first point has implications for resourcing needs and the second affects the reliability of assessment results. That is, if different processes or approaches are used in successive assessments it can be difficult to compare the conclusions, meaning that trends may not be evident in the data over time. An iterative and systematic approach should produce outcomes in which "the findings are repeatable and the conclusions are true" (Johnson, 2014, p. 304).

Multiple methods in assessment

The data collected in an assessment activity can be quantitative, qualitative or a mix of the two. As noted above, the data required to answer a question will vary and, in some cases, such as Burrows et al. (2020), quantitative data is important. If an assessment question seeks to understand user perceptions relating to services and collections then qualitative data is needed. In many situations, the use of multiple methods is the best option because they "will counterbalance one another's weaknesses" (Saponaro & Evans, 2019, p. 183).

In a discussion about total library assessment, Luther (2016, p. 161) outlines the rationale for using multiple or mixed methods in an assessment:

- "to view a single question from different angles"; and
- "to explore fundamentally different questions about a single target".

These different purposes for using multiple methods are evident in the chapters of this book. For Goulding (Chapter 3), the use of data collected by the storytelling approach can complement quantitative data. That is, the richness of stories can *bring life to the communication of key messages through statistics*, so that the human side to quantitative data is presented. Similarly, Choemprayong (Chapter 4) discusses deploying various tools to *gain empathy and insights*. On the other hand, White (Chapter 7) and Haddow (Chapter 8) suggest using multiple methods to answer different questions about a particular phenomenon. An assessment of institutional repositories (Chapter 7) benefits from gathering quantitative data that indicates extent of use and also qualitative data about challenges to that use.

Multiple methods are an important feature of Wells' assessment of materials availability (Chapter 5) and the assessment of collection use by Payne and others (Chapter 6). Both describe using multiple tools to answer a range of questions relating to the assessment being performed. Their chapters highlight the benefits of this approach, which enabled the assessment teams to identify the most useful methods for answering their assessment questions and refining those methods as the assessment progressed.

Information professionals who address the four points discussed above – planning, taking a systematic approach, implementing iterative processes and using multiple methods – in the development of an assessment programme will reap the benefits. These will manifest in a number of ways, but feasibility and relevant data are chief among them. Like research projects, assessment activities create opportunities for learning; in this case about a collecting institution's services and/or collections, and about the process of assessment itself.

The four common topics that have been presented to this point also relate to assessment of impact, which is the subject of the discussion to follow. It is a focus in this chapter because of its growing importance for collecting institutions and because impact assessment was not specifically discussed in the preceding chapters.

Impact assessment

Impact can be challenging to determine because it relates to change at individual, institution and community levels. Some examples of questions related to impact are:

- How has access to a collection contributed to student success?
- To what extent have health outcomes improved as a result of information literacy services?
- How has the digitisation of cultural artifacts influenced societal attitudes?

According to Creaser (2018, p. 87), impact assessment gained importance in the early 2000s, as libraries needed to "demonstrate their value to stakeholders and justify their funding", and this has only continued to grow. As indicated in the quote, *value* is a key term when considering impact, and the need to assess impact is not limited to the library sector (see, for example, King, Stark & Cooke, 2016). By discussing a range of impact assessment projects in this chapter it is hoped that information professionals will take the next step in evaluation: assessing value.

Impact assessment plays a key role in information practice today as organisations acknowledge that it is not only what they *do* do well or not so well, but what difference they make to the individuals, communities and environment they *do* for. The quote below is from the Global Libraries strategy of the Bill & Melinda Gates Foundation (2021), and it exemplifies the rationale and challenges involved in undertaking impact assessment:

> The most successful public libraries around the world are proactively engaging with their communities to understand local needs and customize services to address community problems. What's missing are the

facts and data about how libraries directly improve people's lives—including impact that advances the global Sustainable Development Goals. Without tangible proof to back up what library leaders intuitively know to be true, libraries will be forever fighting an uphill battle for recognition and resources.

Although limited to public libraries, the Global Libraries strategy provides an excellent starting point for this discussion, and the work of Sharon Markless and David Streatfield is central to it. These authors published the first edition of their book, *Evaluating the Impact of Your Library*, in 2006 and have been involved in the Global Libraries since at least 2009. Impact is a key theme in their work, which includes publications from the early 2000s relating to impact evaluation in public, school and university libraries, and in relation to information literacy programmes. Impact assessment, or impact evaluation, has been defined in different ways for different purposes, but Streatfield and Markless (2009, p. 134) use the definition, "… any effect of the service [or of an event or initiative] on an individual or group". They remind the reader that effects can be negative or positive and might manifest as changes across a range of indicators. The Global Libraries initiative presents impact as several levels of changes, rather like Maslow's Hierarchy of Needs. They are changes to:

knowledge and skills …
attitudes and perceptions …
behaviour …
quality of life …
broader social or economic change.
Bill & Melinda Gates Foundation (2015, p. 4)

Impact assessment at the first level is relatively simple to determine because knowledge and skills can be tested. However, assessing impact at the higher levels, such as quality of life and social change, is more challenging due to the number of potential contributing factors. An impact assessment needs to be able to demonstrate a connection or likely connection between the service or collection and those changes.

In 2001, Markless and Streatfield outlined why the data gathered by many collecting institutions is inadequate for assessing impact: "these statistics usually tell managers more about whether the library is working efficiently than about how well it is serving particular groups of people and what effect this is having" (p. 172). Impact assessment in practice, therefore, requires a different approach that focuses on specific targets, such as digital inclusion, and tracks services to "the outcomes they help individuals and communities realize" (Bill & Melinda Gates Foundation, 2015, p. 29).

To determine the targets for impact assessment, a collecting institution must identify what their services are aiming to achieve as impact. For example, access to a large, digitised collection of heritage materials could facilitate collaboration between research communities, which in turn produces richer research. An academic library might provide study skills programmes that enable students to achieve better outcomes in their coursework. A public library's community programmes may have an impact on individuals' sense of social engagement. The targets will be context dependent and, like the discussion above about assessment more generally, require consideration of resourcing and expertise needs. They will also align with the strategic plans of the collecting institution and its parent organisation.

Measuring impact, the extent to which impact targets have been achieved, involves several levels of data. Some of these will be quantitative data, such as inputs like staff hours. However, impact cannot be measured in numbers alone, and qualitative data are required to explore the links between a service and a change for an individual, group or community. In many cases these data are gathered through surveys and direct discussions with the target population.

Three terms are commonly used in relation to impact assessment data: inputs, outputs and outcomes.

- Inputs are what the collecting institution expends to implement and run a programme – for example, staff time, space use, ICT resources.
- Outputs are the activities that are aiming to achieve impact – for example, organising book clubs, providing study skills training, facilitating metadata and content sharing.
- Outcomes are the changes that eventuate for individuals, groups and communities as a result of the outputs – for example, social value, academic success, innovation in the cultural sector.

It is important to note that slightly different terminology is used across the impact assessment literature. An example is the use of 'outcome measures' by Matthews (2015), whereas the *Global Libraries Impact Planning and Assessment Guide* (Bill & Melinda Gates Foundation, 2015) refers to 'outcome indicators'. However, these differences are in name only and the main processes involved in impact assessment are consistent, as the examples discussed below illustrate.

Guides to impact assessment

Before discussing some examples of impact assessment in practice, it may be useful to point to some resources that will help information professionals starting out on an impact assessment exercise. For public libraries, the Bill & Melinda Gates Foundation's *Global Libraries Impact Planning and Assessment Guide* (2015) is invaluable. This resource describes impact targets, processes and terms, and provides examples of assessment activities. The explanations are clear, as are the steps required to achieve a realistic understanding of impact.

Less literature is available about the GLAM sector, however Europeana released an impact strategy document in 2014 that outlines how collecting institutions can realise impact. This work, although written for the Europeana context, identifies areas of potential impact and the different audiences that a digital collection and 'digital service infrastructure' may effect change for. For those managing archival collections, an excellent discussion about their impact on social justice is provided by Duff and others (2013), while Hooper-Greenhill (2004) discusses learning outcomes as an impact. An earlier publication takes a broader view and discusses impact for museums, archives and libraries (Wavell et al., 2002). This resource outlines examples of the potential for the different collecting institutions to have social and economic impact, and the evidence that is available to conduct an impact assessment.

Assessing the value of academic and school libraries is covered in some depth by Oakleaf (2010), who describes a range of factors that lend themselves to impact assessment. It is not a guide to conducting an impact assessment exercise, rather it provides a strong base from which information professionals can draw impact targets. Matthews (2015), on the other hand, presents several models of impact assessment that are applicable to collecting institutions generally, and includes a model for research impact that may be relevant to academic libraries. Finally, Markless and Streatfield (2008) describe the approach used in the Impact Initiative, which involved 22 university library teams. They reflect on the outcomes and how to go forward in future impact assessment activities.

Examples of impact assessment

For information professionals who are considering initiating an impact assessment in their collecting institution it is useful to read about how other organisations like theirs have conducted an activity. There are numerous examples available in the literature, and as noted in the first chapter of this book, there are some go-to resources, such as the journal *Performance Measurement and Metrics*, conference proceedings from *LibPMC* and its sister event the *Library Assessment Conference*, as well as the publications available through The International Federation of Library Associations and Institutions' (IFLA) Statistics and Evaluation Section. In this section of the chapter a few examples are highlighted to provide a starting point for a deeper exploration of the topic.

Public libraries are the subject of most impact assessments. This is logical given their focus on communities and their acknowledged contributions to those communities (Bill & Melinda Gates Foundation, 2021). The *Global Libraries Impact Planning and Assessment Guide* (Bill & Melinda Gates Foundation, 2015) lists examples of impact studies, however a more comprehensive collection of public (and national) library impact studies is provided by Streatfield and others (2019a; 2019b). These two papers describe the aims of impact assessment and the specific methods used to collect data in several countries involved in the Global Libraries initiative.

A wealth of detail is provided in the Suffolk Libraries report (2019), which explored the social impact of a selection of library services. This in-depth report demonstrates that impact assessment can shed light on the value of public libraries services in qualitative and quantitative terms. Using qualitative approaches, Calvert and Goulding (2015) investigated impact assessment and the perceptions of it in New Zealand – in public, school, special and academic libraries. Academic libraries have also been the focus of more quantitative studies that have examined the impact of library use on student success outcomes (for example, Haddow, 2013; Rodrigues & Mandrekar, 2020). In these studies, impact is qualified because establishing a direct link between an academic library's resources and services and the success of students is difficult to do.

In the archives and large digital collections sector there is evidence of the importance of impact assessment, however less literature about specific activities is currently available. The evidence lies in strategic plans, such as the DARIAH Strategic Action Plan (DARIAH-EU, 2019), which includes an objective devoted to enhancing impact, and the Europeana Strategy document (Europeana, 2014). Hughes, with others (2015), evaluated the use and impact of a digital collection of Hansards from the Northern Irish Parliament using the JISC 'Toolkit for the Impact of Digital and Scholarly Resources'. Combining quantitative and qualitative methods, the assessment enabled the researchers to "develop strategic reflections on the value of the resource" (Hughes et al., 2015, p. 197). A notable study by Caswell, Cifor and Ramirez (2016) explored how the South Asian American Digital Archive (SAADA) impacted on South Asian Americans. These authors step through the stages of the study and present findings that indicate SAADA had impact in areas such as feelings of inclusion.

Reflection in practice

Reflective practice and critical reflection are related concepts that stem from educational theory and are widely used in the health and social care sectors. In the information sector, reflective practice can "contribute to the development of a learning culture" (Greenall & Sen, 2016, p. 138). It is also considered an important component of professional development for individual information professionals.

The practice of critical reflection is described by the Australian Children's Education & Care Quality Authority (n.d.) as, "Closely examining all aspects of events and experiences from different perspectives". Reflective practice is about thinking about a process or activity by examining:

- what was done;
- why it was done a certain way;
- in what ways it was successful;
- how it could be improved; and
- what changes should be implemented.

For those involved in an assessment activity, reflective practice can be conducted after each assessment activity is implemented or at a set point in the assessment schedule, either by one individual or with a group of people. Reflective practice is important for understanding how to develop and grow an assessment programme and for considering improvements to the programme over time. Assessment and reflection are iterative and continuous, and together they will lead to a deeper understanding of how collecting institutions serve their communities and how those communities benefit from the collections and services they use.

In conclusion, effective assessment programmes evolve from a series of planned and systematic assessment events. Incorporating iterative processes and embedding assessment activities in a collecting institution's regular planning cycle will contribute to a culture of ongoing improvement. However, an institution engaging in an assessment exercise also needs to engage in ongoing reflection on what has been learnt and what needs to change in the future.

Bibliography

Australian Children's Education & Care Quality Authority (n.d.). What is critical reflection? Quality Support Program Toolkit. https://www.acecqa.gov.au/sites/defa ult/files/2019-07/WHAT%20IS%20CRITICAL%20REFLECTION%20-%20NO% 20EDITS.pdf.

Baker, S.L. & Lancaster, F.W. (1991). *The Measurement and Evaluation of Library Services.* 2nd ed. Information Resources Press.

Bill & Melinda Gates Foundation (2015). Global Libraries Impact Planning and Assessment Guide. http://www.publiclibraryadvocacy.org/wp-content/uploads/2015/ 06/IPA-Guide-2015.pdf.

Bill & Melinda Gates Foundation (2021). Global Libraries. https://www.gatesfounda tion.org/our-work/programs/global-development/global-libraries.

Borrego, Á. (2020). Measuring the impact of digital heritage collections using Google Scholar. *Information Technology and Libraries*, 39(2). doi:10.6017/ital.v39i2.12053.

Burrows, T., Pinto, N.B., Cazals, M., Gaudin, A. & Wijsman, H. (2020). Evaluating a semantic portal for the "Mapping Manuscript Migrations" project. *DigItalia*, 2. http://digitalia.sbn.it/article/view/2643.

Calvert, P. & Goulding, A. (2015). Narratives and stories that capture the library's worth: A qualitative approach to measuring value and impact in New Zealand's libraries. *Performance Measurement and Metrics*, 16(3), 276–288. doi:10.1108/PMM-05-2015-0016.

Caswell, M., Cifor, M. & Ramirez, M.H. (2016). "To suddenly discover yourself existing": Uncovering the impact of community archives. *The American Archivist*, 79(1), 56–81.

Covey, D.T. (2002). Academic library assessment: New duties and dilemmas. *New Library World*, 103(1175/1176), 156–164.

Creaser, C. (2018). Assessing the impact of libraries – the role of ISO 16439. *Information and Learning Science*, 119(1/2), 87–93. doi:10.1108/ILS-05-2017-0037.

Dahler-Larsen, P. (2012). *The Evaluation Society.* Stanford University Press.

DARIAH-EU (2019). DARIAH Strategic Action Plan II 2019–2022. https://www.dariah. eu/wp-content/uploads/2020/05/DARIAH-Strategic-Action-Plan-II-2019-2022.pdf.

Duff, W.M., Flinn, A., Suurtamm, K.E. & Wallace, D.A. (2013). Social justice impact of archives: A preliminary investigation. *Archival Science*, 13, 317–348. doi:10.1007/s10502-012-9198-x.

Europeana (2014). Europeana Strategy 2015–2020, Impact. https://pro.europeana.eu/post/europeana-strategy-2015-2020-impact.

Greenall, J. & Sen, B.A. (2016). Reflective practice in the library and information sector. *Journal of Librarianship and Information Science*, 48(2), 137–150. doi:10.1177/0961000614551450.

Haddow, G. (2013). Academic library use and student retention: A quantitative analysis. *Library & Information Science Research*, 35, 127–136.

Holden, D.J. & Zimmerman, M.A. (2009). *A Practical Guide to Program Evaluation Planning: Theory and Case Examples.* Sage.

Hooper-Greenhill, E. (2004). Measuring learning outcomes in museums, archives and libraries: The Learning Impact Research Project (LIRP). *International Journal of Heritage Studies*, 10(2), 151–174. doi:10.1080/13527250410001692877.

Hughes, L.M., Ell, P.S., Knight, G.A.G. & Dobreva, M. (2015). Assessing and measuring impact of a digital collection in the humanities: An analysis of the SPHERE (Stormont Parliamentary Hansards: Embedded in Research and Education) Project. *Digital Scholarship in the Humanities*, 30(2), 183–198. doi:10.1093/llc/fqt054.

Johnson, P. (2014). *Fundamentals of Collection Development and Management.* American Library Association.

King, L., Stark, J.F. & Cooke, P. (2016) Experiencing the digital world: The cultural value of digital engagement with heritage. *Heritage & Society*, 9(1), 76–101. doi:10.1080/2159032X.2016.1246156.

Luther, M. (2016). Total library assessment. *Journal of Library Administration*, 56(2), 158–170.

Markless, S. & Streatfield, D. (2001). Developing performance and impact indicators and targets in public and education libraries. *International Journal of Information Management*, 21, 167–179. doi:10.1016/S0268-4012(01)00008-1.

Markless, S. & Streatfield, D. (2008). Supported self-evaluation in assessing the impact of HE libraries. *Performance Measurement and Metrics*, 9(1), 38–47. doi:10.1108/14678040810869413.

Markless, S. & Streatfield, D.R. (2017). How can you tell if it's working? Recent developments in impact evaluation and their implications for information literacy practice. *Journal of Information Literacy*, 11(1), 106–119.

Matthews, J. (2015). Assessing outcomes and value: It's all a matter of perspective. *Performance Measurement and Metrics*, 16(3), 211–233. doi:10.1108/PMM-10-2015-0034.

Oakleaf, M. (2010). The value of academic libraries: A comprehensive research review and report. Association of College & Research Libraries. http://www.ala.org/acrl/sites/ala.org.acrl/files/content/issues/value/val_report.pdf.

Rodrigues, M.C. & Mandrekar, B. (2020). Impact of academic library services on students success and performance. *Library Philosophy and Practice*, 4246. https://digitalcommons.unl.edu/libphilprac/4246.

Saponaro, M.Z. & Evans, G.E. (2019). *Collection Management Basics.* 7th ed. ABC-CLIO.

Streatfield, D. & Markless, S. (2009). What is impact assessment and why is it important? *Performance Measurement and Metrics*, 10(2), 134–141. doi:10.1108/14678040911005473.

Streatfield, D.*et al.* (2019a). Innovative impact planning and assessment through global libraries: Sustaining innovation during a time of transition. *Performance Measurement and Metrics*, 20(2), 74–84. doi:10.1108/PMM-03-2019-0010.

Streatfield, D.et al. (2019b). Global Libraries impact planning and assessment progress: Part 2. *Performance Measurement and Metrics*, 20(2), 85–104. doi:10.1108/PMM-03-2019-0007.

Suffolk Libraries (2019). A predictive impact analysis. https://www.suffolklibraries.co.uk/assets/pdf/suffolk-libraries-a-predictive-impact-analysis.pdf.

US Government Accountability Office (GAO) (2012). Designing evaluations. https://www.gao.gov/assets/gao-12-208g.pdf.

Wavell, C., Baxter, G., Johnson, I. & Williams, D. (2002). Impact evaluation of museums, archives and libraries: Available evidence project. The Robert Gordon University. https://www3.rgu.ac.uk/file/dorothy-williams-impact-evaluation-of-museums-archives-and-libraries-available-evidence-project.

Zaugg, H. (2020). The development, design and implementation of a library assessment framework. *Journal of Library Administration*, 60(8), 909–924. doi:10.1080/01930826.2020.1820277.

Index

Aabø, S. 53, 72
Aarhus Public Libraries, adoption of service design approach 61
Acquisition Error for non-availability 85, 86, 87
action research 13–14; data collection in 22; purpose 15–16, 25
Adams, B., & Noel, B. 92, 105
agile approach in systems design 66
Agostino, D. & Arnaboldi, M. 29, 48
Ahonen, P., Buckless, B., Hafford, C., Keating, K., Keene, K., Morales, J., & Park, C. C. 34, 48
algorithms in bibliometrics 122
allowing failures, as benefit of iterative processes 66
Altmann, K. G., & Gorman, G. E. 92, 105
altmetrics for assessing repository usage 110–111
Andrés, A. 124, 130
Appleton, L. 47, 48
Application Programming Interface (API) 102
ArcGIS, for spatial data 101–104
ArcMap 103
arts-based storytelling techniques 42–43
assessment: components of 2–3, 134; in contemporary contexts 6–10 (*see also* collection assessment approaches; digital repository assessment; impact assessments; service design; storytelling, as an assessment tool); criteria for digital libraries 4–5, 133–136; definition 12–13; history of 3–5, 77–79, 108–111; iterative nature of 13, 112, 134–135, 141; ongoing sustainability 1, 3, 8, 25, 77, 87, 132; planning 2–3, 8, 133–134; purpose 2–3, 8, 15, 25; vs research 8, 12–26; types of 5–6
assessment-oriented action research 12; *see also* action research
assessment plans 2–3, 8, 133–134
audience, identifying when scoping projects 15, 25–26
availability error messages 83–85; *see also* non-availability categories in materials availability assessments
avoiding major mistakes, as benefit of iterative processes 65
avoiding misunderstanding, as benefit of iterative processes 66

Baker, S. L., & Lancaster, F. W. 2, 3, 4, 5–6, 10, 130, 132, 134, 141
Bank of Thailand Learning Center library, adoption of service design approach 63
Basaraba, N., Conlan, O., Edmond, J., & Arnds, P. 47, 48
Baú, V. 30, 48
Baughman, S., Roebuck, G., & Arlitsch, K. 108, 109, 110, 115
Becvar, K., & Srinivasan, R. 17, 26
Belter, C. W., & Kaske, N. K. 120, 130
benefits of iterative process in service design 64–66
Betts, D. A., & Hargrave, R. 130
Bibliographic Error for non-availability 83, 85, 86
bibliometric indicators 120, 121–122, 123
bibliometrics: approaches to collection assessments 118–130; case study 9–10, 125–128; data analysis 127–128; data collection 120–122, 124–125, 126–127; history of development 119–120; limitations 129; provisos and

considerations 128–129; tools and techniques 120–122
Bilandzic, M., & Foth, M. 53, 72
Bill and Melinda Gates Global Libraries programme 45, 136–137, 138, 139
Bishop, B., & Mandel, L. 92, 105
Blodgett, A. T., Schinke, R. J., Smith, B., Peltier, D., & Pheasant, C. 44, 48
Boote, D. N., & Beile, P. 25, 26
Bordonaro, K. 53, 72
Borin, J., & Yi, H. 92, 105
Bornmann, L., & Daniel, H-D. 122, 130
Borrego, Á. 141
Boulware, L. E., Barnes, G. J. II, Wilson, R. F., et al. 111, 115
Bradley, W. B., & Mandel, L. H. 105
Brittain, J. M., & Line, M. B. 129, 130
Brody, T., Carr, L., & Harnad, S. 110, 115
Buckland, A., White, H., & Szydlowski, N. 107, 115
Buckland M. K. 79, 88
Burrows, T., Pinto, N.B., Cazals, M., Gaudin, A. & Wijsman, H. 133, 135, 141

Calvert, P., & Goulding, A. 45, 48, 140, 141
Canhenha, P. 63, 64, 68, 70, 72
Carnegie Corporation, standards for college and university library assessments 3–4
Carrigan, D. P. 6, 10
case studies, bibliometric analysis 9–10, 125–128
Castro, F. G., Kellison, J. G., Boyd, S. J., & Kopak, A. 112, 115
Castro, R. C. 92, 106
Caswell, M., Cifor, M. & Ramirez, M.H. 140, 141
catalogue problem reporting 86–87
catalogue transaction analysis 79, 86
Catalogue Use Error for non-availability 84, 86, 87
Cavino, H. M. 35, 48
CEDA repository 108
Chaudhry, A.S., & Ashoor, S. 79, 87, 88
Chelimsky, E. 30, 48
Chen, X. 67, 70
Chicago Public Library, adoption of service design approach 61
Choemprayong, S., & Siridhara, C. 63, 72
Chouinard, J. A., & Cousins, J. B. 34, 49
Choy, S., & Lidstone, J. 41, 49

Cieslik, K., Dewulf, A., & Buytaert, W. 33, 36–37, 49
Ciliberti, A., Casserly, M., Hegg, J., & Mitchell, E. 78, 88
Ciliberti, A., Radford, M. L., Radford, G.P., & Ballard, T. 79, 89
circulation data analysis and visualisation 92, 94–104
citation frequencies 119, 120, 129
citations vs downloads 110
Clandinin, D. J., & Connelly, M. 30, 49
Clobridge, A. 108, 115
co-creative design principle 56–57, 59
coding and themes 23–24, 114; *see also* data analysis
collecting institutions: definition of 1–2; history of assessments 3–5, 77–79; impact assessments 3–5, 6, 10, 136–140
collection assessment approaches: bibliometric approaches 9–10, 118–130; inquiry-based approaches 9, 91–105; materials availability approaches 9, 76–88
collection size analysis and visualisation 94–99
college and university library assessments, Carnegie Corporation's standards for 3–4
computer scripting language 102–103
Conrad, S. K. 47, 49
continuous improvement, as aim of assessments 9, 13, 14–15, 53, 92
Cooper, S. 34, 41, 49
cost-benefit as measure of assessment 5, 6
cost-effectiveness as measure of assessment 5, 6, 10, 118, 125
Costantino, T. E. & Greene, J. C. 31, 35–36, 37, 44, 45, 49
Council of Australian University Librarians (CAUL) 80
Covey, D. T. 8, 10, 134, 141
Creaser, C. 1, 3, 6, 10, 136, 141
creation as service design phase 59
Creswell, J. W. 13, 17, 23, 26
Creswell, J. W., Plano Clark, V. L., Gutmann, M. L., & Hanson, W. E. 112, 116
Critical Incident Technique 40–41, 47
critical reflection, as element of assessment 140–141; *see also* reflective practice
Cronin, B. 129, 130
Cronin, B., & Barsky Atkins, H. 120, 131

146   *Index*

Cross, N. 54, 72
Crow, R. 108, 116
Crum, J. 79, 89
Cullen, R., & Chawner, B. 109, 116
cultural heritage digital collections, development of evaluation frameworks 1–2, 5, 139; *see also* GLAM sector
Curtin Materials Availability Survey (CMAS) 82–88
Curtin University Library, materials availability assessments 76, 77, 79–88

Dahler-Larsen, P. 1, 2–3, 6, 7, 10, 132, 134, 141
Daigle, B. J. 53, 72
Dando, P. 45, 49
DARIAH Strategic Action Plan 140
data analysis 17, 133, 134; in bibliometric analysis 127–128; qualitative 23–24, 114; quantitative 23–24, 109, 114; in repository assessment 109, 114; in storytelling 30, 37–38, 43–45
data cleansing 9, 23–24
data collection 17, 22–23, 133, 134, 135; in bibliometrics 120–122, 124–125, 126–127; in materials availability assessment 85–87, 88; in repository assessments 109, 113–114; in storytelling 30, 33, 35, 38–43
data collection instruments *see* questionnaires; survey instruments
data repositories 108, 109
data sources: in inquiry-based assessments 94, 97–99, 102–104, 126–127; selection of in bibliometric analysis 124, 126
data storage and management 21, 25
data visualisation: as aid to analysis 24; for library collections 9, 91–105; tools 24, 92
Davies, R. 41, 49
Davis, P., & Connolly, M. 109, 116
De Bellis, N. 119, 131
De Prospo, E. R., Altman, E., & Beasley, K.E. 78, 89
define phase of service design 58–59
deliver phase of service design 58–59
democratising evaluations 34–35; *see also* participatory approaches to evaluation
demonstrating progress, as benefit of iterative processes 65
Dempsey, L. 87, 89
descriptive statistics 23, 109, 112, 114

design phases 58–60; *see also* service design
design-thinking tools for service design 60, 61
Detlor, B., Hupfer, M. E., & David, H. S. 47, 49
develop phase of service design 58–59
Dhaliwal, J. S., Macintyre, M., & Parry, G. 56, 72
digital humanities, emergence of term 4–5
digital libraries, need for unique assessment criteria 4–5, 133–136
Digital Library Federation, concerns about assessment 7–8
digital repository assessment 9, 107–115; data analysis 114; data collection 113–114; methodology 112; narrative building and sharing 112, 114–115; purpose 112–113; steps for development 112–115
digital storytelling techniques 42–43, 47; *see also* storytelling, as an assessment tool
Dill, E. & Palmer, K. 108, 116
discover phase of service design 58–59
Dobreski, B., & Huang, Y. 53, 72
document delivery requests, as measure of availability 87, 88
documentation 65; of data collection processes 95–97; importance of 25, 112, 134
domain repositories 108
Double Diamond framework for service design 58–60
downloads, as metric for assessing repositories 110–111
Drew, C. 67, 71, 72
Dryad repository 108
Duff, W. M., Flinn, A., Suurtamm, K. E., & Wallace, D. A. 139, 142
Duff, W. M., & Harris, V. 46, 49

Edwards, S. 120, 131
effective assessment, criteria for 133–136
effectiveness as measure of assessment 5, 6, 29, 77
Eicher-Catt, D. & Edmondson, M. 45, 49
Eigenfactor score 121–122
Eisenhower Library 94, 95, 104
Elliott, J. 35, 49
Emanuel, E. J., Grady, C. C., Crouch, R. A., Lie, R. K., Miller, F. G., & Wendler, D. D. 20, 26

empowerment of staff, in iterative processes 71
error types and remediation in materials availability 83–84, 85, 86, 87
Erway, R., Horton, L., Nurnberger, A., Otsuji, R., & Rushing, A. 25, 26
ethics committees and research oversight 19–22, 94; *see also* privacy considerations in research
ethnography 18–19, 47
Europeana 2, 139, 140
evaluation *see* assessment
Everall, K., & Logan, J. 62, 73
evidencing design principle 57
Excel, role in visualising collections data 92, 96, 97, 98, 99–101, 105
exploration in service design 59, 64

factors influencing assessment activities 7–8, 133, 138
Fadlallah, R., El-Jardali, F., Nomier, M., Hemadi, N., Arif, K., Langlois, Akl, E. A. 35, 45, 49
failures, allowing, in iterative processes 66
feedback, as benefit of iterative processes 65
Feng, Y. 47, 49
Fidel, R. 83, 89
fields, in bibliometric research 123
First Nations participants in GLAM evaluations 34–35, 42
Fischer, IV, B. A. 20, 26
Flanagan, J. C. 40, 49
Fleming-May, R. A. 128, 131
floor plans, graphic representation of 97, 99–101, 103–104, 105
focus groups 18, 19, 62, 77, 87, 88
formative assessment 6, 32, 67, 71
formulaic approach to collection evaluation 92, 94
Foster, N. F., & Gibbons, S. L. 18, 26
Fowler, Jr, F. J., & Cosenza, C. 24, 26
Franceschet, M. 122, 131
Fuks, H., Moura, H., Cardador, D., Vega, K., Ugulino, W., & Barbato, M. 46, 50
Fulfilment Error for non-availability 84

galleries, libraries, archives and museums sector *see* GLAM sector
Garfield, E. 120, 131
Garfield, Eugene, founder of impact factor 120, 121

Gaskill, H. V., Dunbar, R. M., & Brown, C. H. 77, 89
generalisability of results 12, 14, 15, 17, 36; *see also* generalisations
generalisations 12, 13, 29; *see also* generalisability of results
Geographic Information Systems (GIS), role in visualising collections data 92, 94, 101–104, 105; *see also* ArcGIS, for spatial data
Giesecke, J. 116
GLAM sector: evolution of assessment practices 1–2, 5, 132, 139, 140; impact assessment strategy 139, 140; storytelling as evaluation tool 8–9, 29–52
Global Libraries Impact Planning and Assessment Guide 138, 139
Global Libraries strategy, Bill and Melinda Gates Foundation 45, 136–137, 138, 139
Global Library Data Atlas 45
Gomez, M. 120, 131
Gooding, P. 4, 11
Google website activity tracking products 110
Gouke, M. N., & Pease, S. 79, 89
Goulding, A. 29, 32, 50
Government Accountability Office (GAO) US, guidelines for evaluations 133
Graham, J. B., Skaggs, B. L., & Stevens, K. W. 108, 116
Grant, M. J., & Bogroth, A. 25, 27
Greenall, J., & Sen, B. A. 140, 142
Gregory, D. J., & Pedersen, W. A. 79, 89
Gross, P. L. K., & Gross, E. M. 3–4, 11, 119, 131
grounded theory 13
group interviews 38–40; *see also* focus groups; interviews
Groyecka, A., Witkowska, M., Wróbel, M., Klamut, O., & Skrodzka, M. 53, 73
guides: for impact assessments 138–139; for planning evaluations, GAO 133
Guijt, I. M., Brouwers, J. H. A. M., Kusters, C. S. L., Prins, E., & Zeynalova, B. 29, 50
Gureev, V. N., & Mazov, N. A. 120, 129, 131

h-index 122
Hacker, K. 17, 27

Haddow, G. 120, 121, 131, 140, 142
Harris, M., & Garner, I. 78, 89
Hatch, J. A. 13, 27
heat maps as visualisation tool 95–97, 99–101
Heath, F. 3, 6, 11
Hee Kim, H., & Ho Kim, Y. 109, 116
Heidorn, P. B. 109, 116
Hendley, M. 106
Hewett, T. T. 67, 73
Hicks, A., & Lloyd, A. 47, 50
high-fidelity prototypes 64, 67, 68; *see also* prototype development and testing
Hirsch, J. E. 122, 131
history of assessment 3–5, 77–79, 108–111
Holden, D. J., & Zimmerman, M. A. 133, 142
holistic design principle 57–58
Hooper-Greenhill, E. 139, 142
Horava, T. 92, 106
how questions 91, 93
Huck, S. W. 17, 27
Hughes, L. M., Ell, P. S., Knight, G. A. G. & Dobreva, M. 11, 140, 142
human-centric approach, in service design 55
human-human interactions in service design 55
human-machine interactions in service design 55
human-object interactions in service design 55
human research, definitions of 20; *see also* ethics committees and research oversight
Human Research Ethics Committees (HREC) (Australia) 20
Hunter, O., Leeburg, E., & Harnar, M. 42, 50

IDEO, global design company 61
idiographic approach to evaluation, benefits of 32–33, 36–37
impact assessments 3–5, 6, 10, 136–140; examples 139–140; guides for information professionals 138–139
impact factor, in bibliometrics 120, 121, 122
Impactstory 111
implementation as service design phase 59, 60

in-house usage data analysis and visualisation 94–99
Inappropriate Result Error for non-availability 84, 87
Inappropriate Search Error for non-availability 84, 85, 86, 87
incremental improvement, as benefit of iterative processes 64–65
indexing coverage, journals 121, 122, 127, 129
Indigenous participants, role in evaluations 34–35, 42
individual interviews 38–40; *see also* interviews
Indrák, M., & Pokorná, L. 53, 73
inferential statistics 23, 109, 114
inquiry-based approach to library collections assessments 9, 91–105
Institute or Museum and Library Service project 109
institutional repositories 108; *see also* repositories
Institutional Review Boards (IRB) (US) 20
integrated library system (ILS) data 97, 101, 102; limitations of 91, 93, 101
integration with other approaches as benefit of iterative processes 66
International Federation of Library Associations and Institutions (IFLA) 2, 5, 139
interpretation of results 24–25; *see also* data analysis
interpretivist research paradigm 17; *see also* qualitative approaches to assessments
interviews 19, 38–40; in repository assessments 109; *see also* focus groups
iterative approach to service design 54–72; assessment 66–71; benefits of 64–66; guidelines for library settings 68–71; *see also* service design
iterative nature of assessment 13, 112, 134–135, 141
Ivy Plus Libraries Confederation (IPLC) data 97–98

Jantti, M., & Heath, J. 29, 50
Jiang, T., Fu, S., & Song, E. 47, 50
Johns Hopkins University libraries, collection assessments approach 91–105
Johnson, P. 2, 4, 11, 118, 131, 133, 135, 142

Index 149

Johnston, A. L. 34, 50
Journal Citation Reports (JCR) 121, 123

Kantor methodology 77–79, 80, 83
Kantor, P. B. 77, 78, 81, 89
Kaplan, N. 128, 131
Kaske, N. K. 78, 89
Keene, K., Keating, K., & Ahonen, P. 34, 36, 37, 39, 43, 44, 50
Kendall, K. E., & Kendall, J. E. 55, 73
Killick, S., & Wilson, F. 12, 13, 27, 83, 89
Kim, J. 114, 116
King, L., Stark, J. F. & Cooke, P. 136, 142
Knievel, J. E., Wicht, H., & Connaway, L. S. 92, 106
Kohl, L., Bénaud, C.-L., & Bordeianu, S. 92, 106
Kress, N., Del Bosque, D., & Ipri, T. 79, 89
Krueger, R. A. 37, 50
Krutt, H., Dyer, L., Arora, A., Rollman, J., & Jozkowski, A. C. 42, 50
Kushner, S. 31, 34, 50

Lal, S., Donnelly, C., & Shin, J. 42, 50
Lanclos, D. M. 47, 50
late mistakes, avoiding, through iterative processes 65
law of scattering, in bibliometrics 120
Lawson, B. R. 54, 73
lean process in systems design 66
legitimacy: of assessment outcomes 6, 7; of storytelling approach 31, 36–37; *see also* research rigour
Leorke, D., Wyatt, D., & McQuire, S. 53, 73
less documentation, as benefit of iterative processes 65
LibAnswers 86
LibPMC 139
LibQUAL+ assessment tool 5, 15, 18; *see also* questionnaires
libraries, adoption of service design approaches 60–63
Library Assessment and Data Analytics committee 94
Library Assessment Conference 139
library assessment criteria 4–5, 133–136
Library Process Error for non-availability 84, 85, 87
library rings and space heat maps 95–97
Lilley, S. 17, 27

limitations: in bibliometric analysis 10, 129; of datasets in visualisation approaches 101, 104; need to identify 133; in service design approaches 59
Line, M. B., & Sandison, A. 120, 131
list-servs as source of data collection instruments 23
listening, importance of in iterative processes 71
literature reviews 92–94; role of 13, 16, 25, 93, 94
low-fidelity prototypes 64, 65, 67–68; *see also* prototype development and testing
Lumley, R. M. 53, 73
Lunenburg, F. C., & Irby, B. J. 17, 27
Luther, M. 135, 142
Lynch, C. A. 108, 116

macroevaluations 132; as benchmarking 5
Mager, B. 55, 73
Mager, B., & King, O. 55, 73
Mann, S. 79, 89
Mann, S., & Sutton, S. 79, 89
Mansbridge, J. 76, 77, 89
Mansour, A. 47, 51
Māori culture, example of programme evaluation 35
mapping approach to collection evaluation 94, 95–97, 99–104
Margolis, R. 46, 51
Markey, K., Rieh, S. Y., St. Jean, B., Kim, J., & Yakel, E. 109, 116
Markless, S., & Streatfield, D. 137, 139, 142
Marquez, J., & Downey, A. 61, 73
materials availability assessments 9; data collection 85–87, 88; history of approaches 77–79; in hybrid print-electronic world 79; mixed-methods approach 82–88
Mathison, S. 42, 51
Matthews, J. 138, 139, 142
Matthews, J. R. 13, 24, 27
measures of assessment *see* metrics, selection of
methodology 16–19; in materials availability assessments 77–79, 80, 83; relationship with data collection techniques 22; relationship with metric 16–17; for repository assessment programme 112; *see also* mixed methods approaches

metrics, selection of 6, 16, 22–23, 26, 88; in repository assessment programmes 9, 110–111
Meyerson, J., Galloway, P., & Bias, R. 46, 51
microevaluations 132; as diagnostic tool 5
Microsoft Academic 121
Millward, P. 70, 73
Milton S. Eisenhower Library 94, 95
minimum viable service, development of 69–70
misunderstanding, avoiding, through iterative processes 66
Mitroff, I. I., & Kilmann, R. H. 33, 51
mixed methods approaches 6, 17–18, 135–136; benefits in GLAM evaluations 31–32, 47–48; for evaluating repositories 112; in materials availability assessment 82–88
Moed, H. F. 110, 116
Montana State University Library, adoption of service design approach 62
Most Significant Change technique 41
Mukwevho, J., & Ngoepe, M. 47, 51

narrative descriptions 23; *see also* data analysis
narrative methods of evaluation, emerging interest in *see* storytelling, as an assessment tool
narrative sharing, in repository assessment programme 112, 114–115
National Center for Education Studies (NCES)(US) 19
National Health and Medical Research Council (NHMRC) (Australia) 20
national repositories 108
nested mixed methods approach 112; *see also* mixed methods approaches
Neylon, C., & Wu, S. 110, 116
Nicholas, D., & Ritchie, M. 119, 131
Nichols, D. M., Payntner, G. M., Chan, C., Bainbridge, D., McKay, D., Twidale, M. B., & Blandford, A. 110, 116
Nicholson, K. P., & Seale, M. 17, 27
Nielsen, J. 64, 65, 72, 73
Nilsson, E. M. 46, 51
Nisonger, T. E. 76, 77, 78, 79, 81, 89
Nitecki, D. A. 4, 11
non-availability categories in materials availability assessments 78, 83–84, 85–87

O Brien, P., Arlitsch, K., Mixter, J., Wheeler, J., & Sterman, J. 116
O Brien, P., Kenning, A., Sterman, L., Mixter, J., Wheeler, J., & Borda, S. 116
O Leary, D. 110, 116
Oakleaf, M. 139, 142
Oakleaf, M. J. 13, 27
Oakleaf, M., & Kyrillidou, M. 12, 27
objective vs subjective evaluations 5–6
observation studies 18–19; *see also* ethnography
Office for Human Research Protections (US) 22
Oliveira, S. M. 53, 73
one-and-done approach to service development 53–54, 64
open access publications 108, 109, 110
opportunity cost as measure of assessment 6
organisational environment, as factor in assessment processes 7, 133, 138
organisational storytelling 45–46; *see also* storytelling, as an assessment tool
Osborne, J. W. 23, 27
Ospina, S. M., & Dodge, J. 38, 51
Our Research, researchers' altmetric 111
outliers, identification in bibliometric research 123, 124

parent organisation, effect on assessment processes 7, 133, 138
participants, importance of in iterative processes 70, 72
participatory approaches to evaluation 33–35, 43–44, 46–47; *see also* storytelling, as an assessment tool
Pastor, S. 43, 51
Pastva, J., Davis, B., Gutzman, K., Kubilius, R., & Sorensen, A. 120, 131
performance-based data collection techniques 43
performance evaluation, as benefit of iterative processes 65
Performance Measurement and Metrics (journal) 5, 139
performance measurement, introduction of term 4–5
personal ethical code, influence on research 21; *see also* ethics committees and research oversight
Peters, T. A. 79, 89
photo diary 23
PhotoVoice, as data collection technique 42–43, 47

Pickard, A. J. 13, 14, 17, 18, 21, 25, 27
pilot tests: in bibliometric assessments 127, 129; in data visualisation project 104; of materials availability surveys 80–81, 82
Polaine, A., Løvlie, L., & Reason, B. 56, 60, 74
Poll, R. 31, 51
Poll, R., & te Boekhorst, P. 78, 80, 90
Poole, N. 53, 74
positivist research paradigm 17; *see also* quantitative approaches to assessments
post-assessment review of ethics 21–22
post-positivist research paradigm 17; *see also* mixed methods approaches
pre-existing data, as potential metric 16, 22–23; *see also* usage data analysis
preparation, importance of in iterative processes 70, 72
Price, A., & Fleming-May, R. 109, 110, 116
Priem, J., & Hemminger, B. 110, 117
Priem, J., Taraborelli, D., Groth, P., & Neylon, C. 110, 117
Primo discovery system 80, 86
principles of service design 56–58
privacy considerations in research 19–22, 81, 93–94
projects, defining purpose of 15–16, 25, 26
prototype development and testing 58, 59–60; iterative nature of 63–64, 66–71
publications, selection for bibliometric analysis 123–124, 126
purpose of assessments, need to define 2–3, 8, 133–134; *see also* projects, defining purpose of

qualitative approaches to assessments 4, 6, 9, 17; data analysis in 23–24, 114; examples from GLAM sector 29, 45–47, 132, 135; in repository assessments 112, 114–115; *see also* mixed methods approaches; storytelling, as an assessment tool
quantitative approaches to assessments 1, 3–4, 6, 17, 19, 132; case studies 9–10, 125–128; in collection assessments 118–130; data analysis in 23, 109, 112, 114; dominant approach in GLAM evaluations 29, 31–32; in repository assessments 112, 113–114; *see also* mixed methods approaches
questionnaires 18, 23, 32, 47

questions and prompts in storytelling 33, 38–43

Radford, M. L. 47, 51
Ramsay, A. 65, 74
Ranganathan, S. R. 53, 73
rapid prototyping 63, 68; *see also* prototype development and testing
Reed College Library, adoption of service design approach 61
reflection as service design phase 59–60
reflective practice: in action research 14; as component of iterative assessment 59, 140–141
Rengifo, E. 64, 69, 74
repositories: history of development and assessment 108–111; types of 107–108; *see also* digital repository assessment
Repository Analytics and Metrics Portal (RAMP) 109
representativeness, of storytelling approach 36–37, 38
research: vs assessment 12–26; data collection in 22–23; definition 12, 13; design and methodology 13, 16–19; purpose 15, 25, 26
research ethics 19–22, 81, 94
Research Ethics Committees (REC) (UK) 20
research questions 13, 26; in action research 14; defining 13
research rigour 12, 15, 21, 24; perceptions of in storytelling approach 36, 38
resource sharing and circulation data comparisons 97–99
Retrieval Error for non-availability 84, 87
Rodgers, J. R., & Sugarman, T. 107, 117
Rodrigues, M. C., & Mandrekar, B. 140, 142
Rosenberg, Z. 79, 90
Ross, L., & Sennyey, P. 53, 74
Roughley, A. M. 41, 51
Ruby scripting language 102–103
Rung, M. H. 46, 51
Ryan, K., & Destefano, L. 31, 34, 51

Saldaña, J. 24, 27
Salo, D. 109, 117
Saponaro, M. Z., & Evans, G. E. 3, 11, 135, 142
Sapp, G., & Suttle, G. 92, 106
Saracevic, T. 4, 5, 11
Saracevic, T., Shaw, W. W., & Kantor, P. B. 77, 90

Scaramozzino, J. M., Ramirez, M., & McGaughey, K. J. 109, 117
Schatz, B. 108, 117
Scherle, R., Carrier, S., Greenberg, J., Lapp, H., Thompson, A., Vision, T., & White, H. 109, 117
Scholarly Publishing and Academic Coalition (SPARC) 108
Schopfel, J., Roche, J., & Hubert, G. 53, 74
Schrag, T., Mefford, C., Cottrill, J., & Paley, J. 31, 45, 51
Schroeder, R. 17, 27
SCImago Journal Rank (SJR) 120, 122, 123
Scopus 121, 122, 126, 127
scrapbooking, as data collection technique 43
self-citations, treatment in bibliometric analysis 119, 125
sequential design principle 57
service design: as an iterative process 9, 58, 59–60, 66–71; definition 55–56; key elements of 9, 64; in libraries 55–63; methods and tools 58–60; phases 58–60; principles of 56–58
service quality and impact as measure of assessment 5–6; *see also* impact assessments
Shavelson, R. J., & Towne, L. 13, 17, 27
Sheridan Libraries, Johns Hopkins University, collections assessment 91–105
Sherwood, G. 31, 52
Sipes, J. 62, 74
Smith, C. 53, 74
Smith, L. C. 128, 131
Sole, D., & Wilson, D. G. 31, 52
South Asian American Digital Archive 140
spatial approach to collection evaluation 92, 94, 95–97, 99–104
spiral prototyping 63; *see also* rapid prototyping
StackMap service 102
statistical analysis 17, 23–24, 114; in repository assessments 109; *see also* data analysis
steps in repository assessment programme 112–115
Stickdorn, M., & Schneider, J. 56, 59, 74
story circle techniques 39–40; *see also* group interviews
story quilting, as data collection technique 43

storytelling, as an assessment tool 8–9; case for using 30–31; challenges of 36–38; data collection techniques 30, 33, 35, 38–43; examples from the GLAM sector 45–47; guidelines for undertaking 33, 37; as a participatory collaborative exercise 33–35, 43–44, 46–47; in programme evaluations 29–52
Streatfield, D. et al. 139, 143
Streatfield, D., & Markless, S. 137, 142
Stuart, K., Varnum, K., & Ahronheim, J. 90
subject repositories 108; *see also* repositories
subjective vs objective evaluations 5–6
Suffolk Libraries impact analysis 6, 104
Sukop, S. 36, 43, 44, 52
summative assessment 6, 32, 67, 71
survey instruments 15, 23, 80; *see also* LibQUAL+ assessment tool; questionnaires; surveys
surveys 15, 18; in GLAM sector 32, 35; in impact assessments 138; in materials availability assessments 9, 77–78, 80–82, 85; in repository assessments 109
system-centred assessment criteria 4
System Error for non-availability 84
systematic approach, as key element of assessments 2, 10, 133–135; in materials availability assessments 76, 77; in repository assessments 107, 109, 111–115; in service design 54, 60; in storytelling 38; *see also* assessment plans; methodology

Tableau, role in visualising collections data 92, 104
Tang, K. 80, 81, 90
Tatarka, A., Chapa, K., Li, X., & Rutner, J. 8, 11
Tavangar, N. 60, 74
Taylor, C. 80, 90
technological changes, impact on assessment processes 7
Thailand Creative & Design Center adoption of service design approach 62–63
Thamtheerasathian, L., Choemprayong, S., Teerathammonkol, P., & Srisatriyanon, S. 62, 68, 74
theatre, as data collection technique 43
theoretical framework, as part of research design process 13

Index 153

Thorne, R., & Whitlach, J.B. 79, 90
Tilley, E. 46, 52
time factor, importance of in iterative processes 70
'Toolkit for the Impact of Scholarly and Digital Resources' 140
Town, J. S. 79, 909
transaction log analyses in materials availability assessments 79, 86
Travis, D. 71, 74
Tufte, E. J. 24, 27
Tufte, E. R. 24, 27
types of assessment 5–6

Ulrichsweb 122
understanding as key element of design process 64
University of Michigan Library, adoption of service design approach 62
University of Toronto library, adoption of service design approach 62
usability testing, in repository assessments 109
usage data analysis 19; in collection assessments 92–93, 94–98, 101, 102; in repository assessments 110–111
user and community expectations, as factor in assessment processes 7
user-centred assessment criteria 4; *see also* UX research approach
user-centred design principle 56
user focus, as benefit of iterative processes 66
user satisfaction, as unit of assessment 4
user search experiences, as source data for materials availability assessments 77–78
UX research approach 46–47

Vacek, R., Puckett Rodgers, E., & Sitar, M. 55, 62, 66–67, 74
validation as key element of design process 64
validity of research *see* research rigour
van der Steen, J. T., Ter Riet, G., van den Bogert, C. A., & Bouter, L. M. 54, 74
Van House, N. A., Weil, B. T., & McClure, C. R. 77, 90
van Westrienen, G. & Lynch, C. A. 108–109, 117

views, as metric for assessing repositories 110–111
vignettes, as data reporting tool 36, 44–45
Villaneuva, E. & Shiri, A. 5, 11
visualisations, as aid to collection evaluations 9, 91–105
Voorbij, H. 31, 52

Wagenaar, H. 32, 52
Wallis, J. C., Mayernik, M. S., Borgman, C. L., & Pepe, A. 117
Wang, F. 107, 117
Wavell, C., Baxter, G., Johnson, I., & Williams, D. 139, 143
Weare, W. H., Moffett, P., & Cooper, J. P. 106
Web of Science 121, 126, 127
website activity, as metric for assessing repositories 110
Wells, D. 76, 77, 81, 90
what questions 93–94
where questions 93
White, H. 108, 117
White, H., Aiken, J., & Shapiro, F. 107, 117
White, H., Chen, S., & Liu, G. 109, 110, 114, 117
White, H., & Haddow, G. 114, 117
White, H., & Le, A. 107, 117
who questions 93–94
why questions 91, 93–94
Widdershoven, G. A. 31, 52
Wikipedia, as an example of iterative design 64
Willits, F. K., Theodori, G. L., & Luloff, A. E. 18, 28
Wishlade, K. 58, 74

Xia, J. 92, 106, 109, 117
Xie, I., & Matusiak, K. 74

Yakel, E. & Tibbo, H. 29, 52
Young, S. W. H., Mannheimer, S., Rossmann, D., Swedman, D., & Shanks, J. D. 62, 74

Zaugg, H. 133, 134, 143
Zhai, Y. H., Zhao, Y., & Wang, R. M. 53, 75
Zimmerman, E. 63, 65, 70, 71, 75

For Product Safety Concerns and Information please contact our EU
representative GPSR@taylorandfrancis.com
Taylor & Francis Verlag GmbH, Kaufingerstraße 24, 80331 München, Germany

www.ingramcontent.com/pod-product-compliance
Lightning Source LLC
Chambersburg PA
CBHW061350300426
44116CB00011B/2063